THE NORSE MYTHS
THAT SHAPE THE WAY
WE THINK

THE

# Norse Myths

## THAT SHAPE THE
## WAY WE THINK

CAROLYNE
LARRINGTON

Frontispiece: Edward Burne-Jones, *Gudrun Setting Fire to Atli's Palace* (1897).

First published in the United Kingdom in 2023
by Thames & Hudson Ltd, 181A High Holborn,
London WC1V 7QX

First published in the United States of America in 2023
by Thames & Hudson Inc., 500 Fifth Avenue, New York,
New York 10110

Reprinted 2023

*The Norse Myths That Shape the Way We Think*
© 2023 Thames & Hudson Ltd, London
Text © 2023 Carolyne Larrington

Designed by Matthew Young

British Library Cataloguing-in-Publication Data
A catalogue record for this book is available from
the British Library

Library of Congress Control Number 2022945660

ISBN 978-0-500-25234-5

Printed in China by Shanghai Offset Printing
Products Limited

Be the first to know about our new releases,
exclusive content and author events by visiting
**thamesandhudson.com**
**thamesandhudsonusa.com**
**thamesandhudson.com.au**

# Contents

# Introduction

A cyborg monster sprawls across a desolate heath. His body is armoured with technology, and he controls extraordinary machines that can affect people's emotions. A pretty teenage girl sings passionately about her crush on a handsome man and her worries about her own desirability; the lower half of her body is a stinking mass of decaying corpse-flesh. A ruggedly handsome blond man swings his huge hammer, smashing a ruthless killer-automaton to smithereens. And gaunt-faced figures with icicle crowns and frost-rimed cheekbones march from the north through an endless winter: their aim is to erase and enslave every human in their path. These strange supernatural figures sound like creatures of myth and legend – and that is exactly what they are. Yet they haven't stepped straight off the vellum of ancient Northern manuscripts. Rather, these compelling characters are contemporary reimaginings of mythic or heroic figures from Old Norse mythology. All speak in particular ways to our contemporary hopes and fears, bridging the gap between a vanished medieval past and a vibrant, living present. We'll be making a closer acquaintance with each of them – Fafnir, Hel, Thor and the White Walkers – in the chapters that follow.

**What are the Old Norse myths?**
The Old Norse myths are a body of stories that have survived from the medieval period and were thus first written down by Christians (see pls I, II). They existed for generations in oral tradition, but the pre-Christian North had no tradition of preserving its narratives

in writing. The myths feature gods and goddesses as their protagonists, often interacting with other kinds of beings – giants, dwarfs
and monsters – and, much more rarely, with humans. Alongside
these tales, and often in the same manuscripts, we find stories of
human heroes. Most prominent among them is Sigurðr the Dragon-
Slayer, with his extraordinary ancestors and his treacherous kinsmen by marriage. These are heroic legends rather than myths for,
even though they often have superhuman characteristics, humans
are the most important figures. Some of these stories have been
known and retold for hundreds of years since the Middle Ages;
others are less well known but have come to the fore at different
times in post-medieval history.

The Old Norse myths and legends, as we shall see, offer ways
of thinking about the world, about time, history and fate, that
we do not find in the more culturally central Greek and Roman
myths; they differ, too, in important ways from the tales preserved
in the Celtic languages. It might seem that, as journalists like to
say, Old Norse myths are currently 'having a moment', but in fact,
ever since they were first recorded in writing, and conceivably for
centuries before that, they have been retold over and over again.
They have been understood in many different ways: by audiences
in small Icelandic turf-roofed farmhouses or in grand Norwegian
royal halls, among the stone circles and ship-setting burial sites of
eastern Scandinavia or in the tree groves of Denmark. And after
they no longer played any role in active belief or ritual practice,
they were interpreted as meaningful, and have continued to be
thought about and understood as meaningful, in even more and
various ways. That is the subject of this book.

**Our sources for the myths**
We do not have many reliable sources for the Norse myths and
legends as far as written accounts are concerned. There are a small
number of works, contained in a slightly less small number of

Picture stone from Hunninge, Gotland, Sweden (8th century).

Þjóðveldisbærinn Stöng, reconstructed farmstead, south Iceland.

manuscripts, that give accounts of the major myths and heroic tales, and we also have some more ambiguous evidence from archaeology, ranging from huge picture stones to tiny metal figurines. The most important of the literary treatments of the myths are the two famous texts known as the Eddas. This is a word that means 'great-grandmother', but that could be derived from the Latin *edo*, 'I compose'. The older of the two works is the *Prose* or *Snorra Edda* (sometimes, confusingly, called the *Younger Edda*), a treatise that explains the systems of Old Norse poetics and the information needed to compose and interpret court poetry in the 13th century. It was most likely composed by the Icelandic scholar and politician Snorri Sturluson at some point in the 1220s. In the first main section of his treatise, Snorri offers a systematic account of the gods and goddesses, the creation of the world, its ending and rebirth, the attributes of the divinities and some of the adventures in which they are involved.

Snorri was of course a Christian, for Iceland had converted to Christianity around 200 years before he was born, and he had been

educated at one of the country's main centres of Christian learn-
ing. His interests in this material were scholarly and antiquarian,
but he was also conscious that he needed to frame his account of
the gods very carefully. He did not wish his audience to be encouraged to think that the gods of pre-Christian religion were in any
sense real, that they wielded (or had once wielded) actual divine
power, and he therefore turned to a doctrine known as *euhemer-
ism* to explain their existence. The ancient Greek mythographer
Euhemerus had argued that gods were in fact particularly clever
or charismatic humans who had persuaded others that they were
divine and worthy of worship; their status remained unchallenged
after their deaths. We might think of certain Roman emperors who
proclaimed themselves as gods and were honoured with the building of temples after their deaths. Snorri claimed in his Prologue
to the *Edda* that the Norse gods were refugees from Troy. They
had fled the city's destruction and made their way westwards and
northwards to Scandinavia: the Æsir, the name of the main tribe
of gods, were thus understood as coming from Asia. There in the
North, using their superior knowledge (particularly of magic and
trickery) they supposedly impressed the indigenous peoples, first
achieving rule over them, and then being revered by them after
their deaths.

At the beginning of the second section of his *Edda*, known as
*Gylfaginning* (The Deluding of Gylfi), Snorri creates a framework
for his main story collection. Here he relates how Gylfi, a king of
Sweden, is tricked out of a good deal of land by one of these cunning incomers, a woman called Gefjun. She appeared at his hall in
the guise of a 'travelling woman', became his lover, and then asked
for as much land as could be ploughed in twenty-four hours – not
all that much, so Gylfi gladly granted it. But Gefjun brought down
from Giantlands her four sons, fathered by a giant, and turned
them into oxen. By the end of the stipulated period, they had
ploughed out of Gylfi's kingdom all the land that forms the main

Title page of Snorri's *Edda* illustrated by Jakob Sigurðsson (1764).

Danish island of Sjælland and had left a huge hole in the middle of his realm (what is now Lake Mälaren in southern Sweden).

Justifiably surprised by this development, Gylfi goes to visit the strangers in their hall to question them about their origins, identities and powers, and they entertain him with tales about the Æsir, their ancestors who had come from so far away. When they arrive at the end of their narrative, the hall and its inhabitants vanish, and Gylfi goes home to tell his people what he has learned. And, so Snorri relates, the tricksy people who had explained the myths to the king now decide to pretend to be their remarkable ancestors and to claim their deeds as their own.

One of Snorri's key sources for the first sections of his *Edda* were some poems about mythology that are preserved in the so-called *Poetic Edda*. This is a collection of poems, most of which were compiled around 1270 somewhere in Iceland in a single manuscript that is now known as the Codex Regius, or 'King's Book'. This manuscript contains eleven broadly mythological poems and around twenty-nine heroic poems; conventionally a few other poems composed in a similar mode are added to the Codex Regius collection in modern editions. What happened to this rather unprepossessing manuscript between its writing and its reappearance in the hands of Brynjólfur Sveinsson, the bishop of Skálholt in Iceland, in 1643 is a mystery. Thus we do not know how it came to lose a whole gathering (a number of leaves) that must have contained some key poems about Sigurðr the Dragon-Slayer. Bishop Brynjólfur sent this manuscript – along with the most important surviving manuscript of Snorri's *Prose Edda* – to the king of Denmark in 1662. The two manuscripts entered the royal manuscript collection, hence the name Codex Regius.

Eddic poetry is relatively easy to understand, except where words have been miscopied by scribes. It does not have the complicated riddling metaphors, known as 'kennings', that Old Norse courtly (or 'skaldic') poetry has, nor its complex system of rhyme, half-rhyme and alliteration. The word 'skaldic' comes from the Old Norse word for 'poet': *skáld*. These intricate court poems were in fact the main focus of Snorri's poetic treatise, and he discusses and analyses them in the remaining sections of his *Edda*. The poems – at least the ones that have survived – mainly celebrate the exploits of kingly patrons in battle or mourn their deaths. They do not tend to recount or describe myths. However, one poem, known as *Þórsdrápa* (Thor's Deeds), tells of Þórr's perilous journey to visit the giant Geirrøðr, having unwisely set out without his hammer, Mjöllnir. Certain other sequences describe a shield or a set of carvings on which mythological or heroic scenes are depicted: these include the great set piece of Baldr's funeral, Þórr's terrifying confrontation at sea with the Miðgarðs Serpent (see pl. VII), and the horrific death of the Gothic king Jörmunrekkr, whose severed hands and feet are cast into a fire before his eyes. More often, however, the mythological material in the skaldic poems consists in rather obscure allusions, which can confirm details that we know from fuller versions of the tales or hint at other stories that have been lost.

The sagas, another source for Norse myth, are works written in prose in Iceland from the 13th century onwards. They relate different kinds of tales. Some of the so-called 'legendary sagas' (*fornaldarsögur*) make indirect reference to myths and very often feature mysterious Odinic figures who appear in order to stir up trouble for heroes. Historical sagas, on the other hand, give information about the distant ancestors of royal houses: they frequently touch on mythic themes or tell tales about Óðinn's demonic efforts to thwart the efforts of Norwegian missionary kings. One very important saga, much used by Richard Wagner, is *Völsunga saga* (The Saga of the Völsungs). This tells the history of the Völsung clan, the ancestors of Sigurðr the Dragon-Slayer. Fortunately, the saga can fill in for us the gap in the Codex Regius manuscript mentioned above, as well as recounting the remarkable story of Sigurðr's father, Sigmundr, and Sigmundr's twin sister, Signý (see Chapters 1 and 7).

Also important for later interpretation of the Norse myths are various quasi-historical works composed by writers in Latin. These include the early historian Jordanes, who completed *De origine actibusque Getarum* (The Origins and Deeds of the Goths), usually known as the *Getica*, in Constantinople in 551 CE; the ecclesiastic

Adam of Bremen, who gave an account of Uppsala in Sweden in the latter half of the 11th century and described in detail the great temple that was said to be there; and the Danish monk Saxo Grammaticus, who composed his great work *Gesta Danorum* (The History of the Danes) around 1200. In the early books of the *Gesta*, Saxo discusses a man called Othinus and other figures familiar from the Old Norse myths, taking a strongly euhemeristic line. Othinus and his relatives are definitely humans (and there may have been more than one person taking the name of Othinus); while their exploits involve supernatural figures and elements, they are clearly not divinities. Saxo's treatment of many of the kernels of Norse myth in the *Gesta Danorum* were highly influential in subsequent Danish interpretation of the kingdom's early history.

Archaeological finds, ranging from small portable objects to huge Migration- and Viking-period stone sculptures, are inevitably more difficult to interpret in connection with mythological and heroic tales than is written material. These objects tempt us to assume that, for example, the images we find on stone crosses from the British Isles or picture stones from the Baltic island of Gotland are intended to illustrate the stories that we know rather than the vast number of stories that must have been lost. On one Gotland stone we find an image of a man in a square enclosure surrounded by writhing serpents. Is this the hero Gunnarr, confined in the snake-pit in which he loses his life? If the image had included the harp that Gunnarr used to quieten the reptiles for a brief while we could be more confident in our identification. A woman seems about to enter the enclosure. Aha! Is this Sigyn, Loki's wife, returning from emptying the bowl in which she catches the venom that pours onto her husband's face? Or could this figure be the legendary king Ragnarr Loðbrók ('shaggy-breeches'), perishing in the snake-pit of King Ælle of Northumbria? But if so, who is the woman? And so on. Sometimes the sculptural evidence is unequivocal: two figures in a boat with a fishing line, one with

Rune stone (Ög 224) in Östergötland, Sweden (8th century).

a huge hammer, with a creature snapping at the bait must be the
tale of Þórr's fishing expedition with the giant Hymir, even if
sometimes the giant is missing, or the prey (the Miðgarðs Serpent),
or the hammer; or the detail of Þórr's foot going through the bottom of the boat has been added. Other, smaller finds pose similar
problems: the little metal figurines known as 'Óðinn from Lejre'
(but the statue seems to be wearing female clothes) or 'Freyr from
Rällinge' may indeed represent the deities after whom they have

been tentatively named. But they may have entirely different significations. Archaeological evidence can only tell us so much: it must be treated with caution.

## After the conversion

The North converted to Christianity over a 200-year period. Denmark was Christianized first, followed by Norway and the North Atlantic islands, including Iceland, and finally Sweden. Once Christianity had become the official religion, the telling of mythological stories and their depictions may have been repressed – though in the sculptural heritage of the British Isles we find a good number of stone crosses that combine Norse mythological and Christian details. (As we shall see in Chapter 4, Jesus and Þórr were often set against one another as rival protectors of humanity.) As time passed, the stories came to be understood, in Iceland at least, as having antiquarian and poetic interest, as Snorri's writings show. However, Snorri's treatment of the tales

Left: The so-called 'Óðinn' statuette from Lejre, Denmark (c. 900 CE).
Right: Figurine from Rällinge, Sweden, possibly depicting Freyr (c. 11th century).

is unique, and the fact that the mythological eddic poems survive only in two manuscripts suggests that the old stories were no longer vital in medieval peoples' imaginations.

Iceland became a dependency of Norway in 1262–63, and by the end of the medieval period it belonged to Denmark. The peoples of Scandinavia became increasingly interested in their own histories, though they did not distinguish between actual events and legendary happenings in the way we understand history today. Saxo's Latin history of Denmark, historical sagas composed in Iceland and the tales told by Snorri began to be published in the early modern period, very often accompanied by Latin translations. Once they were available in a language that – unlike Old Norse – was well understood by scholars and intellectuals across Europe, the tales began to travel. References to the Norse gods appear in England in 17th-century historical writings, where their connection with the gods of early medieval England who had given their names to the days of the week is noted. By the 18th century, some mythological poems and sections of Snorri's *Edda* were being translated into English and other European languages. Icelandic scholars, very often working in Copenhagen, assisted with both collecting manuscripts from Icelandic farmhouses and making reliable editions and translations for the rest of the world to read.

## Into the modern world

During the Enlightenment, a time when older received ideas about the world were increasingly challenged by arguments deriving from reason and empirical experience, the Norse myths began to be read in new ways. In Germany in particular, the Roman historian Tacitus's account of 1st-century Germanic tribes in his *Germania* (98 CE) was now being reread. In the Battle of the Teutoburg Forest (9 CE), an alliance of Germanic tribes led by Arminius had ambushed and destroyed three Roman legions. Tacitus set out to describe the tribes whose courage, independence and effective resistance to Roman military might had become a topic of great interest in Rome. Tacitus foregrounded the Germanii's readiness to die on the battlefield rather than experience the shame of retreat, as well as their love of liberty. The 18th-century French thinker Charles-Louis de Montesquieu, who argued fiercely against absolutism as a system of government, held up for admiration the Scandinavians, both ancient and contemporary, as exemplifying the same passion for freedom. Just like their Germanic cousins, they were thought to be 'the font of liberty of Europe'. Montesquieu also espoused a theory, originally proposed by Aristotle, that those peoples who lived in northern climes were temperamentally inclined to martial vigour and independence, precisely because cold climates induced resilience and energy. In the Mediterranean South, in contrast, warmth led to political indolence and an apathetic acquiescence to tyranny. The sturdy self-reliance of Northern Europeans, coupled with defiance of death and a strong belief in an afterlife, meant that such liberty-loving peoples needed fewer laws to keep them in line, he suggested. This argument would prove enduringly popular across north-western Europe, especially (of course) among Scandinavians, but also in those nations that were able to claim kinship with Germanic or Nordic peoples. This included the freedom-loving English. For the English were themselves, at least partly, the Anglo-Scandinavian descendants of Viking settlers who were hailed as epitomizing this spirit. Models of a robust and independent early medieval English polity, one that pre-dated the Norman Conquest, were developed by 18th-century historians, and there was a new emphasis on the Germanic elements in early English law and culture.

The 18th century also saw readers across Europe develop a strong enthusiasm for the Gothic – for dramatic, brooding landscapes and tales of horror, violence and grand passions: hatred, love and vengeance. Thorough-going accounts of Norse mythology, often confusingly labelled as Celtic, began to appear in French and English; the

Old Norse myths and legends translated in such collections offered a range of splendidly barbaric subjects that catered to the growing popular taste. Importantly, too, these Celtic–Nordic myths could be explored as home-grown alternatives to the familiar storyworld of classical myth. Understood in opposition to the idea of Roman-ness (whether embodied by classical Rome or Roman Catholicism) and interpreted as celebrating heroes who were precursors to the free-thinkers of Protestantism, the Norse myths and legends were seized upon as representing something entirely new in the European imagination. Old Norse poems caught the eye of poets such as Thomas Gray and illustrators of the calibre of William Blake (see pl. IV). Reliance on Latin translations could lead authors astray, however. The madly impractical idea of drinking mead from your enemies' skulls derives from an incorrect translation: an Old Norse metaphor that describes a drinking horn as the 'curved wood of the skull' – of course, the skull belonging to an ox or cow – was rendered in Latin as 'the curved beakers of skulls'. The widespread misapprehension fitted very nicely with Gothic notions of Northern fierceness and barbarism, and it persisted, as we shall see, for a very long time indeed – it even turns up in *Asterix the Gaul*.

In the 19th century, nationalist movements in Scandinavia and Germany began to take a renewed interest in the Norse myths. A scientific revolution in the understanding of historical linguistics revealed that English, German and the Scandinavian languages had a common ancestor, known as 'Proto-Germanic' – a branch of the Indo-European family of languages. This shared linguistic heritage made it possible to claim that the English, Germans and Scandinavians must also have had a shared mythology. Particularly popular in Germany, these theories impelled Jacob Grimm (he of the fairy tales) to write a huge, magisterial study of Germanic mythology, first published in 1835. This carefully made the argu-ment that, if the beliefs of the Nordic peoples and the Germans were traced far enough back, they would converge into a single system, one that would give insight into the original mythic consciousness of the Germanic peoples. Had it not been for the relatively early adoption of Christianity in Germany, more evidence for pagan belief and mythology might have survived there. As it was, the later conversion of Scandinavia had proved crucial to the preservation in the North of these ancient tales. Óðinn, Þórr, Frigg, Loki and many of the other gods were thus appropriated into German through Grimm's arguments and were given

Henry Fuseli, *Odin in the Underworld* (1770–72).

Monument commemorating the Battle of Teutoburg, Detmold, Germany (1875).

German names such as Wuotan (Óðinn) and Donar (Þórr). Richard Wagner's great operatic masterpiece *Der Ring des Nibelungen* (*The Ring of the Nibelung*), completed in 1876, takes up key stories from Old Norse myth and heroic legend, melds them together, and adds some material from medieval German epic and folklore. As we shall see, Wagner's inspired reimaginings of Norse myth and legend are not only the 19th century's most important reshaping of the myths: Wagner's vision also shaped future thinking about the stories. The operas were composed between 1848 and 1874. The *Vorspiel* or prelude, *Das Rheingold* (*The Rhinegold*), tells of the origin of the Ring and Wotan's (Óðinn's) building of Valhalla; the second opera, *Die Walküre* (*The Valkyrie*) relates the failure of Wotan's son, Siegmund, to recover the Ring and introduces the magnificent figure of the Valkyrie Brünnhilde. The third opera, *Siegfried*, sees the emergence of the hero who does indeed recover the Ring and recounts his ecstatic union with Brünnhilde. *Götterdämmerung* (*The Twilight of the Gods*) brings the cycle to a close with the downfall of the gods and the tragic deaths of both Siegfried and Brünnhilde. Despite their Scandinavian context, Wagner regarded these myths as central to Germany's early medieval heritage.

Meanwhile, in England, writers and poets were rewriting the same tales. Under the watchful eye of the the 19th-century Icelandic scholar Eiríkur Magnússon, William Morris became the foremost Victorian translator of Norse heroic poetry. Translations of the sagas of Icelanders, with their dramatic family histories, their feuds, outlaws and examples of individual courage in the face of death, caught the imaginations of Victorian readers. The more intrepid and wealthier among them could, like Morris, travel to Iceland with the aim of experiencing at first hand the landscapes that had formed these heroes. The first adaptations of the myths for children were published in English from the mid-century onwards, and proved so popular that they continued to be reprinted well into the 20th century.

Translations and new versions created in Britain were exported across the Atlantic, where they were read by the thousands of Scandinavian immigrants who settled in Canada and the American Midwest in the second half of the 19th century, and their descendants. North Americans were particularly fascinated by the sagas, which claimed that the first Europeans to arrive on the continent were not, in fact, Christopher Columbus and his companions, but rather Leifr 'the Lucky' Eiríksson, along with a mixed crew of Icelanders and Greenlanders. Once the idea of late Viking Age journeys westwards became established in the American imagination, all sorts of fake artefacts began to appear, from rune stones to forged maps and the famous Newport Tower, as we shall see in Chapter 9.

The fortunes of Old Norse myth took a darker turn in the 20th century. In Germany, the nationalist enthusiasm for mythology that had got under way in the 19th century fuelled the Nazis' racist ideology, for it supported the idea of an underlying kinship between the blond, blue-eyed Scandinavians and contemporary Germans. These Northern Europeans were understood as 'Aryans' and were defined by the Nazis as superior to all other races. Nazi theorists argued for an unbreakable connection between the land and the history and beliefs of its inhabitants – the doctrine of *Blut und Boden*, 'blood and soil' – and that German identity could belong only to people of 'pure' German ancestry. Hitler, notoriously, was a keen fan of Wagner's operas, which seemed to him to confirm

May Morris (centre), daughter of William Morris, at Fáskrúðsfjörður, Iceland, in 1931.

19th-century theories about racial identity and its link to the land. The Führer was a regular visitor to the performances of Wagner's works at the Festspielhaus in Bayreuth (although he was almost alone among the party leadership in his passion). This well-known enthusiasm, taken alongside the use made of mythological imagery in Nazi propaganda and some wildly eccentric attempts, sponsored largely by Heinrich Himmler, to revive Wotanism as a new national religion, meant that the Norse myths became widely identified with Nazism. In the post-war United Kingdom and North America, it took a while for these associations to be shaken off. It was not until the 1960s that new children's versions of the myths began to be published; as memories of the Nazi obsession with Aryanism faded, writers such as Alan Garner and Diana Wynne Jones began to incorporate Norse mythological themes and motifs into their stories for children.

More recently still, the myths and legends have become a key part of mainstream children's literature. Their appearance in series such as Cressida Cowell's *How to Train Your Dragon* (2003–15) and in Francesca Simon's *Two Terrible Vikings* (2020) has introduced Norse mythic storylines and ideas of historical accuracy (no horned helmets here!) into exciting and imaginative tales written for very young children. Vikings are studied in school, and children usually acquire a good working knowledge of the Vikings and some of the major myths.

Beyond the nursery and classroom, the myths have also moved into popular culture. Thor, a Marvel Comics hero during the 1960s, has made the transition into Hollywood movies, rubbing shoulders with other superheroes in the *Avengers* franchise, as well as starring in his own movie storyline. Neil Gaiman's 2001 novel *American Gods*, whose principal divine figure is a version of Óðinn, has become a popular television series, and the international phenomenon *Game of Thrones* built its imagined version of the North and the world beyond the Wall using many motifs from Old Norse legend. While Wagner has lost none of his popularity, new operas have been created from mythic material, such as Francesca Simon and Gavin Higgins's 2019 chamber production *The Monstrous Child*. The mythically inspired music of the Icelandic composer Jón Leifs has become internationally popular; so too has Viking death metal music, obsessed in particular with the idea of *ragna rök*, and the more traditional folk-related music of the Norwegian Einar Selvik.

In the 21st century, the myths are more widely known and are made to do more complicated kinds of cultural work than ever before. Ásatrú, or belief in the Æsir, has spread widely across Europe and North America and is to be found even in Oceania; and reverence for certain Norse deities occurs in other neo-pagan faiths, such as goddess worship. The roots of such revivals run back to the race ideologies of the 19th century and, although some varieties of belief have explicitly dissociated themselves from nationalist and racist positions, others have evolved into sets of principles that undergird neo-Nazi and alt-right thinking in both North America and Europe. These often depend on a highly selective and partial reading of Old Norse myth, or else incorporate 19th-century systematizations of such nebulous concepts as rune-magic. One of the aims of this book is to demonstrate the contingent and historically specific nature of various schools of thought about the corpus of Old Norse myths and legends. Although these stories have been made to convey different meanings over the centuries, serving the needs and fuelling the aspirations of a whole range of societies and cultural groups, we must remember that they represent the fragments of a strange and resonant storyworld mediated through the writings of medieval Christians, and that there are limits to the immanent and universal significations that we can ascribe to them. The myths refuse to be tied down to particular ideologies, for when those eddic manuscripts left Iceland back in the 17th century they became part of world literature – and they now belong to us all.

# CHAPTER 1

# Yggdrasill, the World Tree

A GREEN MYTH

I know a tree, says the seeress in the poem *Völuspá* (The Seeress's Prophecy), that stands, eternally green, over Urðr's well. Urðr is one of the Norns, three mysterious women who determine fate. Down the ash tree's trunk flows shining white loam, fresh and fertile. The tree is Yggdrasill ('Steed of the Terrible One'), and it is at the centre of the Old Norse mythic universe. Its branches tower into the heavens; whole worlds are found beneath each of its deep taproots. Deer browse its uppermost branches, raptors perch in its crown, and a nimble squirrel scurries up and down its trunk bearing news from the world above to the world below, including the sinister dragon that crouches beneath its roots. Yggdrasill is not made or planted by the gods, and it is not clear that it will be destroyed at *ragna rök*, the end of the world (see Chapter 10). In the wondrous new cosmos that the gods have created, whether by scooping the earth up out of the sea or by shaping the world from the dismembered fragments of the mighty giant Ymir, Yggdrasill stands at its very centre, growing up and down through the worlds. It harnesses remarkable powers and yet, for it is understood in some ways as sentient, it also experiences pain and suffering, inflicted on it by beasts – and, perhaps, by the gods themselves.

## The centre of the world

The eddic poems and Snorri's *Edda* view Yggdrasill from a number of different angles. In one poem we learn that Valhöll (Valhalla) is situated directly beneath it, and that the goat Heiðrún who lives on Valhöll's roof grazes on its leaves, which may explain why her udders give mead instead of milk ('That's a useful goat,' comments Gylfi, the king of Sweden, when he hears about this). A deer, named Eikþyrnir, also stands on the hall, and water drips from his antlers down into the well called Hvergelmir ('Roaring Kettle') that lies by the tree, from which numerous rivers flow. As well as the animals on Valhöll's roof, there are four more deer who inhabit the tree and nibble at its leaves. An eagle perches on its summit, bearing, strangely enough, a hawk between its eyes. Three great roots hold the tree upright; one leads down to the kingdom of Hel, goddess of death; another to the frost giants; and the third to humankind. The same poem also warns that innumerable serpents gnaw at Yggdrasill's branches, 'more than any numbskull fool can imagine', and that the fearful dragon Níðhöggr lurks beneath its roots. All is not entirely well with Yggdrasill. The sustained offensive of the snakes and Níðhöggr's depredations are wearing at its fabric, and on one side of the trunk decay is manifest. Even this central pillar of the imagined universe is subject to the effects of time and the attacks of predators: entropy is understood to be at work in the cosmos.

Nor is the relation of the tree to other parts of the world of gods and men altogether clear. While we can well imagine the worlds of the dead as subterranean, it is hard to visualize human beings as dwelling below ground – and the giants are more generally said to live in the mountains to the east. Snorri tells us that, in addition to Hvergelmir, Mímir's well also lies at one of the tree's roots – the water source in which lies Óðinn's missing eye. He traded it for a drink from the well, which provides a special kind of wisdom, for it also holds the embalmed head of Mímir, one of the Æsir. Mímir prophesies what is to come and has a particular role to play at *ragna rök*. As we will see in Chapter 10, in the mythic universe conceived by the author Joanne Harris, Mímir (there known chiefly as 'the Oracle') does not only divulge wisdom to Óðinn, he actively manipulates other characters in order to achieve his own mysterious ends.

Óðinn drank this special draught of wisdom from the Gjallarhorn, a horn that functions both as a drinking vessel and an instrument of warning. Heimdallr, the watchman of the gods, will sound it to signal the beginning of *ragna rök*. His guard station may well be beneath Yggdrasill, for in one poem it is said that he has a permanently muddy back, the result of the gleaming white soil that courses down the trunk. Heimdallr's sense of hearing also seems to be submerged in the well's waters. We can imagine it quivering there beneath the tree, finely attuned to signs from across the worlds that the frost and fire giants are on the march; so, too, may Óðinn's eye still be channelling information through the tree's network of roots and branches thanks to a kind of cybernetic connectivity. No wonder, then, that it was upon this tree that the god hanged himself without food or drink for nine days and nights, as he tells us in one eddic poem. Óðinn thus sacrificed himself to himself to gain the knowledge of the runes, which he then plucked up from below where he was hanging: the runes originate from the spaces between the tree roots, perhaps. In poetic metaphor, gallows are often imagined as horses on which the hanged man rides, so the ordeal of Óðinn, whose many names include Yggr, or 'Terrible', may explain how the tree got its name: Yggdrasill, the steed of Óðinn.

One of the tree's roots, says Snorri, points upwards into the sky rather than down towards mankind, and it is there that Urðr's well is located. We know very little about this figure and her two companions, Verðandi and Skuld, known as the Norns. Their names relate to ideas of happening and becoming, in essence: past, present and future. 'Urðr' is connected to the Old English word *wyrd*, also meaning 'fate' – a concept that gives us the Three Weird Sisters in *Macbeth* and our modern term for the uncanny. These women sit by the well cutting wooden strips that determine the fates of humans. Whether they carve runes on these strips, thus writing the future, or shape them in other ways is not clear. Elsewhere in eddic poetry the Norns are said to twist or braid together threads that constitute individual human fates; in Wagner's *Ring* cycle (as we shall see, particularly in Chapter 10) this activity, closely

Óðinn's self-sacrifice, illustration by William Gershom Collingwood from Olive Bray's *The Elder or Poetic Edda* (1908).

connected with the idea that fate is a woven textile, is at first located under the World Tree. The Norns pour water from the well over the tree, water that is charged with healing properties that help to preserve it. Everything that the well water comes into contact with turns as white as the membrane inside an eggshell. Honeydew falls from the tree and nourishes bees. Two swans, equally white, sail placidly on the water's surface: swans and bees have more positive, life-giving associations than the serpents and raptors high up in the tree's branches or beneath its roots.

The Norns, illustration by Franz Stassen from
*Der Ring des Nibelungen* (1914).

What does Yggdrasill mean in Old Norse mythological thinking? It seems to function as a model ecosystem, offering a home and sustenance to all the different animals who live upon it or close to it. It is also an important source of fertility: the liquids that flow from it are life-sustaining. The mud that cascades down its trunk is gleaming and white, not dull brown and sticky. Its luscious dews feed the bees whose honey may be used to make the gods' own drink: mead. The waters that flow from it feed the many rivers that irrigate the land. All these details speak to the idea of the tree as a central source of nutrients, vital for growth and the annual cycles of regeneration.

**Wisdom and the sacred tree**
Yggdrasill also operates as a kind of communications centre, amplifying signals across the worlds. Ratatoskr the squirrel scampers up and down the trunk, bearing news from both below and above. The great taproots, plunging down into the worlds of giants, men, gods and the dead, connect and bind the beings that inhabit the universe. Óðinn's intimate connection with the tree – his sacrifice by hanging upon it, and the submersion of his eye in the well beneath it – suggests that it transmits arcane wisdom in various forms. The symbolism of Yggdrasill and Óðinn is strikingly harnessed in the figure of the Three-Eyed Crow in George R. R. Martin's *A Song of Ice and Fire* novel series and the HBO television show *Game of Thrones*, where he is known as the Three-Eyed Raven. The raven is of course an Odinic bird, as we shall see in the following chapter; and ravens are used to carry messages across the continent of Westeros. Young Bran Stark is summoned by this mysterious figure, who appears to him in his dreams in the shape of a bird. The Three-Eyed Crow or Raven is first encountered in his human form in a cave deep below the Haunted Forest. With long, flowing white hair and, significantly, missing an eye, he is remarkably old and quite immobile. The Crow/Raven is seated on a throne

carved out of weirwood: the sacred tree of the North. Tree roots penetrate his body and grow from his empty eye socket, in the book at least. Through this complex, branching root system the seer remains in touch with all the godswoods, the sacred groves, of the North, able to see past, present and future thanks to the trees' mystical power and interconnectedness. 'Most of him has gone into the tree,' explains Leaf, one of the elf-like Children of the Forest, to Bran. 'Only a little strength remains in his flesh. He has a thousand eyes and one, but there is much to watch.' The Raven's arcane connection with the sacred tree system thus taps into the established bond between the one-eyed god and Yggdrasill in Old Norse myth, for the knowledge that Óðinn constantly seeks out seems to be in part embedded in, partly amplified by, the Cosmic Tree.

There are parallels to Yggdrasill as the Cosmic Tree in various neighbouring historical contexts. Around 720 CE the English missionary Bishop Winfrid, better known in Germany as St Boniface, commanded the destruction of a great oak at Geismar in central Germany. This tree was known locally as the 'Jupiter oak', but it was most probably sacred to the German equivalent of Þórr. Sacred trees could also be represented by tall wooden posts or poles. One such pole, a great 'world-pillar' or 'Irminsul', stood in the midst of a stronghold on top of a mountain in Obermarsberg, Saxony (now Germany), until 772; the Emperor Charlemagne, who was undertaking a military campaign to force the Saxons to become Christian, ordered it to be felled and had a church built in its place. Panarctic cultures, including the Sámi (or Lapps) and many subarctic peoples across Siberia, venerated tall poles; these have been connected with the idea of a 'world axis' around which the world rotates. A shining nail secures its tip to the heavens, anchoring it to the Pole Star.

According to the Swedish archaeologist Anders Andrén, the three-pointed stone settings (arrangements of stones) often found in Scandinavian cemeteries may represent the three roots of the World Tree. Perhaps their position marks the place where an actual holy tree once stood or where a sacred pillar had been erected. Cremations often took place within the three-pointed setting, and sometimes there is evidence to show that the stone setting was the first structure at a site: thus it signified a central spot from which later burials radiated outwards. If Andrén's connection between the idea of the tree and the stone-pattern is correct, it gives us an important clue as to the significance of the tree in pre-Christian ritual. Below there is further discussion of the suggestive combination of tree, well and hall or temple at key Scandinavian cult sites.

## Yggdrasill in the end-times

When *ragna rök*, the end of the world, gets under way, Yggdrasill is deeply affected. It shudders and groans, reacting with just the same emotions that we would ascribe to the terrified humans who become caught up in the cosmic struggle between the gods, giants and monsters. But although the flames generated by Surtr, leader of the fire giants, are referred to as 'branches' ruin', this is a common kenning for fire, and the great tree is not said explicitly to succumb to the conflagration. And although no mention of the World Tree is made in *Völuspá* when the earth rises again from the ocean, in another eddic poem Óðinn learns from a wise giant that humankind will be regenerated after *ragna rök*. A woman and a man, named Líf and Lífþrasir ('Life' and 'Life-thruster'), are found after the fire is extinguished, sheltering in 'Hoddmímir's wood'. Mentioned nowhere else, this does not seem to be an actual forest. Rather, given the firm connection between the great ash tree and Mímir's well at its foot, where Óðinn's missing eye lies concealed, it seems very likely that this is Yggdrasill. For the survivors have been sustained by 'morning-dew', surely the rich, life-giving substance that the tree exudes. And thus the world begins over again, with a new generation of humans ready to inhabit its pristine spaces.

Lorenz Frølich, Líf
and Lífþrasir, from Karl
Gjellerup's *Den Ældre
Eddas Gudesange* (1895).

## Central places and cultic landscapes

The tree forms a central point around which the activities of the
gods are organized. In the poem *Hávamál* (Sayings of the High
One), when the speaker, most likely Óðinn, begins to recite arcane
knowledge – spells, runes and other kinds of wisdom – he claims
to be seated by Urðr's well. This suggests that the well has a ritual
purpose: it is a place where a religious specialist can impart vital
and mystical information. Every day Þórr and the other gods ride
to the tree, crossing the numerous rivers that flow around it in
order to sit there in judgment. Just like human magnates, they
deliberate on cases that come before them, decide on policy and,
increasingly frequently as divine history unrolls, assemble on
their 'thrones of power' to take counsel about developing crises:
the demands of the Vanir gods for a share of the sacrifices made
to them, the destruction of the protective wall that surrounds

their home, Ásgarðr, and other critical moments in the course of their story.

The combination of tree, well and hall recurs at important archaeological sites across Scandinavia. They signal the establishment of a so-called 'central place', a well-established political and religious site where people would gather to worship and sacrifice, but also to conduct the business of making laws, passing judgments and agreeing marriages, and to facilitate trade between different tribal groups. For example, at Helgö ('Sacred Island'), an island in Lake Mälaren near Stockholm, the 'central place' had a kind of terrace where a post was erected. Interestingly, excavations around this post revealed not only the expected sacrificial deposits of animal bones, but also several layers of clay. This suggests a particular ritual practice: the pouring over the post of 'shining loam', perhaps in imitation of the actions of the Norns. A three-pointed stone setting has also been excavated on this terrace area, possibly another representation of the World Tree, located at the island's sacred centre.

In the second half of the 11th century, the ecclesiastic Adam of Bremen composed an account of Uppsala (now known as Old Uppsala), the main cultic centre of Sweden. The country was not yet Christian, and thus Adam's account of what his informant told him is of enormous interest. Adam's description of the great temple at Uppsala has provoked much debate among modern historians. Some scholars have questioned whether the informant had in fact visited Uppsala at all, since the claim that it was ringed by mountains is strikingly inaccurate; others have suggested, however, that he might have been referring to the large Iron Age burial mounds of Old Uppsala, which are indeed prominent (although scarcely mountainous). Adam notes the existence of a huge temple, entirely covered in gold, that contained the statues of three gods: Þórr (placed in the centre), Óðinn and 'Frikko' (most likely Freyr), depicted with a huge phallus. Adam also notes:

Uppsala, from Olaus Magnus's *Historiae de gentibus septentrionalibus*
(History of the Northern Peoples, *c.* 1557); see also pl. III.

Near this temple stands a very large tree with wide-
spreading branches, always green in winter and summer.
What kind it is nobody knows. There is also a well at
which the pagans are accustomed to make their sacrifices,
and to plunge a live man into it. If he is not found, the
people's wish will be granted.

Adam goes on to describe the sacred grove, situated next to the
temple, where the bodies of male creatures – humans, horses
and dogs – are hanged over the course of a nine-day festival that
occurred every ninth year. By the final day, seventy-two sacrifices
would have been made. The bodies were left to hang in the trees
until they were consumed by birds and rats. The ritual seems to
have been compulsory for all Swedes to attend, and was accompanied by splendid feasts in the ceremonial hall. Many bones of
domestic animals have been found in the eastern mound at Old
Uppsala: among them, those of horses, oxen, pigs, dogs and cats.
The last midwinter sacrifice was held in 1084, after which the great
temple was burned down, bringing the ritual to a decisive end.

Alongside achieving victory in war, presiding over the continuing fertility of the land was key to being a successful early king.
A probably 10th-century Old Norse poem, *Ynglingatal* (Tally of the
Ynglings), tells of the legends of the earliest kings of Sweden, who
ruled in Uppsala. Imagined as the descendants of Freyr, many of
them met bizarre fates. One of the most powerfully realized death
scenes is that of Dómaldi, a king who had the misfortune to preside
over a series of poor harvests. The 'harvest-eager' Swedes 'carried
bloody weapons' after they sacrificed the king, says the poem.
While Dómaldi may be an obscure figure, an early 20th-century
painting of his sacrificial death was at the centre of a long-running
scandal. The great Swedish painter Carl Larsson was commissioned
to decorate some huge panels for the upper part of the staircase
in the National Museum in Stockholm. All but one of the panels
were used for a depiction of the great early modern Swedish king
Gustav Vasa, but Larsson chose a heroic subject from Norse myth
for the final panel. Entitled *Midvinterblot* (Midwinter Sacrifice; 1915,
see pl. XI), it illustrated the death of King Dómaldi. The striking
painting shows the king, naked except for a wolfskin cloak he is
shrugging from his shoulder, standing proudly, ready to accept
his fate. Behind him is a temple housing an image of Þórr, just
as in Adam of Bremen's description. A white-clad priest raises
a hammer, ready to smash the king's skull, a red-cloaked figure
holds a knife behind his back, and a group of celebrants sound
their *lurs,* the great, curving trumpets sometimes found in Iron
Age Scandinavian graves. Women dance ecstatically, while the
queen grovels in despair. The sacred tree stands to the temple's
left, a stately evergreen; a number of human and horse skulls are
visible among its boughs.

The work was so different from Larsson's usual subjects, which
were primarily idyllic domestic scenes featuring his large family,
that it provoked a good deal of criticism. The Swedish public
disliked the colour and style, particularly the use of gold, the

archaeological inexactitude (two distinctly Chinese lions flank the temple) and the heightened emotionality of the scene. Politically, too, there were strong objections to the theme of sacrifice and the king's unabashed nudity. The public outcry was highly reminiscent of, but much longer-lasting than, the near-riot that accompanied the almost contemporary reception of the first performance of the Russian composer Igor Stravinsky's *The Rite of Spring* in Paris in 1913 – and a similar primitivism is present in both works. The museum refused outright to buy the painting. Larsson died in 1919, and the furore was thought to have contributed to his death. It was not until 1992 that the institution finally acquired the painting, and in 1997 it was hung in its rightful place, where it remains today.

## Big Ash and Little Ash

Yggdrasill is not the only significant ash tree in Old Norse myth. Three of the gods, Óðinn, Hœnir and Lóðurr (a very obscure figure about whom we know almost nothing), were walking along the seashore one day when they found two pieces of driftwood. From these they created the first humans. The man is made from ash wood and is even given the name Askr, or 'Ash', while his female companion Embla has a name that may well mean 'Little Elm'. This connection between trees, humans and the sacred is deeply embedded in Norse mythic thinking. In the riddling style of skaldic poetry, kennings for men and women consistently play with this belief. A man can be denoted as 'the maple of the fire of the arm' (gold) or 'tree of the stallion of the foam' (ship); women are described as 'the young pine of ribbons' or 'the linen-oak'.

In *Hávamál* (Sayings of the High One), Óðinn imparts different kinds of wisdom to his audience. In one verse, celebrating generosity and the pleasure of receiving gifts, he tells how, along the road, he met two 'wooden men' to whom he gave his clothes; 'champions they thought themselves when they had clothing,' he adds. This comment suggests that wooden idols may have been

Embla depicted in a relief by Dagfin Werenskiold, Oslo City Hall (1950).

important in pre-Christian Norse religion. Some such figures are mentioned in the historical sagas, where they come to life and fight with Christians intent on preaching the new religion. People would bring them food as a sacrifice; the idols seemed to consume the offerings, but it is revealed that it is really the rats and mice, lurking in the back of the temple, who feast on the provisions. Such idols are soon overcome, destroyed by the missionaries who have been dispatched by the king for that express purpose. In one brief account, found at the very end of the saga of Ragnarr Loðbrók and his sons (see Chapter 8), we hear of a Dane called Ögmundr who lands on the Danish island of Sámsey (modern Samsø). While they are waiting for dinner to be prepared, Ögmundr and his men go into the forest to amuse themselves. There they find an 'ancient wooden man', forty ells high and all overgrown with moss. This neglected figure recites some verses in which he laments how once he used to 'rule over the settlements'. In those days, the sons of Ragnarr used to visit him in order to perform sacrifices that would ensure 'the deaths of men', but now, he says sadly, 'the clouds weep on him, and neither flesh nor clothes cover him'.

In pre-modern Scandinavia, particularly Sweden, farms would often have a 'guardian tree', a tree that symbolized the spirit of the place and that could be very old indeed. There is a good deal of evidence, too, for trees (the ash in particular) lending their names to farms and other settlements in the pre-Viking Age. And, in earlier periods, when bodies were not regularly cremated, a hollowed-out tree was often used as a coffin; such oak coffins were very common in Denmark in the Late Neolithic and Early Bronze Ages, perhaps with the idea of returning the dead person to their original substance. If so, that would suggest that the identification of humans with trees is very ancient indeed.

### The legendary Barnstokkr

There is one more significant tree in the Old Norse tradition: the great tree – variously an oak or an apple tree – known as Barnstokkr (Child-trunk) that grows up through the centre of the hall belonging to King Völsungr, a descendant of Óðinn. According to one legend, King Siggeirr of Gautland, in what is now southern Sweden, comes to wed Signý, Völsungr's only daughter and twin sister of the hero Sigmundr. During the wedding feast a mysterious stranger enters, grey-haired, one-eyed and with his hat drawn down low over his brow. He has a sword in his hand, which he plunges into the tree up to the hilt. He proclaims that whoever can draw the sword out of the tree may keep it – and it will be the best of swords. The man vanishes, and of course all the men in

41

Sigmund's sword in the tree, illustration by Johannes Gehrts from
Felix Dahn's *Walhall: Germanische Götter- und Heldensage* (1888).

the hall must now compete to pull out the sword. Only Sigmundr
proves capable of this feat; his new brother-in-law Siggeirr covets
the splendid weapon and offers him three times its weight in gold.
But Sigmundr refuses; if the sword had been meant for Siggeirr
it would have responded to his touch. This refusal sparks off a
long and complex vendetta between Siggeirr and his in-laws that
occupies the first half of *Völsunga saga* (The Saga of the Völsungs).

The sword appears also in the second opera of Richard Wagner's
*Ring* cycle, *Die Walküre*. Siegmund, as he is called here, grasps it
in dire need in the hall of Hunding, his enemy and his sister's
husband. Siegmund intends to use it against Hunding but, as we
will see later, Wotan (Óðinn) prevents him, even though he had

left the sword for his son to use in the quest to recover the Ring. The scene in which Óðinn plunges the sword into the tree is not represented in the opera, but in Melvin Burgess's remarkable retelling of the Sigmundr story, *Bloodtide* (1999; see Chapter 7), the feast that concludes the celebrations in honour of the wedding of Signy to Conor (Siggeirr) is held in the atrium of a ruined London skyscraper, built around a huge transparent lift-shaft in which the Volsons (Völsungs) habitually hang their sacrifices to the gods, particularly Odin. Just before the feast, a mysterious one-eyed man is captured, assumed to be a spy, tortured, and then hanged in the lift-shaft along with the other decaying sacrifices. At the climax of the feast, a huge iron girder is rammed against the shaft, which echoes and reverberates like a triumphal bell:

> One of the dead refused to stay still.
>
> It was the man with one eye. The body was still twisting his head this way and that, with its terrible smears of blood and its one dull eye. His arms seemed to have come loose from the bonds behind his back, and now he was lifting them into the air. He turned his head. Remarkable! Then suddenly he bent at the waist and reached up to seize the beam where his foot was nailed. ...
>
> Val said, 'It's nothing to do with me, man. Don't you see? It's the gods – the old gods coming back among us. You're seeing nothing less than Odin himself.'

The revivified figure walks out of the lift-shaft, produces a stone knife, 'an old, crude, ugly thing, with a stubby, crinkled blade', and 'with a sudden stab, he plunged the blade into the lift-glass'. And, sure enough, the blade cannot be withdrawn by Conor, nor anyone else; only Siggy, Signy's twin, who knows from the way the dead man had looked at him that the knife is meant for him, puts his hand to it: 'the knife and my hand together jumped back and

I held it high above my head'. The supernatural properties of this weapon, which can cut through any substance but cannot harm Siggy, its intended recipient, will turn out to be just as important in *Bloodtide* and its 2005 sequel, *Bloodsong*, as the sword that was plunged into Barnstokkr in *Völsunga saga* and its equivalent, Nothung, in Wagner's *Ring*.

### Yggdrasill as ecosystem

In modern reimaginings of Old Norse mythic material, Yggdrasill appears under several of the aspects discussed above. The great tree also symbolizes a well-functioning ecosystem, with birds, reptiles, beasts and people living on or near the tree and nourished by it. The gods order time by setting the sun and moon in their right places, and then set up forges, halls and temples, smithing civilization into existence – an innocent and peaceful first age during which they can sit on the green plains of Iðavellir and play at boardgames with golden pieces. Some dramatic and not-fully-understood intervention occurs to bring this phase to an end; three giant girls appear, and suddenly the gold has run short and the golden gaming pieces go missing – not to be seen again until after *ragna rök*. There is no clear understanding in the Norse sources that building habitations and forging luxury goods might entail environmental destruction. Yet medieval Icelanders knew at first hand how the habitats of their subarctic home had been irremediably altered by the first generations of settlers; trees were cut down for building timber, and the topsoil they anchored blew away. The incomers' goats nibbled away at new-growing saplings, and the forests, such as they had been, vanished until the great tree-planting initiatives of the 20th century finally replaced them. In modern imaginations, then, Yggdrasill figures nostalgically as a symbol of an unspoiled, well-functioning ecosystem.

In 2011 A. S. Byatt published her lyrical and dramatic meditation on the Old Norse myths, *Ragnarok: The End of the World*. The book

BAXTERS Patent Oil Printing 11 Northampton Square.

YGGDRASILL,

The Mundane Tree.

see p. 492.

Yggdrasill on the frontispiece of Thomas Percy's *Northern Antiquities* (1859 edition).

45

is framed by her autobiographical memories of first encountering the myths in childhood, in the form of *Asgard and the Gods*, the popular English translation of a German introduction to the myths and legends written in the 19th century by Dr Wilhelm Wägner. The 'thin child', as Byatt remembers herself, lives with her mother in an idyllic countryside home while her father, in her mind as bright and beautiful as the god Baldr, is away fighting in the war. He is, or so his daughter believes, no more likely to return than is Óðinn's lost son.

Before the inevitable end-times are unleashed, Byatt's account revels in the vividly described new-minted creation. It is a natural world not yet tainted or ruined by humans or their divine counterparts, and it is understood holistically as a complex, joyful interweaving of abundantly multifarious forms of life. There are endless lists of creatures scurrying and burrowing their way through the natural cycle: from insects and amphibians, congregating at the ponds in the hollows between the tree's branches, to the birds that sing among the leaves, and the eagle and hawk mentioned earlier. All these busy beasts that live on the World Tree 'scraped and scavenged, bored and gnawed, minced and mashed', but there is no suggestion that their appetites are destructive. The ministrations of the Norns – 'gardeners and guardians of the tree', who pour the life-giving water and the *aurr*, that shining mud, over it – maintain its vigour and endless fertility. 'So it decayed, or was diminished, from moment to moment. So it was always renewed,' Byatt writes.

Fecundity characterizes every part of the cosmos in this vision. Below the sea is Byatt's invented underwater counterpart to the World Tree: Rándrasill, the 'Steed of Rán' – Rán being the sea goddess who traditionally catches drowned men in her net. Rándrasill is a huge stand of bull kelp, growing as tall and as fertile underwater as the tree is on land. Among its fronds are the smallest of sea creatures, anemones, shrimp, sponges and starfish; larger fish, too, flick through the trailing tendrils of weed, and endless kinds of crab scuttle through this 'sea forest'. Sea otters, dolphins, whales, squid and every sort of fish live and thrive within the ecosystem. The roots of Rándrasill descend into an underwater mountain; here, at its foot, are 'vents and funnels, through which whistle steam, and spittings of molten stone from the hot centre of the earth'. And it is here, too, that Ægir, the sea god, and Rán sit, Ægir playing on the harp and Rán trawling with her net, hauling in beautiful things to plant in her underwater garden. As the end-times approach, however, Jörmungandr, the World Serpent, with her vast appetite, is seen hoovering her way through the northern oceans like some huge industrial trawler, devouring all the life in the sea and leaving it bleak and desolate: an ecological catastrophe that is already under way in our own world, Byatt implies.

The unspoilt, idyllic wartime countryside that could draw the 'thin child' away from her books is already gone; the rest, Byatt observes, will follow. Her book is a complex meditation on memory, the natural world and environmental collapse, communicated through her adult revisiting of the book that awakened and shaped a fundamentally pessimistic imagination and a strongly northern identity. At the end of the book, after *ragna rök*, the child's father returns from the war and moves the family back to their home in the town. Here he makes a new garden, digging out, planting and tending the neglected ground. But growing by the sill of the garden shed is a wild ash tree, a self-seeded sapling with branches that project patterns onto the child's bedroom ceiling by night. And, singing as he works, her father chops it down.

## Yggdrasill as a new cultic site

The World Tree appears as a site of sacrifice and revelation in Neil Gaiman's 2001 novel *American Gods* (also a television show that ran for three series). Mr Wednesday, a version of Óðinn, is one of the main figures in the novel, the leader of the old gods who arrived in North America along with the migrants who formerly believed in them. Wednesday has been there since the 9th century, predating even Leifr Eiríksson's expedition from Greenland (see Chapter 9). The old gods are opposed by the new gods – figures such as Media, Mr World and Technical Boy (who represents the power and fascination of technology). At a key point in the novel Mr Wednesday is murdered. The novel's protagonist, a man called Shadow Moon, is asked if he will observe the customary vigil, and Shadow consents, not quite understanding what this will entail. Along with some of his divine companions, Shadow brings the body to Ashtree Farm, where there is a remarkable tree, much like the one depicted on Wednesday's silver tie-pin.

> Shadow saw the tree. It was a silver-gray and it was higher than the farmhouse. It was the most beautiful tree Shadow had ever seen: spectral and yet utterly real and almost perfectly symmetrical. It also looked instantly familiar: he wondered if he had dreamed it, then realized that no, he had seen it before, or a representation of it.

Shadow has agreed to keep the nine-night vigil over Wednesday's body. Three sisters who dwell in the nearby farmhouse, revealed later to be the Norns, bind him to the tree, where he hangs, sliding into delirium and madness. Ratatosk the squirrel and the bird that roosts in the tree's crown keep him company; Ratatosk even brings him water in a walnut shell to drink. After some days Shadow senses that his body has become the tree itself, his limbs becoming branches, and he is able to draw up water to quench his thirst from its roots.

> Shadow in his madness was now so much more than the man on the tree. He was the tree, and he was the wind rattling the bare branches of the world tree; he was the gray sky and the tumbling clouds; he was Ratatosk the

squirrel running from the deepest roots to the highest branches; he was the mad-eyed hawk who sat on a broken branch at the top of the tree surveying the world; he was the worm in the heart of the tree.

During his ordeal Shadow is visited by his wife, Laura, who died near the beginning of the novel. She has been magically prevented from parting definitively from life and thus is a kind of revenant. As Shadow finally goes down into the world of death, Laura takes her dying husband's advice to ask the three women at the farmhouse near the World Tree for a drink from their well. 'The water of time, which comes from the spring of fate, Urd's well, is not the water of life. Not quite. It feeds the roots of the world tree, though. And there is no other water like it.' After draining a jug of the water, Laura temporarily regains more plausible signs of life. Mr Town, a henchman of the new gods, is sent by Mr World (of whom we'll hear more in Chapter 5) to cut a branch from the tree. Town hews off a stick and jabs it at the still-hanging body of Shadow, whose side begins to bleed – thus enacting the traditional Odinic double sacrifice of hanging and stabbing. Laura later delivers Town's stick to Mr World, for whom it symbolizes Óðinn's sacrificial spear, Gungnir. Mr World wants the stick or spear to hallow the coming battle between the old gods and the new. 'As the spear arcs over the battle, I'm going to shout, "I dedicate this battle to Odin",' he reveals. Once Laura grasps the weapon's significance, she uses it to slay Mr World, after which she can edge closer to a final form of death for herself.

Gaiman has an extensive knowledge of Old Norse myth, which he develops in ingenious and effective ways in the novel. The section that transposes the myths of sacrifice and rebirth – the tree, the well and the spear – forms one of the novel's emotional and imaginative climaxes. That the Odinic spear should be manufactured out of a branch of Yggdrasill is a detail that Gaiman takes from Wagner: in *Siegfried*, the third opera in the *Ring* cycle, Wotan (the Wagnerian version of Óðinn) relates how he shaped his spear's shaft from a bough of the sacred tree. The spear gives Wotan the power with which to rule the world; runes carved into its shaft express the laws that bind gods and men. In the previous opera, *Die Walküre* (*The Valkyrie*), Wotan had shattered Nothung, Siegmund's invincible sword, with the spear, bringing about his death. Siegfried has reforged his father's sword, and it is now his turn to confront Wotan. Nothung splinters the spear-shaft, and the god disappears. Siegfried's defiance signals the coming end of the reign of the gods: *Götterdämmerung*.

Indeed, we learn in the Prologue to the final opera in the cycle that Wotan's action in hacking off that bough, even before the history related in the *Ring* had properly got under way, caused Yggdrasill, the World Ash, gradually to wither. The imposition of autocratic divine rules that bind together gods and men made a disastrous breach in nature; the tree is in decline, and the holy well at its roots has dried up. The Norns can no longer spin their ropes of fate that determine the future within this degraded landscape. They have removed themselves elsewhere and now work at a spot near the cave where Brünnhilde the Valkyrie and her beloved, the hero Siegfried, are dwelling: at this point in the cycle they seem to represent the best hopes for the future. In anticipation of the coming end, Wotan has ordered the Einherjar, the heroes who inhabit Valhalla with him (see Chapter 2), to chop the tree down and to pile the logs high around his hall, ready for the final conflagration. For, with the destruction of the spear, so the Norns report, 'the contracts of sacred submission lie in ruins'; the bonds between gods and men are shattered, and from henceforth humans will make their own fates in the world, for good or ill.

Anselm Kiefer, *Yggdrasil* (*c.* 1980).

Yggdrasill, then, is a complex symbol at the heart of the Old Norse mythological vision of the cosmos. It links together all the different worlds, while Urðr's well, lying beneath it, gives mystical access to past, present and future through its association with the Norns. Thus the tree and its associated features encapsulate concepts of time and space. The tree nurtures and sustains life, but it is not immune from suffering nor from the entropic effects of time. It marks the centre of the universe, the core from which the gods rule, consult each other and find wisdom; there, too, fate is shaped and prophecies pronounced. Its substance is also the matter from which humans are shaped; its protecting branches will shelter those last survivors who will be parents to humanity in the regenerated world after *ragna rök*. The root system that branches deep down and through the worlds of gods, elves, humans and the dead syphons up many kinds of wisdom; knowledge of life and death, time and memory run in its sap and can be imparted to those brave enough to sacrifice themselves upon it. In its totality, Yggdrasill symbolizes the natural world existing in a state of harmony that nevertheless cannot be taken for granted: a symbiotic system that may – or may not – withstand all the depredations that humanity inflicts upon it.

# CHAPTER 2

# The Valhöll Complex

## THE MYTH OF UNDYING FAME

### The hall roofed with shields

Óðinn is feeling self-assertive. There are 540 doors in his superlative hall, the magnificent Valhöll, he boasts, and 800 mortal warriors will march out through every single one when the time comes to fight the Wolf at *ragna rök*. The mighty hall gleams with gold; the building has spear-shafts for rafters and its roof tiles are shields. An eagle hovers over it, and 'a wolf hangs west of the door' – hanged, perhaps, as a sacrifice to ward off the time when the greatest Wolf of all will attack. Valhöll is situated in a territory called Glaðsheimr (Glad-home), and it is Óðinn's personal domain (see pl. XIV). Here the Einherjar, the heroic dead who have fallen in battle, come post mortem to spend their days in warrior bliss. They fight all day; at night they feast on pork provided by the cook Andhrímnir, who boils up the boar Sæhrímnir in his great kettle. Those who have fallen in the fighting are revivified every day, as is the boar who provides their food. Óðinn himself drinks wine in his high seat and tosses titbits to his two wolves, Geri and Freki (or 'Greedy' and 'Ravener'), whom he keeps by his side as other lords keep hounds. His two ravens, Huginn and Muninn, whose names mean 'Thought' and 'Memory', perch on the pillars of his high seat; they have returned from their daily flight across the world, bringing the All-Father the information he needs. They are the inspiration for George R. R. Martin's use of ravens as message-carriers in his *Song of Ice and Fire* novels and the HBO television programme *Game of Thrones*. (There is more on the ravens in Chapter 3.)

Óðinn's claims about his hall are made in a poem called *Grímnismál* (Grímnir's Sayings). He has come to the hall of King Geirrøðr, disguised as a wanderer and calling himself Grímnir ('Masked One'). He refuses to speak and so has been placed between two fires on the hall floor, without food or drink; there he has sat for eight nights. But on the ninth, the king's son, Agnarr, brings him a horn of drink, and at last the stranger begins to speak. He commences by listing the many splendid halls of the Æsir and Vanir, the two distinct groups of Norse gods – a catalogue that culminates in his description of Valhöll. Elsewhere, particularly in Snorri's *Edda*, we learn more about this establishment. Valkyries, the divine women who ride out over battlefields to choose who will live and who will die, are found there; they serve the drink and arrange the tables and serving vessels. The Einherjar drink mead drawn from the udders of that notable goat Heiðrún, whom we met in Chapter 1. She stands on the hall roof, browsing the leaves of Yggdrasill, alongside the hart Eikþyrnir, from whose antlers fall the waters that flow into the well Hvergelmir and give rise to the many rivers of the Other World.

Valhöll is the home of the elite dead: women, those who die in their beds of illness or old age and, presumably, children go down to the hall of Hel situated in Niflheim ('Mist-world'). In the Norse sources, if not in Francesca Simon's treatment of it in the opera *The Monstrous Child* (2009; see Chapter 5), Hel's realm seems a congenial enough final destination, though it is somewhat disgraceful for a nobleman to end up there rather than with his peers in Valhöll. Baldr, whose death, sustained when a mistletoe dart is thrown at him in a divine game, is Valhöll's chief missing person (as we will see in Chapter 10). Kings, earls and heroes can all hope for admission to Óðinn's hall of fame. In two sagas we hear how one Swedish hero, Hjálmarr – who, together with his sworn brother Örvar ('Arrow')-Oddr, has challenged a band of Viking champions, indeed notorious berserkers, to meet in combat on the Danish island of Sámsey (Samsø) – starts to feel some misgivings when he lays eyes on the ferocious band. Angantýr and his eleven brothers have disembarked and set about slaying the sworn brothers' crew members. 'We'll be lodging with Óðinn tonight,' says Hjálmarr, gloomily – and he is right about his own destination, even if Örvar-Oddr survives the battle and avenges him.

Other heroes display highly equivocal feelings when they arrive in Valhöll. In two memorial poems – one for the famous King Eiríkr 'Bloodaxe' and one for Hákon, the foster son of King Athelstan of England – the heroes are hailed enthusiastically as they approach Valhöll. In *Eiríksmál* (Eiríkr's Poem), Óðinn dreams that a hero is on the way to the hall. He awakens the Einherjar and tells them to prepare by strewing the benches with straw and rinsing out the drinking cups, while the Valkyries should get the wine ready. Bragi, the god of poetry, notes that the hall planks are creaking so loudly it sounds as if Baldr is coming, but he is briskly told not to talk nonsense: it is in fact the mighty Eiríkr. Two heroes – Sigmundr, father of Sigurðr the Dragon-Slayer, and his son Sinfjötli – are dispatched to offer a welcome. Bragi is still curious: why did Óðinn allow this great warrior to suffer defeat? 'Because it cannot be known for certain when the grey wolf will attack the homes of the gods,' replies Óðinn, darkly. In *Hákonarmál* (Hákon's Poem), Óðinn sends two Valkyries to fetch King Hákon, and by verse 9 it is clear that the king's defeat has become inevitable: 'The army was not in good spirits and had to head to Valhöll.' Hákon remonstrates with Spear-Skögul, one of the Valkyries: 'Why did you decide it thus, though we were worthy of victory?' 'Well,' responds the Valkyrie, giving good news to temper the bad, 'you held the field and your enemies fled.' Nevertheless, he must now ride with them to the gods' abode, where the heroes Hermóðr and Bragi himself are sent to welcome him. Hákon, though, is still not happy and doubts Óðinn's goodwill. Bragi consoles him with the promise of warm friendship from the Einherjar and the ale of the gods, not to mention reunion with eight of his brothers, already dead. Hákon is reluctant to put down his weapons and resolves to keep them close to hand, just in case. The poet ends by noting that the end of the world will come and the wolf Fenrir run free before another prince of his stature is born.

Valhöll, then, represents a striking heroic male fantasy of the good life after death. It is telling that a militarized culture should see no merit in finally escaping from violence and bloodshed and living in peace: no finer existence beyond one of male camaraderie, drinking, eating meat and fighting can be envisaged. Humans create their vision of heaven as a glorified and endless version of what they value most in everyday existence, so the fantasy that the afterlife entails joining an elite retinue in a well-appointed hall – with a guarantee that you will not die a second time and that lovely women will bring you as much drink as you like – is bound to appeal. So, too, is the idea that once in Valhöll you can lord it over your defeated enemies. According to the second eddic poem named after Helgi Hundingsbani ('Slayer of Hundingr'), when that hero arrives in the hall, Óðinn appoints him to rule jointly over the Einherjar with him. Helgi seizes the opportunity to humiliate his enemy, Hundingr (who, admittedly, had killed his father): 'Hundingr, you shall fetch the foot bath / for every man and kindle the fire / tie up the dogs, watch the horses / give the pigs slops before you go to sleep.' This is degrading work normally performed only by slaves, and not at all what Hundingr should merit as a hero in his own right.

## Later versions of Valhöll

The concept of Valhöll as a place of eternal glory became popular in 19th-century Germany as the idea that Germany and Scandinavia shared an ancient culture and pantheon gained traction. These arguments were put forward most persuasively in Jacob Grimm's highly influential study *Deutsche Mythologie*, first published in 1835. (The fourth edition, now in three volumes, was translated into English as *Teutonic Mythology* in the 1880s.) The arguments that contribute to Grimm's theories, as well as his own work, were critical in catalysing two remarkable 19th-century German cultural achievements.

The national memorial hall of Walhalla stands in Bavaria, southern Germany, high on the banks of the Danube. Walhalla was the brainchild of Crown Prince Ludwig of Bavaria. After the formation of the German Confederation in 1815, he decided that a pan-Germanic shrine, where the whole culture's heroes would be memorialized and celebrated, would be conducive to the larger project of German unification. When Ludwig became king, construction commenced, overseen by the architect Leo von Klenze. The edifice was built between 1830 and 1842 and is neoclassical in style, resembling a Greek temple. It contains a large number of plaques and busts commemorating distinguished historical figures from 'Greater Germany': in effect, from any Germanic nation, including Scandinavia, the Netherlands, England (Alfred the Great is there, and the Venerable Bede) and Switzerland. The earliest hero to be featured is Arminius, who defeated the Romans at the Battle of the Teutoburg Forest in 9 CE and whose victory is depicted on the building's northern pediment.

Other notable busts include the reformer Martin Luther, the Polish astronomer Copernicus, the poets Johann Wolfgang von Goethe and Heinrich Heine, and composers such as Mozart, Brahms, Beethoven and Brückner. Only three women's busts had been placed in Walhalla up until 1945: all of them were crowned queens or empresses. New figures are still being added: Albert Einstein, the artist Käthe Kollwitz and the anti-Nazi resistance heroine Sophie Scholl are among the more recent accessions. Private persons or societies can nominate new candidates to the Bavarian Academy of Science, usually for excellence in the fields of science or art, or for extraordinary merit in humanitarian activities. Once the nomination has been approved, the nominators pay for the new bust or plaque to be made and installed.

Richard Wagner was admitted to the Walhalla pantheon in 1913. His accession was fitting indeed, for the construction of Óðinn's (or, rather, Wotan's) palace is central to the action of *Das Rheingold* (*The Rhinegold*), the first opera in Wagner's *Ring* cycle. At the start of Scene ii of the opera, Wotan finds himself in a fix. He has commissioned two giant brothers, Fafner and Fasolt, to build a splendid new palace for himself and the other gods, and now the work is finished: 'Strong and beautiful it looks, that splendid, holy building,' he exults. But there is a high price to be paid: it was agreed that the goddess Freia (Freyja) would be given to the brothers. Wotan reneges on the deal; the brothers shall not have

Walhalla memorial, Donaustauf, Germany (1830–42).

The giants kidnap Freia, illustration by Arthur Rackham
from *The Rhinegold & The Valkyrie* (1910).

her after all, and he hopes that Loge (Loki) will find some way of
ransoming her. Loge appears, bearing news of the Rhinegold, the
treasure guarded by the three Rhinemaidens. This has now come
into the hands of Alberich the Nibelung, who has forged from
it a ring of power that will allow him to rule the world. Wotan
covets the Ring, and the two giant builders reluctantly agree that
they will hand Freia back if they are given the hoard, provided it
is substantial enough to conceal Freia's graceful form.

By the end of the opera, the hoard is indeed in the possession
of the two giants. The heaped-up treasure hides all of Freia: her
lovely eyes alone can be seen through a gap. The love-struck Fasolt
is quite ready to leave the gold and take the woman, for Wotan is
disinclined to hand over the Ring to close up the crevice. Finally,
Wotan assents to giving it up: the goddess Erda (Earth) has warned

him that the Ring is accursed. And in truth, as soon as the giants have the treasure, Fasolt is murdered by his brother, who makes off with all the loot and turns himself into a dragon to guard his hoard from all comers. The gods are aghast at the speed with which the curse takes effect, but as Donner (Þórr) swings his huge hammer, clouds and mists disperse, and the glorious palace lies clear ahead on the other side of the rainbow bridge. The gods process into their new home in stately fashion; Wotan grandly pronounces the fortress's name as they do so: it shall be known as 'Walhall', he proclaims.

## Building the fortress

Wagner drew upon two distinct myths for the plot of *Das Rheingold*. One tells the story of how the gods stole the gold to ransom themselves from the consequences of killing a shape-changing otter (we'll examine this in Chapter 7). The other is the 'Tale of the Master Builder', related in Snorri's *Edda*. In this story, the walls of Ásgarðr, the gods' central territory, have been destroyed in their war with the Vanir, the group of gods that includes Freyr, Freyja and their father, Njörðr. These gods were later arrivals in the territories of the Æsir; their demand for a share of the sacrifices caused a war that raged until a truce was agreed and hostages exchanged. The three above-named gods came to live among the Æsir, while Mímir and Hœnir went (temporarily) to live in Vanaheim, the home of the Vanir. A master builder appears and promises to build impregnable fortifications in only three half-years, in exchange for the sun, the moon and Freyja. On Loki's advice, the gods conclude the bargain, negotiating revised conditions: that the project should take only one winter, and that the builder must work alone. The master builder agrees; he will undertake the work single-handed, just with the help of his horse. To the gods' consternation the walls rise rapidly, for the stallion can cart huge amounts of stone. When summer is almost upon them, it becomes evident that they will have to forfeit the goddess of love and beauty – and the heavenly bodies too. The gods all roundly blame Loki and demand that he find a way out. Loki knows that the giant's stallion is key to the construction work, so he changes himself into a mare and entices the stallion away, to his master's fury. Consequently, the walls are not completed quite on time, and the master builder flies into a giant rage. Thereupon, despite all the oaths previously given, Þórr smashes him to pieces with his hammer, and Freyja remains with the gods. (We will meet the eight-legged outcome of Loki's tryst with the stallion in Chapter 5.) Interestingly, the story of the master builder is a well-known international folk-tale, one that often involves the devil in disguise undertaking an unfeasible-sounding construction project. However, tricking the devil – himself the original trickster – does not have the same moral implications as the gods swindling and killing a craftsman just because he has concealed the fact that he is a giant.

This act of colossal bad faith, the sundering of solemnly sworn oaths, is highly significant, both in the mythological world and for the plot of Wagner's *Ring*. Although the gods and the giants seem already to be opposed to one another (probably the result of Óðinn and his brothers having shaped the cosmos from the corpse of the murdered giant Ymir), that hostility now seems to intensify. The giants step up their attempts to secure possession of Freyja, or else to kidnap Iðunn, the goddess who keeps the gods' apples of eternal youth. The swearing and keeping of oaths – or finding ingenious ways to circumvent them – is a powerful theme within the Norse myth system, just as it is in human cultures, particularly those where social interactions depend on men and women giving their word rather than signing written contracts. For the Norse gods, this failure resonates through mythic history. Óðinn's cavalier way with oaths allows him to steal from the giants the sacred mead that inspires men and gods to create poetry; he promises his love to its guardian, Gunnlöð, who allows him three drafts of it in exchange. But Óðinn swallows it all and flies away in bird form. 'How can his word be trusted?' asks the poet who tells the tale. Óðinn's wife, Frigg, manages to persuade all things to swear not to harm their son, Baldr, except that, fatally, she is careless with regard to the mistletoe. This early evidence for Loki's changeableness, and his willingness to connive and betray, as Óðinn also knows, foreshadows his role at *ragna rök*.

Within the *Ring* cycle Wotan continues to be obsessed by the loss of the Ring. He fathers the hero Siegmund who, so Wotan hopes, will kill Fafner and so recover it; the giant now broods over the Rhinegold hoard in dragon form. This feat must be accomplished without direct divine help, for that would constitute further oath-breaking on Wotan's part. After Siegmund commits both incest and adultery with his sister, Sieglinde, he has clearly contravened the sacred oaths of marriage. Wotan's wife, Fricka, insists – for she is the goddess of marriage – that her husband should uphold the moral laws he has established and withdraw his patronage from his son. Wotan concedes the logic of his wife's position: laws must be upheld. Thus he shatters Siegmund's magic sword Nothung with his divine spear, Gungnir, as we saw in the last chapter, and Siegmund falls to his enemy, Hunding, Sieglinde's husband – that same figure ordered to feed the pigs in Valhöll.

In his last conversation with the Valkyrie Brünnhilde, Siegmund at first declares himself willing to follow her to the glory that awaits him, there to be reunited with his father and to be greeted by the other heroes. But when the Valkyrie is forced to admit that Sieglinde will not be there in Walhall – partly because she must remain alive to give birth to the son she is carrying, but also because there is no place in Walhall for women – he refuses to obey her summons. Brünnhilde is deeply moved by his love for his sister-wife and resolves to disobey Wotan's instructions – a decision that fails to save Siegmund and leads to her own loss of immortality, explored further below.

The Midland Grand Hotel, Euston Road, London (photograph *c.* 1890).

What might a modern Valhalla look like? If there were a place where the divine world and the human world touch – where those Norse gods, the ones 'who have fallen on hard times' and who linger out their superannuated lives in the British present, might find themselves feasting once again in the presence of the Einherjar – it would have to be grand indeed. At the climax of Douglas Adams's comic fantasy detective novel *The Long Dark Tea-Time of the Soul* (1988), Odin approaches his domain:

> Beneath the sky ranged a vast assortment of wild turrets, gnarled spires and pinnacles which prodded at it ... High in the flickering darkness, silent figures stood guard behind long shields, dragons crouched gaping at the foul sky as Odin, father of the Gods of Asgard, approached the great iron portals through which led to his domain and on into the vaulted halls of Valhalla.

This is, as we soon come to realize, the faded and unloved Midland Grand Hotel in London, which had also come down in the world and was being used as an office block at the time Adams was writing. (Now fully restored, the hotel's splendid, red-brick High Gothic frontage is once more a worthy portal to St Pancras Station, which lies behind it.) The novel's hero, the detective Dirk Gently, admires both the hotel's scale and its architecture: 'a space this size would make a good feasting hall for gods and dead heroes ... the empty Midland Grand Hotel would be almost worth moving the shebang from Norway for'. Once Gently has made his way onto the station concourse, he discovers that the transformation is complete. This is indeed Valhalla, roofed with shields, where the nightly feasting is in full swing:

> The table he was crouched behind was one of countless slabs of oak on trestles that stretched away in every direction, laden with steaming hunks of dead animals, huge breads, great iron beakers slopping with wine and candles like wax anthills. Massive sweaty figures seethed around them, on them, eating, drinking, fighting over the food, fighting in the food, fighting with the food.

Adams's vision is a comic one. Valhalla is a place of frenzied excess where eagles wheel through the rafters and an axe whistles past Gently's ear. Thor comes to the hotel to confront Odin about recent events, and from hearing their exchange Gently is able to solve his case. He discovers the truth about his client's death and that Odin has made a reprehensible deal with a lawyer and an advertising executive in exchange for a comfortable berth in a luxury care home, where the sheets are of crisp Irish linen. Valhalla fades back into the 'immense, dark and labyrinthine' hotel, and the dishevelled, drunken Einherjar straggle out into the London night, where they vanish unobtrusively among the city's other inhabitants.

## The Valkyries

The Einherjar remain garrisoned in Valhöll, endlessly practising their military skills in preparation for *ragna rök*. The women of Valhöll, the Valkyries, are in contrast much more active: they busy themselves in the human world. As we saw above, Óðinn dispatches them to earthly battlefields to determine who shall win victory and who shall be borne back to Valhöll (see pl. VIII). In some respects, the Valkyries perform the god's will – and they are sometimes called his 'wish-girls'. In other stories, though, Óðinn leaves it up to each Valkyrie herself to determine who shall live and who shall die. In one poem, *Hrafnsmál* (The Raven's Speech), a talkative raven and a Valkyrie meet before a battle. The Valkyrie is called 'the white, bright-haired girl'; the poet adds that 'the aggressive maid considered herself wise as she did not care for men'. She asks the raven where he has come from, with flesh still in his claws and the stink of carrion issuing from his beak. He explains that, ever since he hatched from the egg, he has followed Haraldr Fairhair, the king credited with unifying Norway. The victorious king has fed him – and the other beasts of battle, wolves and eagles – well, glutting them with the corpses of his enemies.

Valkyries are not squeamish; they take a clear-eyed view of the human death and suffering that they themselves bring about. In one vivid poem, a man called Dörruðr notices twelve women riding towards a little hut somewhere in Caithness in northern Scotland. The women disappear inside; when Dörruðr peers through the window he sees that they have set up a loom and are weaving. The loom, whose frame is constructed of spear-shafts, is strung with the guts of men; human heads weight the ends of the warp threads while a sword is used as a beater. The women sing an ominous work song as they weave, invoking the names of many other Valkyries and promising victory to the 'young king'. When the weaving is done, they seize the fabric and tear it into pieces; each woman keeps a fragment, and they ride away, six southwards and six to the north. This sinister scene presages the great Battle of Clontarf, which took place in Ireland on Good Friday in 1014. This poem, *Darraðarljóð* (Dörruðr's Song), was one of the earliest Norse poems to be translated into English. The new Gothic tendency in art and literature, noted in the Introduction, was just beginning to gain momentum when the poet Thomas Gray composed a version of the poem. He called it 'The Fatal Sisters', and it was published in 1768. Gray revels in the gory details:

> See the grisly texture grow,
> ('Tis of human entrails made,)
> And the weights that play below,
> Each a gasping warrior's head.
> Shafts for shuttles, dipt in gore,
> Shoot the trembling cords along.
> Sword, that once a monarch bore,
> Keep the tissue close and strong.

William Blake made a series of illustrative watercolours for the poem in 1797–98, depicting the sisters as looking rather demure before they seize the sword that beats flat the fibres and set about their dreadful task. Another drawing clearly shows the dangling human heads; finally, the sisters, grim-faced, are seen mounted on horseback and preparing to ride to battle, clutching the fragments that determine who shall live and who die that day.

*Darraðarljóð* continues to inspire the dramatic imagination. Lines from the poem can be heard being chanted in a battle scene in a key episode of the Canadian History Channel's hit television show *Vikings* ('Brothers' War'), in which the brothers Ragnar and Rollo find themselves ranged on opposing sides in a conflict between King Horik and Jarl Borg. The battle soundtrack is produced by Trevor Morris; the women's baleful words are chanted and sung by the Norwegian musician Einar Selvik, of the band Wardruna, who also plays the fiddle as an accompaniment. This episode marks the beginning of Selvik's long musical involvement with the series, and his conception of what Viking music might have sounded like informs the soundscapes of the remainder of the show. Selvik also composed original songs for the videogame *Assassin's Creed: Valhalla*. The game is discussed in Chapter 6, while *Vikings* is central to the account of Ragnarr Loðbrók in Chapter 8.

### Death as female

Valkyries tend not to have any particular emotional or erotic interest in their prey (Brynhildr/Brünnhilde is an important exception; see below). In *Hákonarmál*, Spear-Skögul leans dispassionately on her spear in her conversation with the aggrieved Hákon and tells him that that's just how things are. Other supernatural female figures take a livelier interest in kings and heroes, however. In the early Norse poem *Ynglingatal* (Tally of the Ynglings), in which we learned of the sacrifice of King Dómaldi (see Chapter 1), a number of other Norse rulers meet their bizarre ends through the actions of female death-spirits. One is trampled by a *mara*, the night demon that crushes men in their sleep; the goddess Hel gathers a second

Stephan Sinding, *Valkyrie*, Copenhagen (1908).

into her embrace; a third is on his way to sacrifice to the *dísir* (who are probably collective female ancestor-spirits) when his horse stumbles and he dashes his head against a stone and dies. In other eddic poems, troll-women and the *dísir* are blamed when men take rash decisions to kill an innocent person. That death should be so consistently imagined as female makes sense in a warrior culture where men have to accept the idea that they could die violently at any moment. Just as a man's mother gives him life, nurtures him and cares for him in his early days, the warrior's last hours or minutes are imagined as a willing surrender to the loving embrace of a woman who may do what she will with his body as she carries him off to the next world: death and sex are powerfully intertwined.

## Brünnhilde and her sisters

Wagner's Valkyries are by a long way the most famous of all modern reimaginings of the Old Norse figures. They are Wotan's daughters by Erda and, like their earlier counterparts, they ride to battle to ensure defeat or victory for the warriors involved, their war cry 'Hojotoho! Hojotoho! Heiaha!' pealing out across the mountain tops where they assemble. The *Ring* cycle Valkyries are obedient daughters, ready to fulfil Wotan's commands, and Brünnhilde is both their leader and her father's favourite. Following Wotan's volte-face over Siegmund's fate, Brünnhilde defies her father by refusing to grant victory to Hunding. Once the god has shattered Nothung mid-battle and Siegmund is dead, Wotan sets off to punish Brünnhilde. He decrees that she must lose her divine nature and marry a mortal. All her sisters protest in horror at this fate. Brünnhilde bargains for her future: if she must wed, her husband cannot be just the first man who happens to come along. She will sleep on a mountain top surrounded by a wall of flame until the bravest of all heroes finds her. In a climactic emotional scene, Wotan kisses away his beloved daughter's divine nature and departs, summoning the fire god Loge to kindle the protective flames.

Gaston Bussière, *Brunnhild* (1899).

Illustration by Emil Doepler, from *Walhall, die Götterwelt der Germanen* (c. 1905).

Brünnhilde is a gruelling role to sing, both in *Die Walküre* and in *Götterdämmerung*, the final opera of the cycle. As we shall see in Chapters 7 and 10, Brünnhilde is the true hero of the *Ring* cycle. She is fearless and sympathetic, moved by the love and courage of Siegmund and Sieglinde, and she dares to defy her father, whose will she knows better than he does. Following the fateful combat, she rescues Sieglinde and bears her away to safety (along with the fragments of Nothung). These actions safeguard the unborn Siegfried who, unbeknownst to Brünnhilde or Wotan, will recover the Ring and keep it out of the hands of the evil Alberich, who had forged it from the Rhinegold. The farewell that Wotan takes of his dearly loved daughter is extraordinarily moving, yet, as ever in the *Ring* cycle, Wotan's immediate desires are frustrated by larger moral imperatives: her disobedience must be punished.

At the beginning of Act III of *Die Walküre*, Brünnhilde's Valkyrie sisters, fresh from battle, assemble on the mountain tops. As they

Amalie Materna as Brünnhilde in Richard
Wagner's *Der Ring des Nibelungen* (1876).

put their horses to graze, they identify the corpses who hang
over their saddle-bows, laugh about how their steeds greedily
jostle one another and wonder why Brünnhilde should be missing; they dare not return to Walhall with their slain heroes until
she is with them. The music that expresses the glorious energy
of their ride, with their wild and jubilant war song, is the most
recognizable tune from the whole opera cycle. 'The Ride of the
Valkyries' became particularly famous in the popular imagination
when it was used in the 1979 Vietnam War film *Apocalypse Now*,
directed by Francis Ford Coppola. Near the beginning of the film,
Captain Willard (Martin Sheen) is given a clandestine mission:
to sail up the River Nung into Cambodia to find Colonel Kurtz

(Marlon Brando). Kurtz has gone rogue, possibly mad, and must be 'terminated with extreme prejudice'. First, however, Willard and his men have to navigate the river mouth, held by the Viet Cong, in order to start their voyage. Colonel Kilgore (Robert Duvall), who commands a helicopter-borne air assault unit, agrees to help. The flamboyant Kilgore mounts a raid to clear out the Viet Cong forces. In an unforgettable sequence, the tense soldiers check their weapons, then the helicopters fly in low in tight formation over the turquoise sea as the sun rises behind them. 'Put on Psy-War-Ops and make it loud,' orders Kilgore; the men grin at one another as speakers strapped to the outside of the machines begin to blare out 'The Ride of the Valkyries'. The soundtrack abruptly cuts out as the scene switches to the village centre, where people are quietly going about their early morning business. Dogs bark

The Valkyries, illustration by Arthur Rackham from
*The Rhinegold & The Valkyrie* (1910).

and children's voices are heard. A Viet Cong soldier runs shouting into the marketplace as an alarm bell rings – and suddenly the music is heard above the sound of the rotor blades. The Vietnamese flee in panic as aerial death swoops in from above; the squadron strafes them with machine-gun fire and rains down napalm until the village is completely destroyed. The squadron lands safely on the beach and the death-dealing helicopter Valkyries come to rest among the carnage. Willard's expedition can now get under way.

## Shield-maidens and warrior women

The women who keep the warrior dead company in Valhöll have never been ordinary mortal women. But there is another kind of Valkyrie who is human and as a result thoroughly enmeshed in the complexities of belonging to a family. In the Norse sources, these women are sometimes called 'shield-maidens'. Although they seem to have freely chosen the Valkyrie life for themselves, they nevertheless remain subject to their fathers' or brothers' patriarchal control – and it is these male kinfolk who decide when it is time for the shield-maiden to get married and settle down, and whom she shall wed. One such girl, Sigrún, and her Valkyrie companions appear to the hero Helgi in *Helgakviða Hundingsbana* I (The First Poem of Helgi Hundingsbani) as he and his men are encamped on a beach after a raid: 'Byrnies drenched in blood and beams blazing from their spears'. Sigrún announces that she loves Helgi, that she had a hand in his recent victory and that her family want to marry her to a king whom she despises. Helgi must go into battle against him if they are to be together. Helgi and his men sail off to attack Sigrún's intended husband. Victory is theirs, aided by the Valkyries, but in the heat of the battle not only the spurned fiancé, but also Sigrún's father and brothers, fighting alongside him, are killed. One brother, Dagr, alone survives; oaths of reconciliation are sworn, and Helgi and Sigrún are wed. But trouble lies in store: abetted by Óðinn, Dagr murders his brother-in-law

Figurine from Hårby in
Denmark possibly representing
a Valkyrie (? 9th century).

and Sigrún dies of grief, though not before spending a splendidly
Gothic night with her dead husband in his burial mound.

The shield-maidens ride through the air like other Valkyries but
do not fight directly – rather, they magically influence the course
of battle. A limited number of other women in heroic poetry
and sagas do captain ships, take up swords and shields, and lead
Viking warbands, until the time comes when they have to marry
and resume women's clothing and occupations, such as textile
manufacture, housekeeping and childbearing. It is this kind of
human shield-maiden that has captured the modern imagination.
The television show *Vikings*, which ran from 2013 to 2020 across
six seasons, featured several shield-maidens. The most notable of
these is Lagertha (played by Katheryn Winnick), the first wife of the
protagonist, Ragnar. She not only fights to defend herself and her
daughter from rapists, but persuades Ragnar to let her accompany

him on an expedition to England. Later she will rule over the earldom of Kattegat in her own right, fight alongside her husband and
the other Vikings when they besiege Paris, cede her earldom to
her son, and travel to England, where she flirts shamelessly with
Ecbert, the king of Wessex. Eventually she is killed by her stepson,
more or less by accident. It is noteworthy that Lagertha is quite
clear in her own mind that she is destined for Valhöll after death;
nor does she imagine that there she will be co-opted into serving
horns of mead and ale to her male peers. Lagertha trains some
of the show's other key shield-maidens: among these, Astrid has
the most prominent storyline. For a while she is both Lagertha's
second-in-command and lover, but then she is kidnapped by Harald
Finehair, king of Norway, and forced to become his queen. Astrid
is determined to resist this domesticated future, for the only life
she wants to live is as shield-maiden at Lagertha's side. Torvi also
holds the rank of Lagertha's second-in-command for a while; she
has a series of relationships with Ragnar's sons and survives to
the end of the narrative.

The idea that historical Viking Age women might have fought
side by side with men gained some traction when, in 2017, a
research paper was published that re-evaluated archaeological
evidence from a grave at Birka, a settlement on the Swedish island
of Björkö in Lake Mälaren. The grave, known as Bj. 581, contained
a skeleton; the remains of two horses, one of which was bridled
ready to ride; a good number of weapons; and gaming pieces and
a gaming board placed on the dead person's lap. The individual
was unusually dressed, in clothing that is more common on the
Eurasian steppes. The grave itself was an underground wooden
chamber-grave, located on the western edge of the settlement,
and originally marked with a boulder. The burial was particularly
remarkable for the number of weapons it contained – a sword,
an axe, lances, fighting knives, shields and arrows – as well as the
gaming board and pieces. When the grave was first excavated in

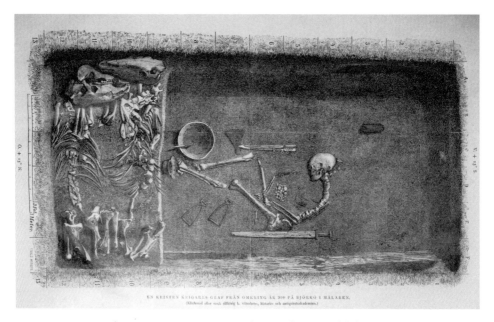

The Viking-era grave Bj. 581 in Birka, Sweden, as published in 1889.

the late 19th century, it was naturally assumed that the body was that of a high-status warrior, and therefore male. But in 2017 the bones were subjected to new investigation: genome sequencing and investigation of mitochondrial DNA proved that the dead person had been biologically female. This, the researchers argued in the original paper and again in 2019, showed that women could indeed have been warriors in the Viking Age. This woman, they said, was a highly regarded war-leader in her own right. The theory went viral, and the story in the media was often illustrated with images of Lagertha from *Vikings* or her shield-maiden colleagues.

This was undoubtedly an exciting and provocative interpretation of the grave findings, and it stimulated lots of argument among archaeologists, historians and Norse literary specialists. (I was interviewed by the *Guardian* newspaper on the topic, even though I am not an archaeologist.) Surely all those stories about shield-maidens from the sagas, poems and Latin histories must have had some basis in reality, people asked. Could the woman in Bj. 581

have been a real-life Lagertha? The jury is still out on this matter, for several good reasons. First, it is important to remember that people do not bury themselves; it is the rest of the community that decides what items are appropriate to place in a grave. An assemblage of weapons in a grave does not necessarily mean that the dead person made regular use of them. Second, it is possible that the dead person did not identify as a woman in life – that they were what we would now call transgender and had a specific social role that was not clearly aligned with their biological sex. And finally, although in the 19th century a grave containing weapons was automatically understood as belonging to a 'warrior', we now understand enough about the complicated social roles operational in Viking Age society to realize that social identities were not necessarily stable and fixed throughout a lifetime.

The Valhöll complex, then, is a myth with several fascinating elements. Within the Norse mythological system, it functioned to endorse the predominant social values of individual heroism, mitigating fear in the face of death and assuaging anxiety about how future generations might remember you. It also offered a comforting vision of life after death for the warrior, placing him in a great hall with plenty of companions to feast and fight for eternity – a preferable alternative to an afterlife in the much less exciting halls of Hel. The role of the Einherjar also gave humanity a stake in the last battle at *ragna rök*, for the wolf Fenrir has people in his sights as well as the gods who chained him up; as one poet warns, soon 'unbound, the wolf will journey to the homes of men'. In 19th-century Germany, Valhalla was rebuilt as a shrine to national glory, a temple on the banks of the Danube where a more broadly defined set of heroes is celebrated. During the same period, Wagner raised questions about the price to be paid for the gods' grandiose palace and the relationship between divine authority and human free will. What kind of heroism is it, asks Wagner, that will prevail in the modern world?

Vikings have become a staple of popular historical fantasy in film and television, as we shall explore further in Chapter 6. Modern transmedia franchises understand that, if you want to maximize your audiences, you need to have plenty of strong female characters and give them something important to do. The shield-maiden has been reclaimed and repurposed as a powerful figure with whom women can identify; while Lagertha fights ruthlessly and continually challenges patriarchal assumptions about women's roles in Viking society, she also contends with rape, miscarriage and infertility, as well as sexual jealousy and being displaced in her husband's affections. This new popular stereotype – the woman who fights like a man but feels like a woman – intersects with academic, archaeological analysis of Viking Age grave finds, complicating our understanding of women in the radically strange early medieval past.

# CHAPTER 3

# Óðinn

## THE MYTH OF THE WANDERER
## IN SEARCH OF WISDOM

We have heard quite a lot about Óðinn in earlier chapters, in particular his relationship with human warriors and his rule over Valhöll. But there are several other facets to this major figure in Old Norse myth and legendary history. The poetic tradition tells us that Óðinn and his mysterious brothers Vili and Vé were descended from giants; Óðinn's mother was called Bestla and was the daughter of the giant Bölþorn. His father was Borr, the son of a male being who was licked out of the melting ice by Auðhumla, the cow whose milk nourished the first of all beings, the giant Ymir. Borr's sons act together in the Norse creation myths; either they raise the earth up out of the sea and set about establishing the courses of the sun and moon, or they kill Ymir and fashion the cosmos from his body parts. After this, Vili and Vé vanish from the stories, leaving Óðinn as the leader of the Æsir, the principal tribe of gods. As we have seen, Óðinn is deeply interested in some humans, recruiting heroes and, relatedly, choosing and supporting kings. He is also responsible for bringing the mead of poetry, kept shut up in a mountain by the giant Suttungr, to gods and men, liberating this precious cultural good for everyone's benefit. And he walks among men, gathering knowledge of different kinds: while he is very much concerned with establishing and verifying

Óðinn and Sleipnir on the Tjängvide picture stone (G 110), Gotland, Sweden.

accounts of the coming of *ragna rök*, he can also advise on much more mundane matters.

### The migrant king

In his *Edda*, Snorri explains that the 'real' Óðinn was a refugee from Troy who travelled to the North and gained prestige and authority over its inhabitants with his superior cultural knowledge. Snorri enlarges on the Æsir–Asia connection in the early chapters of another work attributed to him: *Heimskringla* (The Disc of the World). Here he gives further details of the powers the Æsir possessed and their journey from the East, from their city of Ásgarðr (not, interestingly, identified as Troy here). Led by Óðinn, they migrated first into Garðaríki (Russia) and then south into Saxland (Germany). Óðinn, we learn, took control of large parts of Saxland, then journeyed onwards into Denmark and Sweden, where his associate Gefjun tricked King Gylfi into allowing her to plough away the land that now forms the Danish island of Sjælland. Óðinn and Gylfi came to terms, Snorri relates, and the newcomer established himself at Sigtuna in Sweden, where he gave out lands to the other Æsir who had followed him.

After Óðinn's death, Njörðr succeeded him, and then Freyr, who became the ancestor of the Swedish royal line; Freyr's sister, Freyja, was the last survivor among the 'gods', and she maintained the custom of sacrifice. Óðinn's son with Njörðr's former wife, Skaði, named Sæmingr, was the ancestor of an important dynasty in northern Norway. Gefjun had married a son of Óðinn called Skjöldr, and their children – the Skjöldungar – would rule over Denmark. To this legendary history, Snorri added a full description of Óðinn's magical powers and the cultural customs he established: cremation, the erection of burial mounds, sacrifice and taxation. This tale of eastern origins and migration across Europe came to be crucial in the conception of the Æsir in post-medieval thinking; understood at first literally, then symbolically, it suggested an underlying cultural continuity between parts of Russia, Germany and Scandinavia, and even the British Isles.

## The Goths

The historian Jordanes, mentioned in the Introduction, completed his work *De origine actibusque Getarum* (The Origins and Deeds of the Goths), usually known as the *Getica*, in Constantinople in 551 CE, or so he tells us. Jordanes relates that the Goths (from whom he reckoned to be descended) originated in a huge northern island called Scandzia, located in the Arctic. This region, he claimed, deserved to be called 'a hive of races or a womb of nations', for the Gothic people migrated from there to Scythia – a large region lying to the north of the Black Sea, bordering on Germany to the west, northwards far into the Siberian steppes, and beyond the Caspian Sea to the east. It was these Goths, later moving (or returning) westwards, who became the Ostrogoths – who raided extensively in the Roman Empire and later conquered Rome – and evolved into the Visigoths, who achieved dominance in the Iberian

Peninsula. Jordanes' claims about the origins of the Goths are highly disputed: the Gothic language, for example, is East, rather than North, Germanic. Archaeological evidence suggests that a culture based on the southern shores of the Baltic did indeed migrate to the shores of the Black Sea in the early centuries of the first millennium; whether they were related to the tribe known as the Götar or Geats who lived in southern Sweden (the tribe to which the early English hero Beowulf belonged) remains unclear.

Jordanes' claims that the Goths – the conquerors of Rome, no less, and early converts to Christianity – had their origins in this particular region of the North were taken up with enthusiasm by early modern Swedish historians. The Goths, claimed the Swedish writer Johannes Magnus, had occupied Sweden as soon as Noah's flood had receded and had built a mighty civilization, one that predated Troy, Greece and Rome. Japheth, the son of Noah, had taken control of Europe, and his son, Magog, had seized Scandinavia. In turn Magog's sons Suenno, Ubbo and Siggo had founded Sueonia (Sweden), Uppsala and Sigtuna respectively. As direct descendants of Noah, these generations of course had a clear knowledge of God, but as the years passed their understanding became corrupted and the Swedes fell into idolatry, just as Adam of Bremen had noted in his description of the great golden temple at Uppsala, with its mighty statues of Óðinn, Þórr and Frikko (probably Freyr). This imaginative account traces the rulers of Sweden down to the contemporary Swedish king Gustav Vasa, and names Óðinn as king in the ninth generation after Magog. Published in Rome in 1554, this Latin work proudly announced Sweden's view of its prominent place in early world history.

One of the more eccentric treatments of mythological history was the claim of another Swede, Johannes Rudbeck, that Sweden – that 'cradle of the nations' – was in fact Atlantis, the lost civilization whose story is told by Plato in two of his dialogues (c. 360 BCE). Rudbeck's great four-volume work *Atlantica*

(1679–1702) notes the parallels between Atlantean religious practice as described by Plato and the accounts of Snorri and Adam of Bremen. Sweden–Atlantis was not, said Rudbeck, destroyed by a great flood sent by the sea god Poseidon. Rather, the deluge should be understood metaphorically as signifying the vast numbers of people who flooded into the country because it was such a desirable territory to live in. Plato's references to the elephants of Atlantis were to be interpreted as a kenning-type description of the largest and most dangerous beasts of the North: wolves. Finally, the runic futhark writing system, or so Rudbeck claimed, was exported from Sweden to Greece, where it formed the basis of all the alphabets of the classical world.

Rudbeck's theories, unsurprisingly, did not gain much currency outside Sweden. In the century that followed, however, other writers would take up the idea that Scandinavia was indeed 'a hive of nations', as Jordanes had claimed. In addition to the

The Gefjun Fountain in Copenhagen, designed by Anders Bundgaard (1908).

Goths, the Celts had also migrated westwards from Scythia, ending up in the British Isles, and so they too could be designated as 'Gothic'. Thus, when the Swiss diplomat and scholar Paul-Henri Mallet, who was stationed in Copenhagen, decided to write his *Introduction à l'histoire de Dannemarc* (Introduction to the History of Denmark) in 1755, he supplemented it a year later with a work entitled *Monumens de la mythologie et de la poésie des Celtes et particulièrement des anciens Scandinaves* (Monuments of the Mythology and Poetry of the Celts, and in particular of the Ancient Scandinavians). Mallet's work, which gives a detailed account of Norse mythology, was based on the first edition of Snorri's *Edda* and associated the myths not with religious history, but rather with poetry and the literary imagination, foregrounding Óðinn in his twin roles of god of poetry, war and wisdom, and as the resourceful leader of the Scandinavian ancestors who had migrated from the East to the Northern lands.

Mallet's work was quickly translated into a range of European languages, achieving immense popularity. Representing the Norse mythological material as a record of 'Celtic' belief was very much in tune with a new cultural turn that had got under way in the British Isles from 1760 onwards. The Scottish poet James Macpherson had begun to publish poems purportedly by a Celtic bard, Ossian. These were partly reconstructed from Gaelic oral compositions, partly invented by Macpherson, and they found an enthusiastic readership, ready to admire the untamed, 'primitive' sentiments of Ossian's verse. This primitivism chimed strongly with the poems contained in Mallet's collection. For, like much of the Ossianic material, Mallet's versions of the Norse myths were of a fierce and strange temper; they related tales of courage, endurance, fatalism and fearlessness in the face of death. Bishop Thomas Percy translated Mallet's *Monumens* into English as *Northern Antiquities* (1770), a work that remained in print for decades in successive editions. Seven years earlier Percy had published *Five Pieces of*

*Runick Poetry*, kickstarting the enthusiasm in Britain for the Norse 'Gothic' – a genre taken up also by the poet Thomas Gray, as we saw in the previous chapter. Although none of Percy's 'pieces' is strictly mythological, he did translate the poem *Hákonarmál* ('The Funeral Song of Hacon', as he called it) and is thus responsible for introducing the concept of Valhöll and the Valkyries – 'the beautiful nymphs of war' – into English.

## The Wanderer

Back in our mythological stories, Óðinn is to be found wandering still, alone this time rather than leading his tribe across Europe. Although his ravens gather information for him when they fly across the world each day, bringing him the latest news in his high seat, Hliðskjálf, the god also likes to find out things for himself. Typically wearing a cloak and a broad-brimmed hat pulled low over his brow to disguise his missing eye, he appears as an ordinary human. In one saga, under the odd name of 'Horse-Hair Grani', he becomes foster-father to the orphaned hero Starkaðr, who later enters the service of King Víkarr and fights alongside him for a good while. One night, Horse-Hair Grani suddenly appears, rows Starkaðr out to an island in the nearby fjord and brings him to a council of the gods. Here Grani throws off his disguise and reveals himself to be none other than Óðinn. Þórr is angry with Starkaðr because his mother had chosen a giant as husband rather than Þórr himself, and heaps curses upon him. Óðinn cannot undo them, but he can offer counterbalancing blessings. As a reward for his support, the god explains, Starkaðr needs to give him a sacrifice: his beloved king. The next day, Starkaðr persuades King Víkarr to take part in a mock sacrifice. But this is just a pretence: the loop of calf guts lying loosely around the king's neck tightens into a deadly noose, and the slender reed that Starkaðr jabs him with transforms into a lethal and very Odinic spear. Víkarr is off to Valhöll, but Starkaðr is made an outcast for his treachery.

Here Óðinn is playing a clever long game: to recruit Starkaðr into his service and to win Víkarr for the Einherjar. At other times he will appear to counsel or warn; it is not a good idea to ignore his advice but, as we know, it does not necessarily bring victory. In Wagner's *Ring*, Wotan assumes the identity of the Wanderer once he has decided to cease interfering directly in mortal affairs. His attempt to regain the Ring by fathering and supporting Siegmund had foundered on the hero's incestuous passion for his sister, so thereafter Wotan maintains only a watching brief among mortals. Thus, in the cycle's third opera, *Siegfried*, he appears in the second scene of Act I to find out from Mime, Siegfried's foster-father and Alberich's brother, what is going on. Mime does not like the look of the Wanderer and tries to refuse him hospitality, but the visitor wagers his own head on a wisdom contest, as he does in the eddic poem *Vafþrúðnismál* (The Sayings of Vafþrúðnir; discussed below). He easily answers Mime's three questions – which incidentally allow for a resumé of the history of the Ring – and then, since the Nibelung accepted the head wager, claims that now Mime's own head is at stake unless he can answer three questions in turn. Mime's answers confirm that Siegfried is alive and well, and destined to kill Fafner and recover the Ring – but only if the fragments of Siegmund's magic sword Nothung can be hammered into a new weapon. Mime cannot answer the final question: 'Who will forge that sword?' He himself has tried many times, but Siegfried is so strong that he breaks every sword he wields. This is enough for the Wanderer; he knows that 'the one who knows no fear' – Siegfried himself – will successfully reforge Nothung, and that the Ring will be wrested from Fafner. Smiling to himself, he leaves Mime's head on his shoulders.

The Wanderer now makes his way to Fafner's cave, where he finds Mime's brother, Alberich, the original possessor of the Ring. Alberich taunts Wotan, saying that when he gets his hands on the Ring he will bring down Walhall and the rule of the gods.

Starkaðr and the death of King Víkarr, from *Danmarks Kronike* (1898).

But Wotan is unperturbed: he awakens Fafner and warns him that Siegfried is coming before he summons a storm and rides away back to Walhall. When he next encounters Siegfried, now in possession of the Ring and a magic helmet, the Tarnhelm, that can transform appearances, Siegfried is on his way to seek out Brünnhilde. He is annoyed to find the old man blocking his way.

'Clear off!' says Siegfried disrespectfully, and he threatens to knock out the Wanderer's other eye. Wotan tests his grandson's mettle, describing the fire that surrounds the sleeping Valkyrie, and warns him not to arouse his anger; this spear, he says, is the one that shattered his father's sword. Siegfried simply splinters the spear shaft with one stroke of Nothung, and the Wanderer quietly gathers its fragments and disappears. The rule of the gods has ended, the oaths engraved on the spear shaft are void, and men shall now rule over themselves, he concedes.

**Wisdom**

Wotan learns to welcome the end of his power; in an interview with Erda, Brünnhilde's mother, he reveals that, although he had once relinquished the world to the Nibelung Alberich in furious disgust, now he gladly leaves it to his son, Siegfried, who lacks the Nibelungs' lust for power. Brünnhilde will redeem the world, he prophesies, with Siegfried by her side. As we shall see, however, even as Erda and the Wanderer converse the Norns are spinning quite a different fate for the two lovers from the one that Wotan imagines for them. Here, though, he is content to accept the twilight of the gods; after Siegfried has sundered his spear, we see Wotan no more in the *Ring* cycle.

In the myths themselves, however, Óðinn is often to be found searching for information about *ragna rök*, questioning a seeress who can remember the time before the world was made, and wagering his head with the giant Vafþrúðnir in order to establish what this very wise being knows. What he learns comes as no great surprise, it seems; rather, his incessant questioning of ancient beings confirms what he already knows. Just perhaps, there may be someone who knows a different story, a version of the future in which *ragna rök* can be forestalled. The seeress, whose account in the poem *Völuspá* (The Seeress's Prophecy) opens the *Poetic Edda*, holds out no hope for the survival of most of the Æsir. The wolf is bound but will one day be freed, and the chain of events leading to the downfall of the gods is inexorable. Nothing Óðinn does can forestall it.

Besides his *ragna rök* information project, Óðinn also takes an interest in a more everyday form of wisdom. So, when his wife Frigg claims that Óðinn's protégé King Geirrøðr is so notoriously stingy that he tortures guests who come to his hall rather than offer them hospitality, the god dons his Wanderer guise and takes the name Grímnir ('Masked One') to investigate. Since Frigg has sneakily warned Geirrøðr to beware of a wandering wizard who is on his way to the hall, Geirrøðr does indeed mistreat his guest, placing him between two fierce fires with neither food nor drink to sustain him. When Geirrøðr's son Agnarr finally offers the guest a reviving horn of drink, Grímnir begins to speak. As we saw in Chapter 2, he describes Valhöll in some detail, along with the other gods' halls, and imparts other arcane mythological information, including a long string of Óðinn-names. When Geirrøðr finally realizes who his mysterious prisoner is, he leaps to his feet to rescue him from his agonizing position. But he catches his feet on his own sword and tumbles onto its point; the king receives his punishment, and the more generous-hearted Agnarr becomes king after him.

In one of the legendary sagas, Óðinn again turns up at a royal hall in disguise to take part in a riddle contest with King Heiðrekr. Once more Óðinn wins, using his favourite trick question (revealed in Chapter 10). When the enraged king draws his sword and tries to strike him, Óðinn turns into a falcon and flies away, though not before prophesying that the king will be slain by the worst of his thralls. The riddle contest is fascinating: it preserves the only collection of riddles we have in Old Norse, but it was also J. R. R. Tolkien's inspiration for Bilbo's riddle contest with Gollum in *The Hobbit* (1937). As Professor of Old English and Old Norse at the University of Oxford, Tolkien knew this saga very well – and his son Christopher would later translate it. Tolkien's riddle sequence largely draws upon traditional European folk riddles, but Gollum's fourth riddle echoes one of Óðinn's:

> It cannot be seen, cannot be felt,
> Cannot be heard, cannot be smelt.
> It lies behind stars and under hills,
> And empty holes it fills.
> It comes out first and follows after,
> Ends life, kills laughter.

In a similar way, Óðinn asks, 'What goes over the earth, swallowing up lakes and forest? It is afraid of wood, but not of men, and attacks the sun to harm it.' In both cases the answer is 'darkness'. Although it doesn't have a direct counterpart in the original saga, Bilbo's 'No-legs lay on one-leg, two-legs sat near on three-legs, four-legs got some' is similar in structure to some of the saga riddles, which also describe creatures with unusual numbers of legs, eyes and other body parts. For example, the disguised god asks, 'What has ten eyes, eight legs, and its knees are higher than its belly?' You will have to guess that one for yourself. Like Óðinn, Bilbo too cheats with his final riddle, asking a question to which only he can possibly know the answer: 'What have I got in my pocket?' The answer is, of course, the Ring.

In *Hávamál* (Sayings of the High One), Óðinn gradually reveals himself as the speaker who shares a more everyday kind of wisdom: how to behave in a strange hall (don't eat or drink too much; speak up but do not speak foolishly); make sure you have enough wood in for the winter and good shingles on the roof. Other maxims have a more Odinic quality: 'You must get up early if you mean to take your neighbour's life or property,' he urges, 'for the loafing wolf seldom snatches the ham' (that this is good advice is amply borne out in the sagas). The love of false-hearted women is compared to chasing reindeer over thawing hillsides when you are lame, or trying to ride a frisky, badly broken-in two-year-old horse over ice without spiked shoes – vivid images from lived experience. Wisdom about friendship, generosity, mortality and moderation abounds in the early part of the poem.

It is in this poem too that we learn some of the events surrounding the winning of the mead of poetry, of the nine powerful spells that Óðinn learned from his grandfather, and, importantly, of the ritual by which he won knowledge of the runes, hanging himself on Yggdrasill. The runes seem to emerge from beneath the tree; howling, the god gathers them up, to teach them to gods and men. They must be treated with respect, the god warns; an adept must know how to cut them correctly, how to colour them, what surfaces they may be carved on, and how they should be interpreted.

### Runes and rune-magic

Runes are the writing system used in early medieval Scandinavia and also in England. They derive from a form of alphabet common in Northern Italy and were probably brought to Scandinavia in the Migration Age (c. 300–800 CE) – even if Rudbeck argued erroneously that they were the 'original' alphabet, transmitted southwards from Sweden–Atlantis and inspiring both the Greek and Roman alphabets. Runes consist of straight lines and are designed to be easy to carve on hard surfaces such as rock or wood. The original 'Elder' futhark, or runic alphabet, had twenty-four symbols; these were later simplified to sixteen symbols (the 'Younger' futhark). The word *futhark* comprises the first six letters of the alphabet (*th* is a single character, þ, known as 'thorn'). Each rune had a name that began with the letter that the rune represented, so the letter for M is named *maðr* 'man'; B is *björk* 'birch', and so on.

In the myths, the runes could be used for magical purposes. In one poem, a Valkyrie explains that victory runes should be engraved on parts of a sword; ale runes can protect against poison and should be cut onto a drinking horn; helping runes are scratched onto the palm in childbirth; sea runes are to be set on the prow, oars and rudder of ships. Others work to heal, to give eloquence in lawsuits or to enhance intelligence. Some sagas confirm the runes' magical power; in one, the hero Egill suspects his ale is poisoned, so he pricks his palm with a knife, carves a rune on the drinking horn and smears it with blood. The horn shatters and the lethal drink cascades onto the straw strewn over the floor. Later, a sick girl grows worse and worse. When Egill investigates, it turns out that some healing runes have been carved incompetently by a local man. Once he has shaved them off the piece of bone on which they were carved and burned the shavings, Egill incises the correct ones and places the bone under her pillow. The girl awakens still feeling weak, but sound in mind and body.

The existence of such runic magic is most likely pure invention, particularly the accounts in literary texts written down by Christians. The runes were primarily a writing system, designed to record information, to communicate at a distance and very often to commemorate the dead. The great runic monuments of Scandinavia and the territories colonized by Scandinavians are predominantly erected to honour the memory of family members, and their inscriptions are planned and carved by experts. We are fortunate to have a trove of wooden slips, discovered in a harbourside excavation in Bergen in Norway in 1955. These later medieval finds show that people used runes for such mundane messages as 'Gyða says you must go home' or 'Kiss me!' alongside prayers and even curses. The image on p. 94 shows an early 14th-century rune stick engraved with a passionate, poetic sentiment:

> I so love [another] man's woman that the wide mountains tremble; splendid woman, we love one another so the world will split apart; the raven will turn white as snow before I leave that woman.

The Rök rune stone (Ög 136) in Östergötland, Sweden (9th century).

Rune stick (B 644) from Bergen, Norway (14th century).

The real magic, then, lies in Óðinn's discovery: a means by which time might be circumvented, supplementing human memory and oral storytelling with a technology that would endure long beyond the human lifespan.

The Victorian author and philosopher Thomas Carlyle gave a series of lectures in 1840 in which he defined what makes a hero – and why we need them. Carlyle's first lecture, "The Hero as Divinity', foregrounds Óðinn. He strikes the by now familiar chord that the British are descended from Vikings, noting that Old Norse paganism is 'interesting also as the creed of our fathers; the men whose blood still runs in our veins, whom doubtless we still resemble in so many ways'. His account of Óðinn refuses the idea that he was a god, but is developed from the migrant story that was outlined above. Óðinn must have been an actual historical figure, and thus an ancestor of the British, via their dual Germanic and Anglo-Scandinavian heritage. Thus, Carlyle insists: 'Surely there was a First Teacher and Captain; surely there must have been an Odin, palpable to the sense at one time; no adjective, but a real Hero of flesh and blood!' Carlyle understands the stories of the acquisition of the mead of poetry and of the runes as symbolizing

Óðinn's achievements not just as a military leader, but as a culture hero. For he

> was not only a wild Captain and Fighter; discerning with his wild flashing eyes what to do, with his wild lion-heart daring and doing it; but a Poet too, all that we mean by a Poet, Prophet, great devout Thinker and Inventor, — as the truly Great Man ever is.

Óðinn's discovery of the technology of writing, along with his liberation of the powers of poetry from the giants who kept it to themselves but made no use of it, qualifies him as Inventor, as well as Poet, Carlyle argues.

In the 20th century, however, runes began to play a particular occult role. New Age devotees employ them for divination of the future, attempting to tell fortunes by making creative use of the concepts suggested by the traditional rune names, such as 'wealth', 'man', 'victory', 'riding' or 'joy'. Interpreting those runes whose names invoke nature and natural phenomena – oak, birch, yew, ice, hail – calls for a good deal more imagination. That runes might have magical power was an idea popularized in Germany in the early 20th century, following on from the arguments made by Grimm and his followers that the Scandinavian gods had also been the gods of the Germans and that remnants of their cult had survived in German folklore. A theory that the arcane philosophical doctrine of theosophy developed by Madame Blavatsky could be melded with the idea that Aryans represented a superior, more civilized race emerged in Germany: the ancient, mystical secrets of the Aryans were, in part, encoded in runes. Indeed, some believers thought that each runic letter carried a spell, a magic charge whose power could be harnessed. This ancient religion, so its proponents claimed, had been repressed by Christianity, but Norse myth had preserved vestiges of it. Although the Nazis – apart from Himmler – tended to despise both rune-magic and the revival of

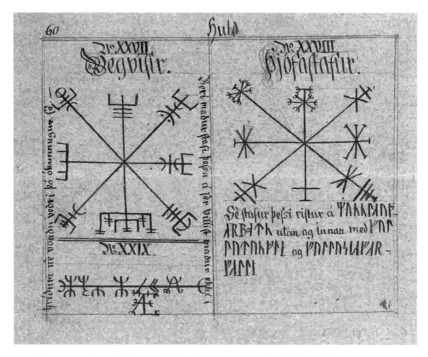

Rune-magic spells in an Icelandic manuscript by Geir Vigfússon (1860).

Wotanism as an alternative pagan religion to Christian belief, runes became important in Nazi iconography – most notoriously in the insignia of the SS, the elite Schutzstaffel corps. More remarkably, some enthusiasts believed that the cosmic powers represented by the runes could be concentrated and wielded through physical postures: runic yoga or gymnastics, forming runic shapes with the hands and fingers, or even, astonishingly enough, runic yodelling.

### Óðinn's ravens

Huginn and Muninn ('Thought' and 'Memory') are the two ravens who are central to Óðinn's communications network. They fly out across the worlds each day and return with crucial information about what is under way. In one poem Óðinn notes that he is afraid that something might happen to them, impairing the basis of his power and rule, adding, cryptically, that he is more

I

*Yggdrasil*, from the Icelandic
manuscript AM 738 4to, f.43r, 1680

II

*Valhöll* and the *Miðgarðsormr*,
from AM 738 4to, f.41v and f.42r, 1680

III

Olaus Magnus's *Carta marina*, 1539, this edition 1572

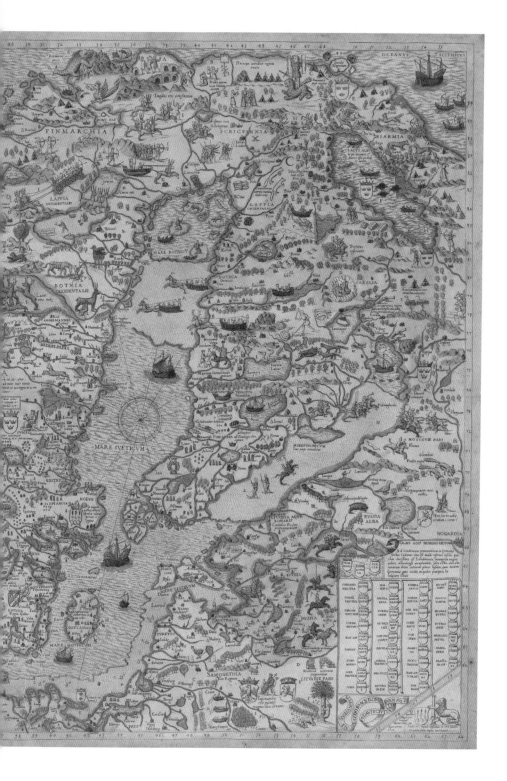

6

IV
William Blake, *The Fatal Sisters*, design 72,
from *The Poems of Thomas Gray*, 1797–98

v

Arthur Rackham, *Brünnhilde Rides Grane into the Flame,*
from *Siegfried & the Twilight of the Gods,* 1924

VI
Mårten Eskil Winge, *Thor's Fight with the Giants*, 1872

VII

Henry Fuseli, *Thor Battering the Midgard Serpent*, 1790

VIII

Peter Nicolai Arbo, *The Valkyrie*, 1869

afraid for Muninn than for Huginn (memory is more vulnerable and unpredictable than other cognitive powers). Wagner gestures at their task as information vectors in the *Ring* cycle. When Brünnhilde is overseeing the preparation of Siegfried's funeral pyre, she senses the presence of Wotan's ravens, spying on what is happening in the human world – and of course keeping track of the Ring for their master. 'Fly home, you ravens!' she calls defiantly. 'Tell your lord what you have heard by the Rhine.' And, she adds, they should go past her fiery mountain top on their way, there to

Óðinn in an engraving after Lorenz Frølich (1845).

summon Loge to Walhall to complete its destruction and to bring rest for Wotan. As she lights the timbers, two ravens do indeed fly up and away, bearing the tidings of the end back to the gods.

In contemporary Norse-inspired novels the ravens not only function as an important symbol of Óðinn, but also very often are characters in their own right. In Joanne Harris's Loki novels (discussed in Chapter 5), Loki is pitted against Odin, or Old One-Eye, as he often calls him: although they are initially blood-brothers, their interests increasingly diverge. During one early disagreement, Loki notes that Hugin and Munin, 'the physical manifestations of Allfather's thoughts in bird form – clicked their beaks and glowered at me'. The ravens spy for Odin but are not above being suborned by Loki, revealing key information in return for cake – for they are, 'like all their kind, fans of sweet and sticky things'. A slice of fruitcake, held out by Loki on Bifrost, the Rainbow Bridge, draws the birds to him. Though it is hard to get the birds to speak clearly when their beaks are stuffed, Munin offers a clue, citing a line from the Oracle's prophecy: 'The ash, Yggdrasill, quakes where it stands.' The birds' confusion of 'cake', 'quake' and 'crawk', their natural call, makes for considerable comedy, but what they reveal is enough for Loki to realize that the quaking of the tree is a portent of the onset of *ragna rök*. Something significant is afoot and is driving Odin's calculations.

Later, after the death of Baldr, Loki is in hiding, and the ravens track him down. Between further hopeful demands for cake, they communicate in menacing terms Odin's threat to punish Loki, reminding him that he has two sons still living in Asgard. Like Mafia hard men, the laconic pair simply pass on the information and, when Loki temporizes, they take off to deliver the news to their master. Just before the final battle of *ragna rök* gets under way, the two ravens appear to Loki again, this time in their human form. Munin is transfixed by a dish of crystallized fruit and has little to say but 'Crawk'. Hugin, who turns out to have a Scottish accent, is more voluble, expanding on Odin's final offer. The prophecy can still be circumvented and *ragna rök* avoided if Loki will call off his alliance with the Seeress, Heid. But although Hugin's hints that Loki is being manipulated by the Oracle make him uneasy, the trickster god remains defiant.

Elizabeth Knox's spectacular fantasy masterpiece *The Absolute Book* (2021) primarily sets the human world side by side with the world of the fairies, but Odin also appears in the human world, where he shadows the heroine's father. He admits particular figures to Mímir's Well, where, if they are worthy, they can obtain wisdom that suits their circumstances and characters, yet bends them towards an as yet unseen fate. The ravens are both female: 'Any wise male god will have female advisors,' notes Shift, one of the supernatural protagonists, when Munin is introduced. 'I suppose it talks,' enquires Jacob, the open-minded policeman. 'Yes,' Shift says, 'but only ever to the purpose.' Talkative and ingenious, the two raven sisters operate freely across the worlds. Bending the rules of time, they communicate vital information and save the situation on more than one occasion. Later, we learn that the ravens came into being as recompense for Odin's sacrifice of his eye at Mímir's Well. Knox recognizes and elaborates on the networked nature of Odin's cognitive system: whatever the ravens know, Odin knows too. Munin is the more important raven, acting at one point as a spiritual messenger, imparting crucial backstory information to Jacob's consciousness as he lies in intensive care. Sometimes she chooses vividly to reveal her raven nature, almost with a wink: 'I for one do not want to sit here twiddling my thumbs,' complains Jacob. In reply, Munin offers to twiddle Jacob's thumbs for him but says she'd have to remove them first. Munin is wise, sardonic and pragmatic by turns; she is one of the most memorably drawn characters in this complex novel.

In December 2020 the Icelandic band Sigur Rós released an album called *Odin's Raven Magic*, based on a highly cryptic Icelandic poem called 'Hrafngaldur Óðins', a pastiche of older eddic poetry probably composed in the 17th century. The poem itself does not mention the birds directly, but the album's tracks as listed refer to various themes and characters mentioned in the poem: Óðinn, the dwarfs, the god Heimdallr, and the horses that draw the sun and the moon. The poem relates how the gods are gathered together, made anxious by the portents of *ragna rök*; a mysterious woman appears, and Heimdallr is detailed to question her about what she knows. She is reluctant to speak, only weeping in reply, and eventually the deities depart in different directions, leaving Óðinn behind. The work was first composed as an orchestral collaboration in the early 2000s and was premiered in London.

## Bait and switch: Mr Wednesday

Shadow's ordeal on the World Tree, keeping vigil over Mr Wednesday's corpse and dying himself, forms a climax in the Odinic storyline of Neil Gaiman's *American Gods*, introduced in Chapter 1. When Shadow agrees to enter Mr Wednesday's employment (a pact sealed with a great deal of mead), Wednesday admits, in response to an accusation, 'Damn straight I'm a hustler.' And that, indeed, is what he is, trading in the deceptions and power games that have always been central to his modus operandi. It takes a while for Wednesday to reveal himself fully as Odin to Shadow, who lags somewhat behind the reader in realizing who his boss really is: '"Odin?" "Odin," whispered Wednesday, and the crash of the breakers on the beach of skulls was not loud enough to drown that whisper.' Odin–Wednesday retains the magical knowledge he used to deploy in the old days; he even recites to Shadow the eighteen spells from *Hávamál*. He knows how to use rune-magic and how to make himself irresistible to women. But, like the other old gods eking out their shabby, down-at-heel lives, he feels that his power is ebbing away from him, for no one believes in him – and, for the gods, belief calls for sacrifice, and sacrifice means blood.

Thus in one of his out-of-time visionary experiences, Shadow finds himself at the great festival at Uppsala, where men, horses and dogs sway from the trees in the dark sacrificial grove that surrounds the wooden temple. Odin's death at the hands of the new gods, noted in Chapter 1, is, unsurprisingly, not a permanent state: 'In the god business it's not the death that matters, but the opportunity for resurrection,' he observes. There's more on Shadow and Mr Wednesday's relationship and the final meaning of the man's ordeal on the tree in Chapter 10; by the end of the novel, however, Shadow's involvement in Wednesday's machinations has set him too on the path of the Wanderer. In Reykjavík, sitting on a grassy bank and looking down at the city, he's approached by an old one-eyed man with a broad-brimmed hat, who speaks to him in Icelandic, asking if Shadow remembers him, and Shadow gives him Wednesday's glass eye, a gift from the new world to the old.

## Óðinn in the Marvel Universe

If Mr Wednesday endeavours to rekindle his waning powers by trying to bring about a battle that has much in common with *ragna rök* in the Marvel Cinematic Universe – comprising four films so far: *Thor* (2011); *Thor: The Dark World* (2013); *Thor: Ragnarok* (2017); and *Thor: Love and Thunder* (2022) – his reign is to all intents and purposes over: he is mostly concerned with managing tricky questions of succession. In the movies' backstory, Odin had waged war against the Frost Giants, seized their Casket of Power and confiscated the Eternal Flame from the fire demon Surtur; he has defeated monsters, conquered the Nine Realms, and brought them peace and stability. His heroic feats are fuelled by his 'Odinsleep', when he withdraws from his responsibilities to rest and recharge: an opportunity for others to make mischief. Odin's daughter Hela had been his chief general and leader of the Einherjar, but she was too committed to violence; after an attempt to usurp his throne, Odin banished her to Hel: 'Odin and I drowned entire civilizations in blood and tears. Where do you think all this gold came from?' And then, one day he decided to become a benevolent king,' Hela later tells Thor. Thor is Odin's son by his wife, Frigga; Loki is also raised as his son, though in fact he is the child of Laufey, the leader of the Frost Giants. Laufey is Loki's father here, though in Old Norse this distinctly feminine name belongs to the god's mother.

At the opening of *Thor*, Odin is preparing to abdicate in favour of Thor. A few rogue Frost Giants have raided the vault where the Casket of Power is hidden but have not succeeded in recovering it. Thor's rage and disobedience – he mounts a retaliatory raid on Jotunheim (the giants' realm) – suggest that he is not yet ready to take the throne of Asgard, and Odin postpones his departure. The struggle for power between Thor and Loki, despite the external threats that Asgard faces, culminates in Odin being exiled to Earth – to the Shady Acres Care Home, in New York, no less. However, once he escapes from this facility (throwing off the spell that Loki cast upon him), he takes up the identity of the Wanderer and travels through the kingdoms of the world before, exhausted, he elects to die in Norway. There he warns both Thor and Loki of the imminence of *ragna rök*, and that his death will release Hela. Now he returns to Valhalla, 'where the brave shall live forever. Nor shall we mourn but rejoice for those that have died the glorious death,' or so Thor declares.

We have seen how the mythological Óðinn fulfils a good range of key functions: as patron of kings, as ceaseless quester after wisdom, as deceiver, shape-shifter and wanderer among people. Óðinn is obsessed by gathering information about *ragna rök*, hoping perhaps to falsify the understanding that he already has of how the world will end. In the modern period, that particular dilemma defines him: the knowledge that the reign of the gods is finite overshadows everything else he can achieve. 'The *Ring*'s drama is made from Wotan's failings,' says the music critic Tom Service; indeed, Wagner's Wotan has realized by the start of the cycle's second opera that he and his kind are already superannuated. He cannot forestall the collapse of his regime, and all that remains to him is to try to prevent – at arm's length – the Ring falling into the hands of Alberich the Nibelung, with his terrifying fantasies of world domination.

For Gaiman and for the Marvel writers, Óðinn lingers as a relic from a time before men turned irrevocably to new gods, or before he grew too tired and his powers became too attenuated to keep in balance the forces of evil, his daughter's unbridled malevolence and his sons' ambitions across the Nine Realms. Óðinn speaks now to a patriarchal order that is played out, to a model of heroic masculinity combined with political pragmatism that no longer convinces in a world where other gods hold sway or where the destiny of mortals lies in their own hands. Óðinn's generation no longer matters, so he is often found fighting an uncompromising rearguard action against a future that holds no place for him.

As we saw in the last chapter, Douglas Adams's Odin had colluded with lawyers and advertising execs to sell out the other gods in exchange for his berth in a luxury nursing home. Óðinn, then, has come to signify the old white man, the outdated patriarch clinging to power and self-interest, willing to fight with any means necessary. Yet he is often underestimated by his opponents; he has reservoirs of power upon which he can draw, and the drama of his eventual defeat extends as far ahead as *ragna rök*. He is still a potent figure, and it is no wonder that he is the favourite of 'the cosmic right', the spiritual leaders of the alt-right movement. In Elizabeth Knox's *The Absolute Book*, the *sidhe* (fairy) woman Neve observes: 'Odin is best left out of this. We're not sure what his intentions are. He's not himself these days. His head has been turned by many new worshippers. Of the wrong kind.' 'You mean white supremacists with valknuts tattooed on their man boobs?' asks Jacob the policeman, but he already knows the answer. Óðinn's son Þórr, on the other hand, occupies a very different imaginative space both in the Norse myths and in modern culture, as we shall see in the next chapter.

# Þórr

## THE MYTH OF THE SUPERHERO

The myths of Þórr recorded in the *Poetic* and *Prose Eddas* are of two related kinds. One shows him as the mighty killer of giants (see pl. VI), often away from the land of the gods, patrolling the eastern borders to make sure that there are no giant incursions – or venturing into Jötunheimar ('Giantlands') to crush skulls and smash bodies; male or female, all are fair game to the god. The other kind tends to depict Þórr in a comic light, poking fun at his masculinity and fierceness, depicting him as more macho than he needs to be and prickly about his strength; the best-known stories of Þórr invite us not to take him entirely seriously. Among them is the hilarious account in *Þrymskviða* (The Poem of Þrymr) of how the god wakes up one day to find that his mighty hammer, Mjöllnir, has been stolen. Only the promise of Freyja as a bride can persuade the thief, the self-regarding giant Þrymr, to return it. But when Freyja refuses to cooperate, there's only one thing for it: to dress Þórr as a blushing bride and pack her off to Jötunheimar, with Loki along to do the talking. Though Þrymr has his doubts when he sees his bride's fiery eyes and enormous appetite, he brings out Mjöllnir to hallow the wedding – and is promptly slaughtered. In another tale, it is Þórr's father, Óðinn, in disguise who makes a fool of his son, refusing him passage over a fjord, riddling with him and taunting him, and finally making him take the long way round.

"AH, WHAT A LOVELY MAID IT IS!"

Left: Edward Burne-Jones, *Thor* (1883–84). Right: Elmer Boyd Smith, Þórr dressed as Þrymr's bride, from Abbie Farewell Brown's *In the Days of Giants* (1902).

In one of the best-known tales, Þórr and his companions set out to visit the mighty giant Útgarða-Loki. On their way to his distant hall, the party is thoroughly deceived by the giant Skrýmir, in whose glove the party spends the night, taking it for a convenient shelter. Skrýmir offers to share his food, but the pack is secured with magic wire, and their annoying companion turns out to be unkillable even when Mjöllnir crashes into his skull as he sleeps. At Útgarða-Loki's court, Þórr's team fail miserably in a series of competitions: eating, running races, drinking from a horn and, with increasing bathos, lifting up a cat. At last – most humiliating of all – Þórr cannot even wrestle the ruler's elderly nurse to the floor. Útgarða-Loki finally admits the truth: that these were all a series of complicated illusions, and that he is so much in awe of Þórr's strength that he will never risk admitting him to his home again. For Skrýmir was Útgarða-Loki in disguise – and would have been annihilated had he not deftly interposed a mountain between himself and Mjöllnir. The opponents in the contests were no less than Fire, who ate up food, trough and all, and Thought, than whom no one is swifter; the end of the horn was submerged in the sea, where Þórr's efforts have given rise to the phenomenon of tides; the harmless cat was the Miðgarðs Serpent in disguise; and the game old woman was Elli, the personification of Old Age herself. None of these revelations quite dispel the sense that Þórr is seen as a figure of fun in this series of adventures.

In another episode, related in *Gylfaginning* as a sequel to the visit to Útgarða-Loki, Þórr, accompanied by the god Týr, goes to visit the giant Hymir in order to gain a huge cauldron in which beer may be brewed for the gods' feasts. Þórr eats Hymir and his family out of house and home, and Hymir suggests that they go fishing the next day to replenish the supplies. The timorous giant does not want to row too far out, for fear of the Miðgarðs Serpent, who lurks in the outer reaches of the ocean. Þórr rows mightily, however, casts his hook (baited with the head of Hymir's prize ox) overboard, and fishes up none other than the serpent itself. God and monster gaze at one another, and it seems likely that Þórr would have slain the creature there and then, giving the lie to the prophecy that the two antagonists would meet and destroy one another at *ragna rök*, had Hymir not drawn a knife and cut the line in sheer terror. In one version, Þórr clouts him over the ear so that he falls overboard and drowns; in another they return home with a couple of whales instead – and Þórr is able to win the cauldron from Hymir too.

When he is away killing giants, Þórr is distinctly brutal. He does not spare women who attack him, and his first resort when provoked is to violence: Mjöllnir is always within reach. Despite having a giantess mother – Jörð, whose name means 'Earth' – he is not keen to socialize with his maternal kindred. We saw how, in Chapter 2, he slaughtered the giant master builder without a care for the previously given oaths, and when he comes home from an expedition to find that Óðinn has invited the giant Hrungnir to drink among the gods, he is so furious he can barely be restrained from annihilating his father's guest. While Óðinn is consistently unfaithful to his wife, Frigg, Þórr seems to be a model husband. Opportunities to stray are limited: unlike some of the other gods, he is not ready to have sex with giantesses, however beautiful they might be – and, of course, given his track record in slaughtering them and their kinsmen, he would scarcely be acceptable. Nor does Þórr's hypermasculinity express itself in affairs with the goddesses. Sif, his wife, may not be quite so exemplary; Óðinn claims that she keeps a lover at home while her husband is out on his patrol of the borders of Jötunheimar. And when Loki mischievously – or aggressively – cuts off all her golden hair, it is unclear quite how he managed to get close enough to accomplish such an intimate act. In the poem *Lokasenna* (Loki's Quarrel), in which Loki systematically insults all the gods one by one at a feast, he mentions that Sif has welcomed him to her bed. Þórr appears at the end of the poem, blustering, swinging his hammer and threatening annihilation. Loki fires off a few choice insults: that Þórr cowered with fear when he camped in Skrýmir's glove; that he could not open the giant's food pack (secured with magic wire); and that he won't be so brave when he has to face the Wolf at *ragna rök*. At last, however, he agrees to leave peaceably, 'for I know you do strike,' he says.

This idea of Þórr as a big, none-too-bright blusterer, roaring and swinging his hammer, is an influential one, as we shall see. Nonetheless, it is clear that the god had a rather different signification in Old Norse religious belief. In Norway and Iceland, he appears to have been the most important god, judging from the evidence provided by place and personal names. In poetry he is called the protector of Ásgarðr, home of the gods, and of Miðgarðr, home of men; some of his other titles refer to him as guardian of the sanctuaries. Besides Óðinn, with his self-serving investment in the fortunes of kings, Þórr is the god most credited with interest in humans. He has two human servants, Þjálfi and Röskva, a brother and sister whom he acquired when Þjálfi disobeyed him in cracking open the marrowbone of one of the magic goats who draw the god's chariot. It is significant that Þórr's two goats can be killed, eaten and reconstituted the next day as he travels onwards; he does not burden his human hosts with demands that they kill their own animals to feast the god. And the final service that Þórr offers to humans is one he points out himself: if he did not keep the population of giants and trolls down, the human and divine worlds would be completely overrun by malevolent creatures.

Carving of the crucified Christ on a stone in Jelling, Denmark (c. 965).

**Þórr and humans**

Þórr was more important than the other gods for the Icelandic settlers, as far as we can tell. Temples to him were established quite early; many Icelanders, men and women, bear his name as part of theirs; and sometimes he is credited with guiding the Norwegian emigrants to the best place for them to settle. Travellers would bring the uprights from their throne-like high seats, often carved with images of Þórr, onboard ship and cast them overboard in sight of land. Following their drift or quite often making landfall and finding the posts already there, as if by chance, was a good omen for making a new life on Iceland. Archaeological evidence points to the god's popularity, if the many 'Thor's hammers' that have survived are anything to go by (see overleaf). Cast in metal, silver or tin, and worn on a thong about the neck, these served as amulets, harnessing the power of the god to protect and aid in all kinds of human endeavours, in particular fishing, travelling and farming. Freyr is credited with bringing fertility to beast and soil, but the weather is absolutely critical to success on both sea and land. Although the myths do not tell us much about human interactions with Þórr – apart from his demand that he be given a farmer's two children as his servants – the sagas are very clear about his importance. When Christian missionaries arrive in Iceland, poems and sagas tell us, the god, the 'White-Christ', they preach is usually compared with Þórr, not usually to Christ's advantage. So when the missionary Þangbrandr's ship is wrecked in a storm, *Kristni saga* (The Saga of Christianity) relates how a woman called Steinunn makes up a couple of derogatory verses. Þórr, she says, pulled the 'sea-beast' out of its place, shook it and beat it and smashed it against the land; in a second verse, she adds that Þórr broke the 'bison of the gull-seat' (the ship), despite the 'bell-guardian' (the priest). Christ did not protect it, and God took little care of the ship – or his priest. One–nil to Þórr.

Gradually, though, as Scandinavia converted to Christianity, Christ does indeed win the victory over Þórr. According to early histories, such as Snorri Sturluson's *Heimskringla*, King Óláfr Tryggvason, the missionary king of Norway, marches into the temple at Trondheim and knocks the statue of Þórr off his throne without more ado. His successor, Óláfr the saint, goes to convert an inveterate heathen called Guðbrandr, who thinks that carrying his people's idol of Þórr in order to confront the king will be effective, especially given the fact that the king's god is invisible. The statue of Þórr is indeed brought to the conference between the farmers of Dalir, led by Guðbrandr, and the king and his men. It is huge, bears a hammer, is adorned with gold and silver, and is hollow inside; offerings of bread and meat are made to it daily. The king tells the assembly to look at the rising sun, and while their attention is directed elsewhere his associate Kolbeinn gives the statue a mighty blow. It keels over and breaks open; rats as big as cats, mice, snakes and toads rush out. Þórr is disgraced and shown to be a mere empty, pest-ridden idol, and Guðbrandr, along with the other men of Dalir, agree to be christened on the spot. This 'debunking of the idols' motif is a popular one (a similar tale is told of an idol representing Freyr), found not only relation to the Old Norse gods but the classical gods as well.

In the wake of conversion, smiths transformed their hammer-shaped moulds into crucifix-shaped ones, and some enterprising craftsmen even manufactured dual hammer–crosses for those in two minds about their divine protector. While Óðinn retained his role as the king who had emigrated from Troy and as progenitor of the Scandinavians, Þórr figures in two different accounts given by Snorri. In one he is a grandson of Priam of Troy called Tror. He is brought up in Thrace, where he kills his foster-parents and seizes the kingdom. In his travels in the northern part of the world, he meets the Sibyl, whom he marries; this is Sif, Snorri explains. Tror defeats giants, berserkers and a particularly fierce dragon before he returns home and has sons by his wife. Many generations later, Óðinn is born and, as we read in the previous chapter, sets out to lead the migration to the North. In another part of his *Edda*, Snorri identifies the Trojan prince Hector with Þórr, proving the connection by noting one of the god's bynames, Öku-Þórr ('Driving-Þórr', a reference to the goat-drawn chariot). Öku-Þórr does indeed sound a bit like 'Hector' or 'Ector', as Snorri tells it. However, one incontrovertible fact about Hector was that he was killed by Achilles. Although his statue might have been venerated in Uppsala, as Adam of Bremen tells us, he does not count as an ancestor of the royal lines of Scandinavia. Thus Þórr goes somewhat out of fashion in post-medieval accounts of the Norse gods, even if his connection with thunder keeps him alive in Scandinavian folklore.

### Þórr returns

In the 19th century, Þórr was rediscovered by poets and writers in Denmark and Germany. They tended to retell the stories of his exploits against the giants; these could be identified with a range of contemporary enemies while the god represented the epitome of Danish or German national identity. In the English-speaking world, Þórr was viewed nostalgically, as recalling aspects

'Thor's hammer' amulet and mould, Denmark (10th century).

of a bygone heroic but flawed age; his eclipse by Christ was understood as inevitable as his followers turned at last to the true faith. An early and stirring poem about the god is the American poet Henry Wadsworth Longfellow's 'The Challenge of Thor' (1863), which revisits the medieval opposition between Þórr and Christ. Þórr begins by proclaiming the various roles with which he is associated, as god of thunder and god of violence:

> I am the God Thor,
> I am the War God,
> I am the Thunderer!
> Here in my Northland,
> My fastness and fortress,
> Reign I forever!

The god brags of how he holds sway among the icebergs, brandishing his hammer, wielding his belt of power and the magic gauntlets that, in one Old Norse poem, he uses to catch a red-hot ball of iron hurled at him by the giant Geirrøðr (deftly catching it, he hurls it back, totally destroying his opponent). Later in Longfellow's poem Þórr presents himself as a deity of huge natural phenomena: lightning flashes from his eyes; the rumble of his chariot wheels causes the thunder; his red beard is the comet that hurtles across the night sky; and when he whirls his hammer, he causes earthquakes. Þórr's credo is one of 'might equals right':

> Meekness is weakness,
> Strength is triumphant,
> Over the whole earth
> Still is it Thor's-Day!

Thor's-Day (Thursday) it may be, but the doctrine of absolute power gives way, in the last stanza, to a less boastful tone. Thor recognizes 'the Galilean' as a god too and challenges him to single combat: 'Gauntlet or Gospel, / Here I defy thee!' Although the power that

Þórr wields is embodied in nature, here he is also depicted as the god of war, and the gentler beliefs of Christ are not elaborated upon. Nevertheless, while a 19th-century audience would have admired Þórr's defiance, they would also know that the Galilean had indeed triumphed. Longfellow, who travelled in Scandinavia in his youth, composed a number of poems about Norse mythic and legendary subjects, as we shall see in Chapter 9.

A contrasting position to that of Longfellow is adopted in an early poem by the American fantasy writer H. P. Lovecraft. He celebrates the idea of *ragna rök* as a final, explosive confrontation in which 'the gentle maxims of the school, / the cant of preachers, and the Golden Rule' will be cast aside in favour of crude and joyful violence: the 'feeble word or doctrine' shall no longer hold sway. Classical philosophy and mild Christian sentiments will be abandoned as men give way to their primordial instincts ('race' instincts, says Lovecraft, himself a notorious white supremacist). There will be a terrible bloodbath in which cries of pain sound like a symphony: 'Slay, brothers, slay! And bathe in crimson gore; /

Hermann Ernst Freund,
*Thor* (1828–29).

114

Let Thor, triumphant, view the sport once more!' proclaims the speaker, as he exults in the idea of death, the destruction of the world and the victory of the Allfather (Óðinn). Lovecraft was writing in the run-up to the First World War: although this poem, 'The Teuton's Battle-Song', was published in 1916, it was composed somewhat earlier. Lovecraft had long believed that Christianity was a religion for weaklings; that the 'Teutonic stock' had found its finest expression in the British Isles, where Northern courage and ferocity were combined with the inherited knowledge of Greece and Rome; and that it was above all the British-descended inhabitants of New England, among whom he counted himself, who best preserved this heritage. The veneer of civilization that characterized the modern European could quickly disappear, for, writes Lovecraft, 'in the heat of combat he [the Teuton] is quite prone to revert to the mental type of his own Woden-worshipping progenitors'. Lovecraft's racialized thinking chimes with the arguments being made in Germany by Nazi theorists around the same time, and it also resonates with contemporary white supremacist beliefs. These frequently include nostalgic claims about 'Viking' ancestry and the legacy of Þórr as authorizing violence against those, like the giants, who are defined as 'Other'.

**Thor the Marvellous**

In August 1962 Þórr's fortunes took a new and unexpected turn when Jack Kirby, Stan Lee and Larry Lieber decided to introduce an all-new character, the Mighty Thor, in an original series for Marvel Comics. Lee had the idea of choosing a Norse god rather than inventing an original superhero, and he came with splendidly distinctive accoutrements: 'I pictured Norse gods looking like Vikings of old, with the flowing beards, horned helmets, and battle clubs,' said Lee in 2002. Kirby, it seems, already knew quite a bit about the Norse gods and so was able to incorporate other characters from the pantheon into the Thor storyline. In the Marvel

Comics version, Thor regains his original affinity with humans when Odin banishes him to Earth in order to learn humility. His memory of his godhood erased, Thor is partly disabled and, as a medical student called Donald Blake, he is also mortal. On holiday in Norway, he wanders into a cave where he finds Mjöllnir disguised as a walking stick; striking it against a rock, he reactivates his divine identity. Mjöllnir not only allows Thor to determine the weather all across the globe, but also enables him to fly – as well, of course, as fulfilling its original function as invincible weapon.

Thor remains on Earth, aiding the sick with his medical skills – assisted by the loyal scientist Jane Foster, with whom he eventually falls in love – and he assumes his divine form to fight off various enemies intent on attacking humanity. Loki launches various assaults on Thor, who is his adoptive brother, summoning a host of antagonists, some of whom derive from Old Norse tradition. These include Surtur the fire giant and Laufey, the leader of the Frost Giants (and Loki's true father). Odin seeks to recall his son to Asgard, but now that he is in love with Jane Thor refuses to return. His affinity with life on Earth is explained by the revelation that his mother is the primal goddess Gaea: the Greek earth goddess. In fact, as we know, in the Norse myths Þórr's mother is the giantess Jörð, or Earth; the scriptwriters stay true to the concept, even if she is given a Greek name.

The comic-book Thor also becomes a member of the Avengers, a team of superheroes including the Incredible Hulk and Iron Man. He meets Hercules, the classical hero, who becomes a firm friend, and over the sixty years of his career he has had an extraordinary range of adventures. He has lost body parts and replaced them with prostheses; he has even been deprived of Mjöllnir and has had to harness huge forces and resources to enable the dwarfs to forge a replacement. Controversially, in one storyline from 2014 Thor loses his capacity to wield Mjöllnir; Jane Foster takes up the hammer in his place, thus herself becoming Thor.

With the loss of the hammer comes a total loss of identity: Thor relinquishes his name, taking on that of Odinson, and his new weapon is the battle-axe Jarnbjorn ('Iron-bear'). Undergoing a huge crisis of confidence, questioning his very identity and purpose, Thor finds himself 'emotionally crippled'. No longer the 'Mighty Thor', but rather the 'Unworthy Thor', the hero finds himself in 'a pretty dark place'. He is a 'darker, more desperate, more driven version', according to Jason Aaron, who created both the 'Jane Foster as Thor' and the 'Unworthy Thor' storylines. In the comic universe, then, it is Mjöllnir that confers the state of 'being Thor' on the person who is capable of wielding the weapon: self-doubt, feelings of unworthiness and guilt for past actions shake up the superhero's idea of himself when that relationship is disrupted. This development produces a profoundly psychological reading of what it means to be a god – or a confident and mature human being – and is the starting point for the fourth Thor movie, *Thor: Love and Thunder* (2022).

### Moving into the movies

This unsettling storyline emerged as the comic books responded to the transfer of Thor onto the big screen. The *Thor* movie series begins where the comics also started: with Thor's exile to Earth for his disobedience to his father. Once there, he mounts a retaliatory raid on Jotunheim in response to the infiltration of Asgard by a couple of renegade Frost Giants. Landing in New Mexico, Thor (Chris Hemsworth) falls in with Jane Foster (Natalie Portman), the astrophysicist, her mentor Erik Selvig (himself of Scandinavian descent; he is played by Stellan Skarsgård) and Darcy (Kat Dennings), the team's comic sidekick. Mjöllnir has followed Thor to Earth and is deeply embedded in a rock in the desert; there it has become a tourist destination as rednecks bring their trucks and barbecues and try to pull the hammer out of the stone, recalling the feat of King Arthur and Excalibur. A shadowy government organization takes control of the area, and Thor must fight his way in to grasp his weapon, only to find that he too is unable to shift Mjöllnir. He is not yet ready, not yet worthy.

Thor will of course eventually learn the lessons afforded by his exile. 'My father was trying to teach me something, but I was too stupid to see it,' he admits to Selvig as the pair sink drink after drink in a bar. The human research team come to realize that Thor and his people are indeed identical to the Æsir of legend and that, as Jane notes, 'a primitive culture like the Vikings might have worshipped them as deities' – for, in the pre-credit sequence, we learn how in early medieval Norway the gods had originally defeated the Frost Giants, driven them back to Jotunheim and saved humanity. When the Destroyer, a monstrous robot-like creature, is unleashed upon the human community, Thor springs to humanity's defence, marshalling the fleeing citizens and then fearlessly facing up to the automaton. Without Mjöllnir, Thor is in grave danger, but thanks to Odin's intervention the hammer is returned to him and he is able to overcome the Destroyer. Once Thor recovers the hammer, he returns to Asgard just in time to defeat an attack by the Frost Giants and he mends fences with his father. 'You'll be a wise king,' Odin (Anthony Hopkins) observes in the final scenes; Thor responds, 'There'll never be a wiser king than you, or a better father.'

In *Thor: The Dark World*, the threat to the Nine Realms is embodied by Malekith (Christopher Eccleston), the leader of the Dark Elves. In this film the battle for the cosmos is waged on Earth – to be precise, in Greenwich, London – where many lines of dark energy cross, including (of course) the meridian. Here we learn about the Asgardians' perceptions of themselves; in response to Loki (Tom Hiddleston), who (in an intervening Avengers film) had tried to unite the people of Midgard in worshipping him 'as a benevolent god', Odin remarks: 'We are not gods. We are born, we live, we die. Just as humans do.' 'Give or take 5,000 years,' ripostes

Loki. In this film, Thor continues to resist the idea of kingship – 'I'd rather be a good man than a great king,' he argues – unlike Loki, who, as we shall see in the next chapter, is obsessed with gaining rule over Asgard and triumphing over his brother.

In *Thor: Ragnarok*, the catastrophe is heralded at the start of the film. Just as Baldr's impending death in the Norse tradition is prefigured by his bad dreams, Thor's sleep has also been marred by nightmares. In the Norse poem *Baldrs draumar* (Baldr's Dreams),

Chris Hemsworth as the eponymous hero in Kenneth Branagh's *Thor* (2011).

Óðinn rides to the edges of Hel's kingdom to discover from a dead seeress that Baldr's arrival is keenly anticipated in Hel's own hall: the ale is brewed in readiness, and the benches strewn with clean straw. So in *Thor: Ragnarok*, while Loki continues to cause trouble, it is the emergence of Hela, the goddess of death and eldest child of Odin, that threatens to annihilate Asgard and its people.

The first *Thor* film was directed by the distinguished actor Kenneth Branagh, and he draws out the Shakespearean themes of family conflict within a royal dynasty: the heir who is not ready for rule, and bitter fraternal rivalry felt by the adopted brother, Loki. The second film, *Thor: The Dark World*, was helmed by Alan Taylor, who concomitantly directed several episodes of *Game of Thrones*; the influence of the television show is reflected in the huge battle scenes, and Thor is reunited with Jane. The third movie, *Thor: Ragnarok*, reflects the vision of the maverick New Zealand director Taika Waititi. While it continues the themes of kingship and family strife found in the earlier films, it is riotously funny and inventive. Very early in the film, Waititi has Mjöllnir, that crucial emblem of Thor's male – and very white – power destroyed. Hela (Cate Blanchett) simply explodes it as she catches it in her grip, for she had once wielded it herself and still retains some affinity with it. Unlike the temporary separation of superhero and weapon in the first of the *Thor* films, this time Mjöllnir stays destroyed – at least for the duration of the film. As a director of Maori heritage, Waititi was acutely aware of the symbolism of the hammer in contemporary 'cosmic right' circles and thus removed it from Thor's arsenal. This is a key element in his general rescripting of the Marvel Universe: one that puts Earth aside, dispenses with well-loved characters such as Lady Sif and The Warriors Three, and that sets a good deal of the action on another planet, Sakaar. Here Thor encounters the last of the Valkyries – Scrapper #142, also known as Valkyrie (Tessa Thompson) – and recruits her to return to Asgard with him.

*Thor: Ragnarok* is also interested in depicting Thor's significant character development. This time when Loki tries to double-cross his adoptive brother at a key stage in their escape from Sakaar, Thor is one step ahead of him. In the course of their tried-and-tested 'get help' ruse, intended to gain them entrance into the space-vehicle garage of the Grandmaster (Jeff Goldblum), Thor has quietly planted an Obedience Disc into Loki's neck and can now paralyse him with a zapper. 'Oh brother,' says Thor, 'you're becoming predictable. I trust you; you betray me. Round and round in circles we go.' By the end of this film, Thor has grown into kingship and learned the true extent of Loki's loyalties; he is now ready to lead the Asgardians into the future. (There's further discussion of *Thor: Ragnarok* in Chapter 10.)

Thor in the movies shares many characteristics with the deity: he is strong, he is not especially thoughtful (at least not at first), and once on Earth he dedicates himself to protecting humankind against the monsters unleashed by his enemies. Thor is always a courageous fighter, temporarily wrongfooted when he is separated from Mjöllnir but not completely powerless. In the myths, when Þórr sets out to visit the giant Geirrøðr, having left his hammer at home, he has to call upon his *ásmegin*, the divine power that is integral to him – and is woven into his belt. It turns out that the belt has also been left at home, and Þórr has to manage without his key attributes. Likewise, when Hela destroys Mjöllnir after materializing in Norway as Odin is dying, Thor must learn that he can cope without this magical prop: 'That hammer helped you control your power, focus it. But it was never the source of your strength,' Odin reveals at the film's climax.

There are some differences in characterization too. Having a human love interest in Jane Foster means that Sif – traditionally the god's wife but here an ally of the doughty fighting trio The Warriors Three – yearns for Thor in vain. Nor does movie-Thor share the huge appetites of the god. Instead it is another Warrior companion, Volstagg (Ray Stevenson), who is the glutton. When Thor is cast out to Earth in the first movie, Volstagg appears unconcerned. Fandral (Josh Dallas), another of the Warriors, is shocked: 'Our dearest friend banished, Loki on the throne, Asgard on the brink of war, yet you manage to consume four wild boar, six pheasant, a side of beef, and two casks of ale!' 'Do not mistake appetite for apathy,' retorts Volstagg, casting aside his trencher and leaping to his feet. There are more adventures in preparation in Hollywood, extending the series with Thor as the focal character, together with films in which he fights alongside the other Avengers. Following the wholesale destruction of Asgard by Surtur (voiced by Clancy Brown) and Hela in the last movie, a new start for the home planet – and possibly the employment of a whole team of master builders, with or without their magical stallions – looks to be necessary. In Waititi's *Thor: Love and Thunder*, Valkyrie becomes ruler of New Asgard, as Thor is absent, battling with the psychological crisis outlined above and coming to terms with Jane Foster's appropriation of his own superhero identity.

**Thor in contemporary novels**

Where the Marvel Thor – particularly, as we have seen, the movie version – matures into the role of hero and king, his avatars in mainstream literature fare less well. He has no role in *American Gods*, having committed suicide forty years before his fortunes would be revived by Marvel Comics. Mr Wednesday reminisces to Shadow:

> 'I just keep thinking about Thor. You never knew him. Big guy, like you. Big-hearted. Not bright, but he'd give you the goddam shirt off his back if you asked him. And he killed himself. He put a gun in his mouth and blew his head off in Philadelphia in 1932. What kind of way is that for a god to die?'

Thor certainly does not share the cunning and duplicity of Mr Wednesday and Mr World, but it is hard to see the Old Norse god killing himself unless he is making the ultimate sacrifice to destroy the Miðgarðs Serpent. Yet the idea of the god as none too clever, easily fooled and mainly interested in violence persists across other literary treatments. For Joanne Harris's Loki, who narrates *The Testament of Loki* (2018), admittedly from a very partial point of view, Thor is 'a muscle-bound oaf with more beard than brain and a love of sports and hitting things'. That Thor is treated as somewhat stupid and violent limits the roles he can play in modern retellings. The most popular of his adventures is undoubtedly the tale from *Þrymskviða* (The Poem of Þrymr) in which Mjöllnir is stolen and can be retrieved only if Freyja will agree to marry the giant Þrymr. As noted above, Freyja refuses, and so the gods dress a heavily veiled Thor as a bride and send him off to Giantlands with Loki to do the talking:

> And that was how, eight days later, the Thunderer,
> dressed in one of Freyja's gowns, drenched in her
> perfume, arms and legs waxed, fingernails gilded, wearing
> Freyja's necklace and an expression of murderous rage
> (happily, hidden under the veil), set off on the road to the
> Northlands with Your Humble Narrator at his side.

Once the hammer is restored to the god during the marriage ritual, he takes his revenge, and soon the hall 'is piled with broken corpses. You had to admit,' opines Loki, 'he was good – not smart, but a death machine on two legs.'

Unlike Óðinn and Freyr – whose offspring, in Snorri's accounts and more widely in Norse tradition, become kings – Þórr has no human descendants; no dynasties trace him as their ancestor despite his popularity in place and personal naming practices. While his sons Móði and Magni survive *ragna rök* and will dwell in the golden hall of Gimlé, where the gods gather to recall the past, nothing further is related of them. In Joanne Harris's young adult novels *Runemarks* (2007) and *Runelight* (2011), the twin-sister heroines, Maddy and Maggie, discover that Thor is in fact their father and Jarnsaxa the giantess their mother: their names are of course feminized versions of Móði and Magni. A human lineage descending from Thor is invented in the *Blackwell Pages* fantasy series (2013–15), set in the US in South Dakota and written by K. L. Armstrong and M. A. Marr. As his surname suggests, the hero, Matt Thorsen, is not only directly descended from the god – he is indeed Thor reincarnated. Matt is charged with the task of preventing *ragna rök*; his cousins, Fen and Laurie, descendants of Loki, are both allies and antagonists across the series. As a type of Thor, Matt is able to summon thunder and lightning at will, and in the final book he finds himself fighting the World Serpent Jörmungandr and almost succumbing to its deadly poison.

In other young adult series, the god simply materializes in the modern world, often to comic – or partly comic – effect. In Rick Riordan's *Magnus Chase* series, in the second novel, *The Hammer of Thor* (2016), Magnus encounters Thor himself and is surprised to find he does not resemble the Marvel hero, 'with bright Spandex tights, a red cape, goldilocks hair and maybe a helmet with fluffy little dove wings'. When Thor's hammer has been stolen and cannot be found even via the god's 'Find my Hammer' app, just as in the Old Norse Loki's help is enlisted, and the god must once again cross-dress (in a frock that he rather admires) if Mjöllnir is to be recovered. In Francesca Simon's *The Lost Gods* (2013), a follow-up to *The Sleeping Army* (2011), Óðinn, Þórr and Freyja, anxious that their powers are on the wane now that humans rarely sacrifice to them, arrive in London in search of Freya, their ally in the previous novel. The gods seek to expand and renew their worship among their followers, and they need Freya's assistance to bring this about. Þórr, huge and red-bearded, lashes out with his hammer whenever he is puzzled by the modern world (the first casualty is

Freya's mobile phone). Watching a television talent show, Freya has an astonishing insight: 'The gods didn't need worshippers. They needed fans.' Indeed, the gods go on to achieve all the success that could be hoped for in celebrity culture: Thor is signed to play football for Tottenham Hotspur, becoming 'the greatest footballer ever to play in the premier league'. The god is greatly taken with his new career ('I love this game ... Even more fun than bashing giants!') and soon he is promoting his own lightning-bolt-branded tracksuit range. The fans' adulation restores the gods' powers, and although the Frost Giants advance on both Asgard and Midgard their defeat depends, as so often, on Thor undertaking to dress as a bride in order to lure all the gods' enemies to Thrym's wedding, where they can be destroyed.

Þórr roars and smashes his way through the Norse myths, but nevertheless he has a powerful bond with humans. He is invoked in personal and place names; he protects seafarers and even visits human homes from time to time. When Óðinn sneers at him that he 'owns the thralls', Þórr does not dissent: the ordinary farmers, sailors and labourers are his followers, and he delivers to them the weather they need. He is imagined as strongly resisting the coming of Christ, and when he re-emerges in the 19th century he is the powerful god of thunder, the hero of Asgard and the bulwark of the gods in the face of the chaos and destruction represented by the giants. Figuring a self-assertive nationalism in Scandinavia and Germany in the early part of the 20th century, he swung his hammer in defence of his people – whoever they might be.

Yet most recent versions of Þórr take him as an at least partly comic figure. He lacks eloquence, swings his hammer instead of speaking, and he is ultraviolent, macho and rather stupid: Harris's 'muscle-bound oaf'. Heroes whose main claim to fame is brute strength have not fared well in an age where other skills are more valued, and Loki's smooth tongue and cunning mind are set in contrast to the thunder god's recourse to violent action. His hypermasculinity, symbolized by Mjöllnir, comes under threat; to lose his hammer is to lose confidence and power, yet the only way it can be recovered when it is stolen by Þrymr is to submit to the charade of dressing up as Freyja, veiled, silent and fuming, as quick-tongued Loki explains away his red eyes and gargantuan appetite as a sign of 'Freyja's' longing to come to Jötunheimar ('Giantlands') to embrace 'her' bridegroom. The episode is a favourite of modern writers: the comic inversions lighten plot lines that tend towards apocalypse. Þórr is humiliated (at least until he regains his hammer); that he might take some pleasure in escaping into another kind of identity, in experimenting with feminine behaviour and performance, is rarely mooted in these retellings.

Þórr still has work to do, though. The enemies against whom he is pitched represent terrifying forces: the frost giants, the dark elves who wish to return the universe to primordial nothingness, the terrible power of fire. The Marvel Thor has a strangely protean identity: he need not be the son of Odin, nor even male; he does not require Mjöllnir, but can simply call upon his divine power (in what looks to be a profoundly American move, his self-belief and confidence will overcome all obstacles). This Thor, the Thor of the movies, is incorporated within a troubled family structure. With his mother and father now dead, his adoptive brother an untrustworthy ally and his love interest living on another planet, he has to contend with human emotions and rivalries, with disappointments, betrayals, triumphs and tragedies that make him a key contemporary fantasy hero: one who is all too human, and thus one who still speaks to us in ways that remain relevant.

# Loki and his Children

## THE MYTH OF THE MONSTROUS BROOD

Loki is perhaps the most intriguing figure in Old Norse myth. We have no idea if he was regarded as a god: there is no evidence that anyone ever worshipped him or incorporated his name into place or personal names. His father was a giant called Fárbauti, and his mother, Laufey, may be one of the Æsir; such an unusual pairing would account for his uncertain status in Ásgarðr. He causes endless trouble, yet he is also extraordinarily useful. Nevertheless, his loyalties are finally aligned with the giants, alongside whom he will fight at *ragna rök*. For now, he remains among the Æsir, insisting on his blood-brotherhood with Óðinn, and he has a wife and children who seem like other gods. He can also change his shape (like his blood-brother), sleeps with giantesses and fathers an extraordinary range of children. When gods go off on adventures, Loki often makes up one of the party: he is both a liability and a good companion in a crisis. And, unexpectedly, his stock has risen in contemporary popular culture – not just in the Marvel Universe, but in other treatments of his story. He has become a figure of sympathetic interest, capable of being imagined with an unusual suppleness. Let us see why.

The Snaptun Stone, showing Loki with his mouth sewn shut (*c.* 1000).

### Trickster or traitor?

Loki's actions range from relatively harmless pranks to orchestrating the murder of the most beloved of the gods, Baldr. Some of his adventures seem playful, if malicious. He cuts off Sif's glorious golden hair, raising the question of how he managed to come quite so close to her. Loki is forced by the gods to restore her lost locks, commissioning a splendid new hairpiece of actual gold from some dwarfs. At the same time they manufacture a series of other marvellous treasures: the ship Skíðblaðnir, which can be folded up and carried in the pocket, given to Freyr, and Óðinn's signature spear, Gungnir. This isn't quite enough amusement for Loki, though; in an elaborate stratagem he dares to wager his head that Brokkr, brother of one of the dwarf craftsmen, cannot make three equally excellent objects. The competitive Brokkr sets to work, and thus are created the golden boar Gullinbursti, which Freyr rides; the gold ring Draupnir, from which eight equally heavy rings drop every nine nights (it is an attribute of Óðinn); and finally Þórr's mighty hammer, Mjöllnir. Loki cleverly changes himself into a fly that stings Brokkr to distract him, and as a result the hammer's handle comes out a little short. Nevertheless, the Æsir judge that Brokkr has won, for Mjöllnir, despite its deficiency, is the best of all the treasures, given its giant-quelling powers. Loki looks set to lose his head, but when he stipulates that Brokkr may not take any of his neck, the dwarf concedes defeat. All the same, he takes an awl and some cord and sews Loki's mouth shut – a lesson about what happens when the cockily self-confident find themselves saying too much. Loki rips out the stitches but is left with scarred lips.

When he goes out and about, Loki's penchant for impetuous actions often gets him into trouble. Poking an eagle that seems magically to be preventing the gods' supper from cooking with a stick proves disastrous. The stick adheres to the eagle (the giant Þjazi in disguise) and to Loki's hands. The eagle flies off with the dangling god; if he wants to win his freedom, Loki has to agree to help Þjazi abduct the goddess Iðunn and her apples of youth. Loki is later suspected of complicity in Iðunn's vanishing, for she was last seen with him. The grey-haired and ageing gods, anxious that the apples that kept them ever young have disappeared for good, seize Loki and force him to rescue Iðunn – a tale that forms the basis for Francesca Simon's novel *The Sleeping Army* (2011), discussed below. This escapade results in Þjazi's death and the arrival of his daughter Skaði in Ásgarðr, fully armed and seeking recompense for her father. She is ready to accept marriage in settlement of the feud, but when she is tricked into choosing Njörðr the sea god rather than Baldr the beautiful, by dint of selecting her future husband on the basis of his feet, she refuses reconciliation. Unless, that is, the gods can somehow make her laugh. Again, it is Loki who finds a solution. He ties his testicles to the beard of a nanny goat and each pulls in a different direction: it's hard to determine who screeches more loudly, notes Snorri. This does indeed make Skaði laugh, and she agrees to the marriage – even if the couple are not well matched and soon separate.

Another time, having borrowed Frigg's falcon skin and flown into Giantlands 'out of curiosity', Loki is captured by the giant Geirrøðr, shut in a chest for three months and released only when he promises to bring Þórr into the giant's territory, minus Mjöllnir

Loki in a manuscript illustration by Jakob Sigurðsson (1765).

and his belt of power. Þórr still succeeds in defeating Geirrøðr and his vicious daughters thanks to a stout staff and a pair of magic iron gloves provided by Gríðr, a helpful giantess. And finally, as we'll see in Chapter 7, a casual stone tossed by Loki at a dozing otter digesting his dinner of salmon precipitates a series of events that has profound repercussions in the human world.

Contrasting with these casual, often improvised moves on Loki's part, where he is often forced to fix problems he is complicit in causing, are some instances where he does act with altruistic motives. When the giant Þrymr steals Þórr's hammer, Loki is instrumental in the negotiations and strategy that enable its return. We might suspect that, although it is Heimdallr who suggests dressing up Þórr as a bride when Freyja proves unwilling, Loki takes considerable pleasure in perpetrating the imposture. He also dresses himself in women's clothes, acting as a sharp-witted handmaiden, and his ready answers win time for the hammer to be returned to Þórr's waiting fist. So too he accompanies Þórr on his visit to Útgarða-Loki and, although we might see that tricksy giant as a double of Loki of Ásgarðr, Loki plays it straight both on the journey and in Útgarðr itself. We saw in Chapter 2 how Loki saved the gods from having to hand over the sun, moon and Freyja to the master builder – admittedly a bad bargain whose acceptance he had earlier urged. Here his gender fluidity is clearly manifested: he does not simply pretend to be female, but transforms himself into a mare, successfully distracting the master builder's helpful stallion.

The trickster, then, is one key facet of Loki's identity. But as mythological history shows, Loki shifts from amusing, if nasty, jokes to shattering the community of the gods, casting aside essential values of kin loyalty and guest behaviour, and aligning himself finally with the giants. From his orchestration of the death of Baldr, his provocation of the gods as related in the poem *Lokasenna* (Loki's Quarrel) and his capture and binding with the guts of his own son to his presence on the ship Naglfari in the company of

James Doyle Penrose, *The Punishment of Loki*, from Donald A. Mackenzie's
*Teutonic Myth and Legend: An Introduction to the Eddas & Sagas* (1894).

the fire giants at *ragna rök*, Loki transforms himself from a nuisance into a deadly adversary: a figure who relies on cleverness and speed rather than strength and far-sightedness to make his way through the worlds of gods and men.

## Óðinn's queer double

Why do the gods permit Loki to remain among them, given the trouble he causes and the knowledge that Óðinn, at least, has of his future role in *ragna rök*? The answer seems to lie back at the dawn of mythic time when, for some reason, Óðinn and Loki swore blood-brotherhood. Loki, as he intimates in his explosive confrontation with all the gods at the feast in Ægir's hall, knows things about Óðinn that should be kept secret, or so Frigg warns. These dark hints seem to have to do with the magical practice known as *seiðr*. We know very little about what this may have entailed, although it seems to borrow some shamanic features from the neighbouring culture of the Sámi, beating on a drum in particular. Women are the main practitioners of *seiðr*: Freyja is credited with its knowledge, and in the sagas the figure of the *seiðkona* (*seiðr*-woman), who can prophesy the future and summon spirits, is a familiar one. Loki and Óðinn both have knowledge of *seiðr*; each accuses the other of cross-dressing, shape-changing and trafficking in hidden knowledge.

Both Óðinn and Loki are sexual adventurers. Óðinn fathers children on human women and does not shirk from disguising himself as an elderly woman to get access to the princess Rindr, who is destined to be the mother of Váli, Baldr's avenger. He also has affairs with giantesses: Jörð, Þórr's mother; Skaði (so it is said); and Gunnlöð, who keeps the mead of poetry and lets him have three drinks of it in exchange for the three nights they spend together. Loki has a wife among the goddesses, Sigyn, who bears him two sons. We know little about her apart from her loyal efforts to save her husband from the venom-dripping serpent hung by

Skaði over Loki's face once the gods have captured and bound him. He also has a liaison with a giantess, Angrboða, the mother of three unusual children: Fenrir the great wolf, the Miðgarðs Serpent and Hel, who rules over the realm of death. If Loki is to be believed (not necessarily a given), he has also slept with a good number of the goddesses: he fathered a child with Týr's wife, was invited to bed by Skaði and Sif – perhaps taking her hair as a trophy – and Iðunn and Gefjun may also be among his lovers.

Where Loki surpasses his blood-brother, however, is in sexual behaviour that we would now regard as queer or gender non-conforming. Óðinn notes that Loki spent eight winters below the Earth in female form, milking cows (a lowly occupation) and bearing children, and we also learn that eating a half-roasted heart belonging to a powerful witch impregnated him, such that he became ancestor (or ancestress) of a line of ogresses. Not only does Loki have this female capacity to reproduce, as we recall from the 'Tale of the Master Builder', he does not shy away from trans-species sex, changing into a mare in order to distract the stallion Svaðilfari and giving birth to Óðinn's eight-legged horse, Sleipnir. The modern Loki, as we shall see – unlike his ageing blood-brother – is often imagined as bisexual or ready for different types of sexual experimentation.

## Loki's monstrous offspring

In addition to his two normal sons with Sigyn and the distinctly aberrant Sleipnir, Loki and Angrboða produced three powerful offspring who play significant roles at *ragna rök*. Until that time comes, the three children are assigned distinctive and crucial functions by the Æsir. Perhaps since Loki's children may share their blood, the gods do not elect to destroy them when they are young, but rather employ them to generate and demarcate boundaries between important and often opposed domains. Fenrir the wolf is reared among the Æsir. Snorri depicts him as quite an amiable animal, talkative and playful, and he is regularly fed by Týr. According to Snorri's detailed account given in *Gylfaginning* (The Deluding of Gylfi), the decision to fetter him rests partly on prophecies that he will harm the Æsir, partly on alarm about his increasing size and appetite. Fenrir does not seem particularly ill disposed towards the gods until they mistreat him; they organize a competition to see if he can break whatever bonds they put on him. Fenrir simply regards this as an opportunity to win honour for his strength. But the wolf is no fool: Fenrir suspects that something is not right about the deceptively soft and silky bond the gods finally offer him, and undertakes to try to snap it only on condition that one of the gods place his hand in the wolf's mouth as a pledge of good faith. Týr, guarantor of law and of solemnly sworn oaths and Fenrir's former caregiver, steps up. The gods'

Steve Fields, *Sleipnir*, Wednesbury, England (1998).

duplicity compromises Týr: the god of justice must swear falsely to the suspicious wolf. As the fetter tightens and the wolf realizes he has been tricked, Týr loses his hand – while the other gods laugh. Now, instead of keeping watchful guard over his master's property, the wolf glares balefully at the civilized world from afar. Fenrir has been turned into a rabid dog, slavering and wild, his jaws painfully propped open by a sword so that rivers of drool run out of his maw. Now he waits in his bonds for the day of his vengeance, gazing keenly at the homes of gods and men and biding his time. He is made to signify time itself, which will come to its end after he gets loose.

The Miðgarðs Serpent (Miðgarðsormr) was cast into the sea by the gods, and there he lurks in the outer ocean, with his tail in his mouth, signifying the furthest limits of space. Men can venture no further than where the Miðgarðsormr lurks – a limit that Hymir the giant recognizes when he advocates a little flat-fish angling in preference to rowing out to the margins where the serpent represents a real danger, the course of action that Þórr nevertheless insists upon (see Chapter 4). And Hel, half attractive woman, half decaying corpse, is sent down to be ruler of Niflheim, the underworld where those who do not die heroic deaths must wait out eternity. There, as the story of Baldr makes clear, she is both hospitable and courteous, seating her newly arrived honoured guest in the high seat, and she offers hospitality too to the gods' messenger, Hermóðr, though she wisely decides to test the assertions he makes about Baldr's universal popularity (see Chapter 10). Although poetic kennings often denote her in terms of her siblings and her father, thus inscribing her, like other women, within her kin network, she has no husband and thus no one to constrain her power. She symbolizes death, which – as we have seen – is imagined as feminine and desiring. Like her father, who is both god and giant, Hel embodies the paradox of 'Both/And', at once living and yet dead. (The dead are a crisis-ridden category in Old

The binding of Fenrir, manuscript illustration
by Jakob Sigurðsson (1760).

Norse belief, where the dangerous deceased very often walk again
and harm the living.) The way to Hel's domain is guarded by female
sentries: giantesses, a dead seeress, and the girl Móðguðr. A hostile
beast – a barking and bloody dog, perhaps also kin to Fenrir – and
high gates bar the road to her realm.

These three children of Loki lurk at the margins awaiting their
moment, the time of *ragna rök*, when their irruption will mark

the end of one version of time, of space and mortality. Yet they are also harbingers of a new heaven and a new earth, signalled as arising anew in the final verses of *Völuspá* (The Seeress's Prophecy). All three have captured the imaginations of later writers; while the wolf and serpent, representing an animal monstrosity, have so far seemed a little less interesting to think with, Hel in particular has featured in a number of recent works, as we'll see below.

## God of fire?

Jacob Grimm and the many scholars who followed his lead regard Loki as a god of fire, for the figure of Logi ('Fire'), Loki's opponent in the eating competition at Útgarða-Loki's, was understood to be an aspect of the god. In fact, apart from this contest, Loki has no clear connection with fire in the mythological sources. Wagner, however, took up Grimm's suggestion in his characterization of Loge in *Das Rheingold*. Here, Loge is not only a fire god, he also fulfils his Old Norse roles of ingenious fixer of the gods' problems and Wotan's (Óðinn's) companion in adventure. When we first meet him in *Das Rheingold*, Loge turns up rather belatedly at the assembly of the gods, displaying some insouciance about the fulfilment of the bargain with Fasolt and Fafner, which requires yielding up Freia. Wotan – 'your only friend among the gods,' as he reminds the fire deity – has charged Loge with finding a means of nullifying the contract. But, reports Loge, the walls are sound, and he can't see a way out. Froh (Freyr) and Donner (Þórr) are furious with him; Froh punningly suggests that he should be called 'Lüge' ('Lies') instead of Loge, and Donner, predictably, threatens to smash him with his hammer. In his defence, Loge claims that he has travelled across land, sea and sky, and has found nothing more desirable than the love of women – which is what the beautiful Freia represents. Only Alberich the Nibelung has forsworn love and thus succeeded in acquiring the Rheingold, the treasure guarded by the three Rhinemaidens who dwell in the mighty river.

Fafner pricks up his ears at this; such a quantity of gold is worth more than Freia to him. As the giants take temporary custody of Freia, the gods begin to age, for they depend on the apples that she cultivates to stay youthful (here Freia has taken over Iðunn's function). This decides Wotan: he and Loge head off to Nibelheim to wrest the treasure and the newly forged Ring from Alberich.

Alberich has made his brother Mime create the Tarnhelm, a magic helmet that confers powers of shape-changing and invisibility. Thus armed, he feels sure that the gold and the Ring cannot be stolen from him. He brags that he will use the hoard to overthrow the gods and rule the world. Although Alberich fully realizes that Loge is not to be trusted, when the god doubts that the Tarnhelm is capable of the kinds of transformation that Alberich brags of, the Nibelung demonstrates its powers. First, he turns himself into an enormous snake, badly frightening Loge – or so he pretends – thus lulling Alberich into a false sense of security. Cunningly, Loge asks if Alberich can make himself very small, so that he can hide from his enemies, and the foolish creature transforms himself into a toad. Wotan promptly traps it beneath his foot. Now the dwarf is in the gods' power and must ransom himself with the coveted gold. Loge takes the Tarnhelm – he clearly grasps how useful it might be – while Wotan demands the Ring. Furious, Alberich places a curse on the Ring. 'Did you hear his friendly farewell?' asks Loge, but Wotan is unmoved.

The gods, as we have seen, duly hand the treasure over to the giants; Loge reluctantly adds the Tarnhelm while Wotan argues about keeping the Ring. When Fafner strikes Fasolt dead and seizes the Ring from him, Loge ironically notes how the Ring benefits Wotan by causing his enemies to destroy one another. But as the gods process into Walhall, Loge hangs back, observing that they are rushing towards their own end. In the past the gods might have tamed him, but now, if their power is waning, he could easily abandon them, reverting to his primal form: 'Who knows what

Loge, illustration by Arthur Rackham from *The Rhinegold & The Valkyrie* (1910).

I shall do?' he muses, keeping his options open for the moment. When Wotan summons him at the end of *Die Walküre*, the next opera in the cycle, to fire up a wall of flame, reminding Loge that he is subject to Wotan's will, fire does indeed leap up around the rock where Brünnhilde will sleep. But Loge himself does not appear. His defection then is an early signal that Wotan and the other gods have yielded the moral high ground and that their rule will not endure.

## Why everyone loves Loki

Loki's fortunes have taken an unexpected turn in the last forty years or so. In post-war retellings of the myths, his development from irritating prankster to the malicious schemer who brought about the death of Baldr was clear; the father of monsters was regarded as the epitome of evil. He begins to be viewed more sympathetically from the 1970s onwards. Thus, in Diana Wynne Jones's novel *Eight Days of Luke* (1975), the hero, David, an unhappy young boy, accidentally releases a charming and unreliable youth called Luke (Loki) from his chains. Very soon some peculiar figures, including Mr Wedding (Óðinn) and Mr and Mrs Fry (Freyr and Freyja), appear in the neighbourhood. The gods bully and threaten Luke, rather as David's own unkind relatives mistreat him. Luke himself is extremely evasive about why he had been chained up with a serpent dripping venom onto his face: 'Somebody did something and they blamed it on me ... they always blame it on me.' David needs to recover a mysterious missing object for Mr Wedding if Luke is not to be chained again; it is said to be in the clutches of Brunhilda and, with Luke's help – for he is also, as in Wagner, the god of fire – David braves the flame wall and retrieves what proves to be Thor's hammer. As he lifts Mjöllnir, he understands at last exactly who Luke is: 'Luke might be lord of fire and master of mischief. He might have done a number of appalling things and be going to do more before he was through. But David was simply very glad to see him.' Nevertheless, there's an uneasy sense of unfinished business at the end of the story, even if Luke is permitted to remain in the human world for the time being. When Mr Wedding remarks that, with the return of the hammer, the gods will be at their full strength when the day of *ragna rök* dawns, David realizes that 'Luke and Mr Wedding were going to be on opposite sides when that final battle came'. Wynne Jones's novel makes Luke sympathetic, while his role in the death of Baldr remains effaced: the knowledgeable reader has the pleasure of being in on the secret of why he was put in chains, while the newcomer to Norse myth is invited to grasp the parallels between the two youngsters, both bullied by their unpleasant relatives.

Loki's likeableness, which is clear when he is reimagined as a troubled youth, foreshadows the many ways in which he is, at least in part, rehabilitated in treatments from this century. His questing intelligence, easy charm, sexual attractiveness and relaxed relationship with ethical questions turn him into a favourite antihero. In contrast with Óðinn, old, unattractive, and restlessly anxious about the coming destruction of the gods, or with Þórr, who is often bumbling and brainless when he is not thuggish, Loki has come out well in many recent versions of his story. In her *Ragnarok*, it is obvious that A. S. Byatt likes him very much: 'Alone among all these beings he had humour and wit. His changeable shapes were attractive, his cleverness had charm; he made her uneasy, but she had feelings about him,' she notes of her childhood self. Loki's coupling with Angrboða, the giantess with a wolf's pelt, claws and sharp white teeth, out in Jarnviðr ('Ironwood') is fierce and violent, yet both take pleasure in the sex, which is performed to a roaring soundtrack of snarls and growls. He is the intellectual's god, wondering, speculating, thinking, endlessly poking at parts of the universe just to see what will happen. The other gods 'hammer and slash', says Loki to his daughter the Miðgarðs Serpent: 'They do not study. I study. I know.' That knowingness fuels Byatt's lasting sympathy with Loki, even when he deliberately brings about the death of Baldr, for he is the god who sets narratives in motion. 'He was the god of endings. He provided resolutions to stories – if he chose to. The endings he made often led to more problems.' Loki's adventures, before he embarks on the trajectory that unleashes *ragna rök*, hint at the chaos to come, keeping him just within Ásgarðr, just about on the gods' team, but with the certain knowledge that one day he will go too far.

Joanne Harris's *The Gospel of Loki* (2014) filters the history of the gods through Loki's consciousness, offering a defiant, often camp, running commentary on grave matters among gods and men. Summoned by Óðinn out of Chaos, the primeval, undifferentiated mass of possibilities, as 'Wildfire incarnate, happy and free', Loki finds himself among the Æsir, where he will never quite belong, smarter than everyone around him and presenting, as he later describes himself, as 'a young man with red hair and a certain *je ne sais quoi*'. Óðinn is his 'brother', but also increasingly an authority that Loki chafes against, and his mischief becomes more destructive. His role in the recovery of the stolen Mjöllnir from Þrymr is the apogee of his popularity in Ásgarðr; as we have seen, the ingenious idea of dressing Þórr as Freyja and Loki's cleverness in handling the situation in Jötunheimar win him much credit, especially since (for a change) Loki was not implicated in the original theft. But as time goes on, he becomes increasingly alienated from the other gods. The fate of his children (see below) distresses him more than might be expected, and he begins to wonder, once Fenrir is bound, how long it will be before the gods find an excuse to chain him as well. And thus a vicious feedback loop of dislike and mistrust is set up, leading, ultimately, to the precursor events of *ragna rök*, discussed further in Chapter 10.

Loki has also become a queer icon. His sexuality is polymorphous, and his nature demands frequent transformation and reinvention. 'He shifted shape as he shifted sex. He was slippery,' notes

Byatt. In *The Testament of Loki*, Harris's 2018 sequel to *The Gospel of Loki*, after *ragna rök* and the fall of Asgard Loki escapes the eternal prison of Chaos by effecting an ingenious move into a quite different world: he is incarnated via a computer game into the body of a young girl called Jumps. Jumps has an eating disorder, self-harms and is tentatively exploring her sexual orientation. Surprisingly, becoming possessed by Loki proves beneficial to Jumps; his casual amorality and lack of hang-ups change the way she feels about herself. Loki had always found it hard to adapt to others' sexual mores: 'When I first joined Asgard, one of the things that confused me most was all the rules regarding sex. No sex with animals, siblings, demons; no sex with other people's wives; no sex with folk of the *same* sex – honestly, with all those rules, it was hard to imagine anyone having any sex at all.' Jumps's nickname points to Loki's own capacity to flip between different kinds of existence (no wonder he settles into a corner of her mind so easily), and by the end of the book she has proved her strength and determination, growing up into an unafraid young woman.

'"You're slow," said Loki, "but you get there in the end." And his lips twisted into a crooked smile and embers danced in the shadows of his eyes.' Low-Key Lyesmith is the former cellmate of Shadow Moon, the novel's principal character, at the beginning of *American Gods*, advising the novice how to survive in jail. Shadow takes his time to realize just who it was who had shared his cell: when at last he meets the apparent leader of the new gods, Mr World, with his 'close-cropped orange hair' and 'scarred smile', that memento of Loki's long-ago risky bet with the dwarfs, Shadow recognizes the former con as Loki's avatar. Gaiman's Loki is the opponent and equal of the novel's Odin figure, Mr Wednesday, like him a grifter and conman as ruthless and amoral as the All-Father himself, for both are playing a long game to refill the reservoirs of blood and psychic energy that the two Norse gods need to survive. While Odin feeds on death, Loki feeds on chaos, Shadow notes, just before the battle between the old gods and the new is about to begin. But Loki has met his match – both in Shadow, as he figures things out and outwits the two gods, and in Shadow's extraordinary and fearless wife, Laura.

The Marvel movie Loki, played by Tom Hiddleston, is enmeshed in a recurrent family drama: he is the adoptive son who does not quite belong, the favourite of neither of his parents who feels himself caught between conflicting identities and loyalties. His storylines recycle a pattern of persuading others – mostly Thor – to trust him, betraying that trust, displaying his opportunism and gaining temporary advantage. And yet, when the stakes are at their highest, he will still fight for Asgard and the survival of its people. He dies – or appears to die – many times, yet still somehow survives, still working at his conflicted relationship with his brother. Loki has betrayed and murdered his real father, Laufey, packed Odin off to an old folks' home so that he can take his place thanks to some crafty shape-changing, and is always ready to leave Thor in the lurch. But in *Thor: Ragnarok* he saves the day by unleashing Surtur the fire demon and setting him against Hela. Although Asgard is consumed in flames, the Asgardians at least escape their doomed planet.

In a Disney spinoff television show, which premiered in June 2021, Loki has jumped into a different time-dimension following the events in the 2019 film *Avengers: Endgame* (and as a result has not followed the redemptive arc of the last movie). The trailer shows Loki as a prisoner in the dock, snorting contemptuously at the tribunal ranged above him and pleading 'guilty of being the god of mischief, yes. Guilty of finding all this incredibly tedious, yes. Guilty of being a crime against the Sacred Timeline? Absolutely not.' Loki has made off with the Tesseract (a key to disordering the sequential flow of time), thus 'breaking reality', according to the Time Variance Authority, a body that exists to make sure that time travel does not distort history. This is the 'multiverse' – a concept borrowed from quantum physics that suggests that multiple universes exist in parallel, distinguished from one another by whether a particular event occurred in any one universe. If it did, then a chain of cause and effect applies; if it didn't, then events in that universe will proceed along a different timeline. The first season of the show was complex, playful and open-ended; multiple Lokis (some of them of a different gender, and one that was a CGI crocodile) switched between timelines. These avatars unpacked the different possibilities inherent in Loki's character, in particular – or so it was claimed by the show's writers and fan commentators – depicting a Loki who was 'gender-fluid'. Loki's antihero status, particularly as characterized against Thor's brand of traditional masculinity, has generated an enthusiastic fandom that is deeply interested in gender identity and sexual difference. As we have seen, the concept of Loki's gender-fluidity is always present in the Norse myths, just as it is in the comic-book universe, where Odin reflects on his children: 'My son, my daughter, and my child who is both'. The show's first season did not develop Loki's character as gender-fluid in any meaningful way, disappointing many fans; the potentialities that other modern versions of Loki have exploited were perhaps too edgy for the Disney market.

*The Witch's Heart* (2021), the debut novel of the American writer Genevieve Gornichec, offers a different slant on Loki by relating the story of Angrboda, Loki's lover and mother of the his monstrous children. Angrboda is a compelling character; witch, prophetess and giantess, she is identified with a good number of the magical female figures who appear across the myths. Her tale as related by Gornichec begins when she has taken refuge in Jarnviðr ('Ironwood'), having been burned alive three times in the hall of the Æsir for her sorcery and her refusal to share her occult knowledge with Odin. Her heart, singed and blackened, was excised in this ordeal, and Loki takes it upon himself to return it to her – as so often, motivated by curiosity. This Loki is a quintessential romance bad boy, misunderstood by his peers, unreliable but charming, and even loving at times. Nevertheless, after he has won Angrboda's heart he stays away from her for months at a time. Despite his prior commitment to the novel's heroine and their children, he marries Sigyn, one of the goddesses. Loki is commendably unfazed by his unusual children; indeed, he has a special bond with Hel, the eldest – for it is no coincidence that he will appear at *ragna rök* captaining the ship of the dead, liberated from Hel's kingdom. The disadvantage of the novel's focus on Angrboda is that, in her exile, she is absent from most of the great set pieces in Loki's career, which are related at second hand by her lover himself or by other witnesses. Yet Angrboda's story not only reflects on difficult relationships – with the perennially absent husband and father, and the rival wife's exchanges with more conventional women such as Frey's wife, Gerd – it also casts a highly critical light on the behaviour of the Æsir, particularly when they come mob-handed to take Angrboda's children away. When the giants have finally had enough, massing at Útgarðr to march against their oppressors in the final battle, the readers' sympathies are strongly aligned with them – in particular with Skadi, who has left both Njord, her erstwhile husband, and Asgard, and relinquished her father Thjazi's hall in the mountains to live with Angrboda as her lover in the last days before the end. In the post-*ragna rök* world, Angrboda makes the ultimate sacrifice for her daughter, as we'll see in Chapter 10, enabling her, now that the old gods are gone, to build a rewarding life with a mortal family within a new kind of normality.

## Loki's children in modern retellings

Loki's five children (or six, if you count the monstrous horse Sleipnir) have captured the imagination of later writers to varying extents. His two sons by his wife, Váli and Narfi (or Nari), meet a grisly end: Váli is turned into a wolf and rips his brother to shreds;

Narfi's guts are used to form Loki's magical bonds. Who knows where Váli goes after that: as a brother-slayer he can scarcely rejoin the other gods, and he probably attaches himself to the pack of wolves who throng the last days of the world. The three monstrous children borne to Loki by Angrboða are rewritten in more interesting ways, however: Fenrir the Great Wolf; Jörmungandr, the Miðgarðs Serpent; and, most fascinating of all, Hel, goddess of death, who features in books, movies and even an opera.

As a gigantic wolf, Fenrir is less easy to recast imaginatively than his sister. In *The Witch's Heart* he can at least speak, although as he grows he becomes increasingly fierce and uncontrollable. Joanne Harris makes him into a surly teenager in human form. At first, he is 'a cute little werewolf', but then Loki brings him into Ásgarðr, where he behaves like an objectionable adolescent: 'To be fair, young Fenny was going through a bit of a rebellious phase, characterized by grunting, bad smells, obscene language, loud music in his rooms late at night and a generally uncouth approach to anything of the opposite sex.' Fenrir is a nuisance yet as in Snorri, rather than reasoning with him or trying to reform him, the gods, aware of the prophecy that he will kill Óðinn, chain him up, a move that further alienates Loki from the divine cohort. Elsewhere he is depicted as a large, troublesome and unpredictable dog, but not as particularly wicked; nevertheless, the gods always bind him painfully, with that agonizing sword propping open his jaws. His giant rage is produced by his mistreatment rather than his being innately evil: the prophecies of *ragna rök* are in some ways self-fulfilling.

The serpent too is hard for the modern imagination to bring up to date. Byatt makes Jörmungandr female and eternally hungry, hoovering up the fish, plants and animals of the ocean as she grows, powerfully figuring contemporary degradation of the marine environment. Jörmungandr becomes increasingly bad-tempered, particularly after her run-in with Þórr, when he fishes her up on Hymir's boat and strikes her a mighty blow with his hammer. Following this incident, she finds in the lowest depths a 'wavering form, lumpen and twitching', and bites down savagely upon it. But it is her own tail, for she is now so huge that she girdles the Earth. And there she lies in the outer ocean, biding her time, 'where there was living kelp to rest her head, where there was food and more food for her vast appetite'. Harris's Loki never comes to terms with this particular child: 'So shoot me. I can't stand snakes,' he quips, even if he is ready to make use of Jörmungandr's enormous size to escape from his prison in Chaos at the start of *The Testament of Loki*. The snake-brother, consigned to the ocean, is less easy to make likeable than a wolf or even the half-human Hel, goddess of death.

Revealed as a surprise elder sister to Thor, Hela makes her appearance in *Thor: Ragnarok*, released from confinement at the death of Odin: 'Hela, my first-born, your sister. Her violent appetites grew beyond my control. I couldn't stop her, so I imprisoned her,' their father explains. Played by Cate Blanchett, Hela effortlessly smashes Mjöllnir to pieces and then sets out to take over Asgard. Here she is horrified to see that the old history of how father and daughter conquered the Nine Realms has been effaced; in the good old days, 'Odin and I drowned entire civilizations in blood and tears.' The new murals that celebrate her father's victory tell a different tale: 'Has no one been taught our history? Look at these lies!' she snarls. 'Goblets and garden parties? Peace treaties?' History and its narratives, who gets to write them, and which truths are promoted and suppressed, are in fact one of the film's major themes. Hela's destruction of almost all the Valkyries is a memory that has been culturally erased, but is then replayed for the last of them at Loki's command. The usual dynamics of the Marvel movies are thrown off course in this film: Hela is, as she points out, 'not a queen or a monster' but 'the goddess of death', and thus indestructible. Only the reincarnation of Surtur, the great fire demon, and the Asgardians' abandonment of their home planet save them from certain destruction by Hela and her army of the revivified dead, her 'Butchers', raised up from the crypts of Old Asgard.

Hel's childhood and adolescence are treated in Francesca Simon's *The Monstrous Child* and in Genevieve Gornichec's *The Witch's Heart*. In both these books (and in Simon and Gavin Higgins's opera), Hel is disabled from the waist down; her lower half is dead and corpse-like, and her legs 'moulder and stink, blotched with gangrene ... reeking and putrefying'. In the *Monstrous Child* opera, we witness Hel's birth: she is brought forth from her mother as a puppet with a perky, red-cheeked face, but her lower body is a dangling, useless tangle of strings. By the time she is sent down to Niflheim, she is a pretty, anxious teenager with bold blue hair, whose upper half protrudes from a shapeless brown mass from which she cannot escape. The gods' treatment of the disabled girl, exiling her to the hall of the dead, is heart-rending: 'They entombed a living child in a gigantic grave mound.' Simon's heroine is distraught when she finds herself exiled from sun, sky and grass, consigned to a dark realm populated by insubstantial, unhappy wraiths. She misses Baldr in particular, who has always been kind to her, and with whom she is in love. She builds herself a hall, and makes a kind of friend in Modgud, warden of the bridge Gjöll, across which the dead must march to enter Niflheim.

Harris's Hel is split between living and dead on a vertical axis: 'She looked at me askance', says Loki, 'through her single living eye (the other one was dead as bone under a wisp of white hair).' She had, her father notes unsympathetically, developed a 'bad case of puppy-love towards Asgard's favourite Golden Boy, aka Balder the Beautiful'. As in *The Monstrous Child*, this powerful, unreciprocated passion foreshadows, even motivates, Baldr's eventual journey to Hel's hall, his death a key precursor of *ragna rök*, as we shall see. For while Harris's Loki is callously indifferent to his

Hel Puppet and Hel, from Francesca Simon and Gavin Higgins's
*The Monstrous Child*, Royal Opera House, London (2019).

daughter's plight, in Gornichec's *The Witch's Heart* the wayward
god has always felt a strong attachment to his first-born child, and
his plotting against Baldr is largely motivated by his wish to give
his daughter her heart's desire.

We will see more of Loki's children in the run-up to and events
of *ragna rök* in Chapter 10. Meanwhile, their progenitor enjoys
an unparalleled popularity, eclipsing Þórr and Óðinn as the
most admired of the Norse gods. He is a flawed antihero, amoral
and witty, shrewd and yet, somehow, not beyond redemption.
His outsider status, his alienation from the gods' – particularly
Óðinn's – priorities, and his determination to act as he pleases,
to enquire and experiment, recast him as the surrogate for the

novelist who seeks to explore the imaginative world of the Norse gods and as the catalyst for the best stories and the most modern of deities. At the same time, Loki possesses many of the attributes of the classic American hero: the wisecracking lone wolf, who answers to no one and who sets out to shape his own destiny – for good or ill.

# CHAPTER 6

# Vikings and Berserkers

MYTHS OF MASCULINITY

## The Vikings of history

We all think we know about Vikings. Everyone now knows, of course, that, as recent historical studies have firmly established, they never wore horned helmets – indeed, Viking Age helmets are remarkably rare (and horned helmets are extremely impractical). 'Viking' is in fact a job description rather than an ethnic identity: 'going Viking' was, unsurprisingly, a young man's occupation. From the 750s onwards, if he were well born and wealthy enough or could get backing from a patron or his family, a young Norwegian, Dane or (later) Icelander might kit out his own ship and set off across the North Sea. If he were Swedish, he would more likely go raiding in the Baltic or sail down the great rivers of Russia to Miklagarðr (Constantinople). One Scandinavian speaker graffitied the name 'Halfdan' in runes on a marble balustrade high up in the city's great cathedral of Hagia Sophia. If he were less well off, a young man might take service with a sea king, a war-leader with a whole fleet of vessels, and take his chance on gaining a decent share of plunder from the towns, monasteries and estates that the crew would attack. If he lived long enough, he could retire with those gains to live a peaceful life back home, taking over or buying a farm or practising a useful craft such as smithing or rope-making, or he might continue the sea-borne life but spend his days trading goods rather than risking his life in smash-and-grab raids. The 8th- and 9th-century rune stones of Sweden commemorate many a man who did not make it home, having lost his life *vestr* (west) in the British Isles or *austr* (east) on the European mainland. His companions would bring the news home to his grieving family, probably along with his share of the crew's reward, thus providing the wherewithal to pay the local rune-master for carving his epitaph on the monumental stone that commemorated him.

Other Scandinavians came to the British Isles and to Normandy in modern France not to raid but to settle, to find land to farm or to expand towns such as York (*Jorvík*), where they set themselves up as traders, merchants or craftsmen. In Britain these people intermarried with the local communities, creating an Anglo-Scandinavian population in parts of the North and East, where their legacy still lingers. Their stone sculptures, which are often hybrids of Christian and pagan elements, survive to testify to that blending of cultures; the great 10th-century Gosforth Cross in Cumbria, for instance, displays recognizable mythological scenes on a Christian stone cross. Distinctive place names, ending in *-thorp*, *-by* or *-thwaite*, for example, are part of their legacy; so, too, are the many streets in York called *-gate*. A good number of Scandinavian words were adopted into the English language, among them such key words as *die*, *egg*, *law*, *window*, *skirt* and *scum*. Many more are preserved in Northern dialects including Yorkshire, Cumbrian and Geordie.

The Scandinavian immigrants did not always succeed in integrating peacefully in their new homeland. On St Brice's Day, 13 November 1002, King Æthelred ordered the execution – in reality, a series of massacres – of all 'Danes' living in England. In practice, this could hardly have been put into effect in the Danelaw, where those of Scandinavian descent were a majority: it was in

Detail of the
Gosforth Cross,
Cumbria, England
(10th century).

frontier towns such as Oxford where townsfolk heeded the call.
A royal charter from 1004 relates how the terrified Danes took
refuge in the church of St Frideswide, the patron saint of Oxford;
their attackers promptly burned it down. In 2008, at my own
Oxford college, St John's, the skeletons of between thirty-four
and thirty-eight young men were discovered during excavations.
Most of them had serious injuries caused by a range of weapons,
and there was some charring of the bones. Evidence of healed
injuries suggests that they were probably professional fighters,
and some of them had certainly grown up in Scandinavia. These
remains have been dated to a period between 960 and 1020, so are
consistent with the date of the massacre. It seems that they had
been hacked down then dragged to the edge of the city (by the

Scandinavian skeletons uncovered in 2008 at St John's College, Oxford.

north gate), where an attempt had been made to burn the bodies. Our St John's 'Vikings' bear testimony to the continuing strife between Scandinavian mercenaries attracted to the opportunities provided by the turbulent conditions of the early 11th century, and the English who encountered them.

### Rediscovering the Vikings

By the late 11th century, 'going Viking' was no longer viable as a trade. The conversion of Scandinavia to Christianity, the growth of towns, the region's closer integration with other parts of Europe, and the dramatic defeat and death of King Harald Hardrada of Norway at the Battle of Stamford Bridge in 1066 all served to discourage the raids and full-scale invasions that had occurred in earlier centuries. The myth of the indomitable Viking resurfaced in the 17th and 18th centuries, fuelled by sensationalist writing based on newly rediscovered histories and literary sources.

The Dane Thomas Bartholin wrote an extremely influential text in Latin that explored the timeless Danish courage and spirit. Its English title is *Three Books on Danish Antiquity and the Reasons for the Heathen Danes' Contempt for Death* (1689). Bartholin explains the vividly imagined Viking fearlessness in the face of death, drawing widely on the newly available mythological and literary sources to make his arguments. He stresses the importance of post-mortem reputation and notes how it interacts with the myth of Valhöll and its offer of eternal life spent fighting, feasting and drinking. The human chieftain Óðinn and his associates from Asia are represented as having cleverly devised this belief to encourage suicidal bravery in their followers. Bartholin also adduces, as evidence for this fearlessness, many instances from the sagas of wisecracks made in response to terrible injury. A favourite, repeated across more than one saga, is the injured man's observation: 'I was never very handsome, but you haven't improved things,' along with 'The Danish ladies of Bornholm won't be so keen to kiss me now' – this as his lower jaw is near severed. Bartholin is also responsible for popularizing the erroneous belief that Vikings drank from their enemies' skulls, a misapprehension that only magnified their reputation for savagery.

The increasingly widespread idea that Vikings laughed defiantly in the face of death drew sustenance from two important poems translated into English by Bishop Percy in his *Five Pieces of Runick Poetry* (1763). Percy also consulted an earlier English version made by the well-known Oxford scholar George Hickes. The first of the original poems, *Krákumál* ('The Speech of the Crow' or 'The Dying Ode of Regner Lodbrok'), will be discussed in Chapter 8. The second, known as 'The Incantation of Hervör', preserved in *Hervarar saga ok Heiðreks* (The Saga of Hervör and Heiðrekr), introduced a fearless Viking heroine to the English-speaking world.

### Not like other girls

Hervör's tale is a welcome reminder that women might also 'go Viking'. They accompanied the Great Heathen Army that ranged across England in the mid-9th century and, as suggested in Chapter 2, they might have taken up weapons on their own account. The idea of the fighting woman is a staple of Old Norse myth and legend and was explored with enthusiasm not only by Thomas Percy in his prose accounts, but also by the poet Anna Seward, 'the Swan of Lichfield', in a poetic paraphrase of the saga's Hervör episode, published in 1796. In the original saga, Hervör runs away to sea dressed in men's clothing, where she commands a crew of Vikings. They sail to the island of Samsø in the Baltic, where Hervör's father, Angantýr, and his eleven brothers – notorious berserkers all – had met their deaths in a famous fight against two heroes (Örvar-Oddr and Hjálmarr, whom we met in Chapter 2). Angantýr owned a magic dwarf-forged sword, Tyrfingr, that is destined to kill every time it is drawn from its sheath – and Hervör wants her inheritance. The poem relates how, all alone, she goes boldly among the grave mounds and summons her dead father:

> 'Hear from thy dark sepulchral hall!
> Mid the forest's inmost gloom,
> Thy daughter, circling thrice thy tomb
> With mystic rites of thrilling power
> Disturbs thee at this midnight hour!'

Angantýr emerges from his burial mound, but he prevaricates: he does not have the sword, he says, and he unleashes eerie flames that play around the mounds, where all the dead now stand at the doors. Hervör insists, threatening her father and uncles with the curse of unquiet rest. Angantýr reveals that the sword is itself accursed, and that she will bear a son who will kill his own brother with the weapon: 'When in blood of millions dyed, / It arms an

ireful fratricide.' Finally, Angantýr concedes, not without express-
ing admiration for his fearless daughter. In the Old Norse poem,
he says:

> 'Young girl, I declare you are not like most men,
> hanging around mounds by night,
> with an engraved spear
> and in metal of the Goths.'

Sewell renders this rather grandly as:

> 'Young maid, who as of warrior might,
> Roamest thus to tombs by night,
> In coat of mail, with voice austere.'

The sword is handed over with further warnings, and Hervör
leaves the island in triumph, bidding the dead to sleep in peace.

Hervör is indeed not like most people, either male or female,
in her fearless defiance of the dead and the sword's curse. The
poem wonderfully illustrates all the traits in Norse heroic legend
that appealed to the Gothic imagination: the dead and their bod-
ily decay; uncanny and unholy places; women faced with terror;
eternal curses; and remarkable courage. Hervör's story continues
to capture the imagination: in 2016 the composer Melissa Dunphy
created a song cycle based on the tale, which can be heard on
Maren Montalbano's album *Sea Tangle: Songs from the North* from
the same year.

## Victorians and Vikings

The earliest citations found under 'Viking' in the *Oxford English
Dictionary* use the Old Norse word *víkingr* instead of the modern
term. These instances, quoted from historical texts from 1807 and
the 1830s, perpetuate the already widespread idea of the Viking as a
merciless, piratical raider. While Sir Walter Scott's 1822 Shetland-set
novel *The Pirate* does not use the word 'Viking', it does distinguish

between the savage 'Berserkars', 'who used to run like madmen on swords', and the noble war-leaders, ancestors of the Shetlanders, 'the old Norsemen, who swept sea and haven with their victorious galleys, established colonies, conquered countries, and took the name of Sea-Kings'. Over the course of the 19th century, however, as noted in the Introduction, new conceptualizations of British, particularly English, nationalism foregrounded the Anglo-Saxon and Viking past as integral to shaping the national spirit. Adventurousness, stoicism (the famous stiff upper lip), love of liberty, courage, loyalty and the ideal of 'grace under pressure' that accorded with the well-established 'contempt for death' trope were all ascribed to the influence of Northern blood. That the country's ruling dynasty, the House of Hanover, was closely associated with Germany, by descent and by Victoria's marriage to Albert, and the growing influence of the work of Jacob Grimm helped to establish the idea that the Vikings were ancestors worth reclaiming and celebrating.

Interest in medieval Scandinavian history and literature grew apace in England as more and more translations of key texts became available. One of the most important translators active during this period was Sir George Webbe Dasent, who translated Snorri's *Prose Edda* into English in 1842. Dasent spent four years in Sweden, working in Stockholm as secretary to the British envoy. He was a friend of the poet Matthew Arnold and of Thomas Carlyle; indeed, he dedicated his translation to Carlyle, whose lectures *On Heroes, Hero-Worship and the Heroic in History* had been published the previous year (see Chapter 3). The *Prose Edda* was followed by his translation of the great Icelandic *Brennu-Njáls saga* as *The Story of Burnt Njal* (1861). Dasent's knowledgeable and authoritative translations of the Norwegian folk-tales collected by Peter C. Asbjørnsen and Jørgen E. Moe and, later, of *Gísla saga* (The Saga of Gísli) did much to popularize narratives from the North. An important late work was his translation of the mammoth sagas of medieval Orkney, published between 1887 and 1894 under the umbrella title *Icelandic Sagas and Other Historical Documents Relating to the Settlements and Descents of the Northmen of the British Isles*. The Scandinavian settlement was now understood as a central strand in British national history. Understandably, Dasent was much feted when he visited Iceland in 1862 in the wake of the publication of *The Story of Burnt Njal*, and a public banquet was even held in his honour in Reykjavík.

Dasent was by no means the only British traveller to sail across the northern seas to the land of ice and fire. During the 19th century enthusiasm for Scandinavian literature and history developed in tandem with the exciting possibility of travel to Iceland. The noted physician Sir Henry Holland went on an expedition to Iceland as early as 1810 and again, astonishingly, in 1871, at the age of 83. William Morris too visited Iceland in 1871 and 1873, in the company of the Icelandic scholar and his partner in translation Eiríkur Magnússon. In his journal, Morris notes ironically as he arrives at the geothermal site of Geysir that it was not its literary heritage but the geological wonders of Iceland that had made the country 'famous to Mangnall's Questions [a well-known school text] and the rest, who have never heard the names of Sigurd and Brynhild, of Njal or Gunnar or Grettir or Gisli or Gudrun'. Morris and Magnússon would continue to produce translations of Old Norse for many years, creating a Saga Library that augmented Dasent's work. There is more on Morris's interest in Sigurðr and Brynhildr in Chapter 7.

The 19th century's most highly regarded Viking tale was *Friðþjófs saga*, the subject of an epic poetic paraphrase by the Swedish bishop Esaias Tegnér. It was published as *Frithjofs saga* in Tegnér's native language in 1825. This is a late saga with a strong love story at its centre, featuring a villain who is dedicated to the worship of the old gods, and some ideas about 'natural religion', anticipating Christianity, emerge towards the end. Tegnér's poem enjoyed enormous success and was widely translated from Swedish; it was particularly popular in Germany and England and was highly instrumental in the establishment of the Norwegian tourist industry. Set in the scenic Sognefjord, *Frithjofs saga* became a favourite of the German emperor Wilhelm II, who regularly took holidays at the little village of Balestrand in the west of Norway.

Max Unger, *Frithjof* (1913), now in Vik, Norway.

He commissioned sizeable statues of King Bele – the father of Ingebjörg, the tale's heroine – and of Frithjof himself. Both were erected in Sognefjord in 1913, somewhat to the dismay of the locals, who were uneasy about the implicit claim the Kaiser was making upon their Norwegian and Icelandic heritage. *Friðþjófs saga* has fallen out of favour in the 20th century; its romantic themes and swashbuckling hero seem old-fashioned in contrast to the timeless tragic dramas of the classic Icelandic sagas.

The popularity of *Frithjofs saga* encouraged late 19th-century British novelists to write original novels about fictional Viking Age heroes. These often promoted a moralizing view of their protagonists, as notable exemplars for the young men who would themselves be setting out to cross the seas in the service of the empire. They might one day need to 'plunge off the high bulwarks of a vessel to save a sister, or mother, or child, with as little thought about yourself as if you were jumping off a sofa', as R. M. Ballantyne urged in *Erling the Bold* (1869). H. Rider Haggard, the author of rousing adventure fiction such as *King Solomon's Mines* and *She*, wrote the Iceland-set saga-like tale *Eric Brighteyes* in 1889, dedicating it to Queen Victoria's daughter, the recently widowed empress of Germany. Eric's life story is that of many saga heroes: he is born and dies in Iceland but spends three years in exile, during which time he takes part in Viking expeditions where he has to establish his leadership over his unruly and once treacherous crew:

> Now it were too long to tell of all the deeds that Eric and his men did. Never, so scalds sing, was there a viking like him for strength and skill and hardihood ... Wherever Eric joined battle, and that was in many places, he conquered, for none prevailed against him, till at last foes would fly before the terror of his name, and earls and kings would send from far craving the aid of his hands. Withal he was the best and gentlest of men. It is said of

Eric that in all his days he did no base deed, nor hurt the weak, nor refused peace to him who prayed it, nor lifted sword against prisoner or wounded foe.

Like Ballantyne and Haggard, Charles Kingsley and Sabine Baring-Gould also produced stirring novels of the Old North in the latter half of the century. These tales featured daring hand-to-hand combats, storm-tossed sea voyages, dramatic ship funerals (with or without the longship being set aflame) and tender maidens waiting for their heroes at home. The heroes largely adopt Eric's ethical stance, functioning as powerful models for English manhood: courageous adventurers, fearless voyagers and perfect gentlemen all.

Lancelot Speed, cover design for Henry Rider Haggard's *Eric Brighteyes* (1908).

## Vikings for children

The Victorian tendency to rewrite heroic stories of the medieval past as moralizing instruction for children continued into the 20th and 21st centuries. Gentle tales such as Oliver Postgate's *Noggin the Nog* books (published 1965–77) and the British television series *The Saga of Noggin the Nog* (broadcast 1959–65) offered a reassuring glimpse of a Northern realm, ruled at first by King Knut of the Northmen. Alas, Knut is dying, and unless his son Noggin can find a queen within six weeks he will not inherit; instead, the throne will fall to his dastardly mustachio'd uncle Nogbad the Bad. Graculus, a green talking cormorant, brings Noggin an ivory dagger carved with a portrait of Nooka of the Nooks, an Inuit princess from the Land of the Midnight Sun. With the help of his crew of faithful friends, led by the redoubtable Thor Nogson, Noggin wins Nooka's hand, just in time. Noggin and Nooka have a son, Knut, named after his grandfather, in line with good saga principles. The resonant opening lines, intoned at the beginning of most episodes, did much to kindle young viewers' enthusiasm for Viking adventure: 'In the lands of the North, where the Black Rocks stand guard against the cold sea, in the dark night that is very long, the Men of the Northlands sit by their great log fires and they tell a tale ... the Saga of Noggin the Nog.'

Aimed at older children were classic adventure stories including Henry Treece's much-loved Viking Trilogy (1955–60) or Rosemary Sutcliff's *Blood Feud* (1976). These historical novels make use of Viking characters to explore universal themes of adolescence, maturing and identity. *Blood Feud* relates the life of Jestyn, who, as a child, is kidnapped by Vikings and sold as a slave in Dublin. Freed by Thormod, his Viking owner, Jestyn takes ship to Denmark with him. Once there, Thormod discovers that his father has been murdered and swears the vengeance that gives the novel its title. The killers are pursued down the rivers of Russia, as far as the court of Grand Prince Vladimir at Kiev. Jestyn finds himself caught between several worlds and value systems: the Christianity of his childhood in Britain, the pagan values of his friend, and the Greek customs of Constantinople, where he ends up. Sutcliff expands the canvas of the Viking world in line with contemporary historical research to emphasize the eastward extent of Scandinavian influence – the central role of the Viking Rus' in the foundation of what would come to be Russia.

The protagonist of Kevin Crossley-Holland's more recent, beautifully written novels *Bracelet of Bones* (2011) and *Scramasax* (2013) follows a similar route to Sutcliff's hero. Set in the early 11th century, when belief in the Norse gods was still alive in Norway, *Bracelet of Bones* tells of the quest of young Solveig for her father. He has slipped away from their farm in a dark Norwegian fjord to join the future king Harald Sigurdsson in far Byzantium, breaking the promise he made to take her with him. Crossley-Holland's decision to make his heroine a 14-year-old girl allows him to evade the ceaseless battles and violence of other Viking novels, although many other dangers beset Solveig on her quest. The novel vividly evokes the tense atmosphere in trading towns such as Birka in Sweden and the now Russian settlement of Stara Ladoga, where merchants deal in glossy, deep-piled furs, 'hunks of wax, boardgames of draughts and chess, boxes of salt, two wooden platters glistening with honey scooped out of one of the barrels', and the artefacts that Solveig, herself a skilled carver, manages to shape from walrus ivory and other bone. Solveig makes the demanding, perilous journey along the great rivers of Russia and across the Black Sea to the gleaming city of Byzantium, and comes to find a substitute family, including both enemies and allies, among the ship's crew. In an afterword, Crossley-Holland notes that he was inspired by the runic graffiti carved high up in Hagia Sophia: indeed, he gives the Norse name Halfdan to his heroine's father. *Scramasax* continues Solveig's adventures in Constantinople, where the brutal Empress Zoe now rules with the support of Harald and his fierce mercenaries, including Halfdan. In this melting-pot of a city, where Christians, pagans and Saracens mingle, Solveig has to learn to decide for herself who is friend and who is foe.

**Critiquing the Viking past**

Solveig's doubts about the ethics of the Viking way of life are shared by the Icelandic Nobel laureate Halldór Laxness, whose Viking Age novel *Gerpla* (1952) was recently translated by Philip Roughton as *Wayward Heroes* (2016). Laxness retells the story of *Fóstbrœðra saga* (The Saga of the Sworn Brothers), with several invented embellishments. Funny and horrifying by turns, it is a deadpan account of two sworn brothers, difficult and unlikely heroes. The psychopathic Þorgeir Hávarsson is raised by his mother to think only of achieving glory by killing every opponent worthy of the name. The other hero is Þormóður Bessason, a poet and ladies' man. The two sworn brothers vow lifelong friendship, but Þorgeir's violence drives them apart quite early in the novel. Nevertheless, despite achieving a lyrically described happiness with his wife, Þordís, and their daughters, Þormóður will not eschew the obligation to avenge his friend when Þorgeir is killed. His adventures – in Greenland and Norway, invented or elaborated beyond the saga source – begin anew. Laxness is scathingly ironic in his treatment of his main characters' bullish stupidity, although compassion sometimes moderates the author's savagery. The crazed pursuit of outmoded heroic ideals is not his only target. Opportunistic priests and bishops, hopelessly superstitious Irish monks, even Óláfur the Stout (the future St Olaf, patron saint of Norway) betray their cynically pragmatic beliefs whenever they open their mouths. Sensible peace-loving Icelandic farmers concur with the criticisms voiced by the hard-boiled narrator. 'Harm and misfortune alone result when killers and skalds [poets] come together, and landless liegemen should concern themselves more with honing their skills in hooking flounder and hunting seals than in sword-rattling and palaver,' advises one. Laxness is sceptical not only about the values of the Viking past, its senseless violence and narrow-minded worship of honour, but also about the ways in which the Iceland of his own day derived so much of its nationalist self-confidence from the medieval sagas as its proudest cultural achievement.

## Movie Vikings

The Hollywood idea of the Viking engages with particular kinds of masculinity and male group identity epitomized by the Viking warrior band and its members. The tradition arguably begins with *The Vikings* (1958), starring Kirk Douglas and Tony Curtis, which features some extraordinary stunts. The most famous involves Douglas as Einar running the oars of his longship, leaping from one oar held horizontally to the next as the ship was being rowed along a Norwegian fjord. No one had seen this feat performed in a thousand years, marvelled the director, Richard Fleischer. In the film, the character of Erik (Curtis) has to discover his true lineage as the son of an English king and reassert his innate civilized values in the face of Viking barbarism – even if he kills his adoptive father and brother on the way. *The Vikings* is discussed in more detail in Chapter 8.

In *The 13th Warrior* (1999), directed by John McTiernan, Antonio Banderas plays Ibn Fahdlan (or Fadlan), an actual historical figure. The original Ibn Fahdlan was a 10th-century Arab who wrote a detailed account of his meeting with a group of apparently Scandinavian warriors performing the funeral rites for their dead chieftain on the River Volga in what is now Russia. The movie Ibn Fahdlan, the product of a highly civilized culture with which he has become profoundly disillusioned, encounters a Viking band who force him to join them. He returns with his new companions to their distant homeland to rescue a settlement from attack by the terrifying 'Eaters of the Dead' – enemies who cannibalize their victims and who are consequently even less civilized than the

Norsemen. During this adventure he comes to value his Viking friends, admiring their courage, loyalty and zest for life, and he learns important lessons about masculinity and its proper performance. In the epilogue, a voiceover asks Allah to 'bless the pagan Northmen, who shared their food and their blood, and who helped Ibn Fahdlan to become a man'. *The 13th Warrior*, then, as one critic writes, involves 'manly men doing manly things in a manly way': the covert ideological aim of many Viking movies.

Terry Jones's comedy fantasy *Erik the Viking* (1989) parodies the 'manly men' and a range of familiar tropes from Viking movies, as we shall see below. The film's berserkers' feast harnesses a good number of Viking-movie clichés: roaring drunkenness; dangerous games such as throwing axes at a pinioned, flaxen-haired maiden, parodying a similar scene played straight in *The Vikings*; and considerable touchiness about personal honour. As is traditional in Viking movies, women are annoyingly critical of men's posturing; they represent a voice of common sense that can earn them a punch in the face, usually from a secondary male character.

Still from John McTiernan's *The 13th Warrior* (1999).

The History Channel show *Vikings*, discussed in Chapters 2 and 8, capitalizes on contemporary ideas about Viking identity, but it also demonstrates the ways in which post-medieval stereotypes about Vikings interact with modern scholarship on the Viking period. Robert Eggers's 2022 film *The Northman*, co-written by Eggers and the Icelandic writer Sjón, is a reworking of the story of *Hamlet* (itself originally recorded by the Danish writer Saxo Grammaticus). As Eggers revealed in an interview, he 'was working with the finest Viking historians and archaeologists consulting on the film'; thus the film draws upon the latest research into Viking fighting techniques, clothing and self-modification. One particularly striking make-up detail is the reproduction of the grooves that some fighters would file into their teeth and colour with dye. Starring Alexander Skarsgård as the hero Amleth, Anya Taylor-Joy as Olga, a captive Slav, Nicole Kidman as Gudrun, Amleth's mother, and Björk as a blind seeress, the film makes much knowing play with the conventions of Viking films. The opening scenes include a subdued version of the Viking feast, and Amleth himself is a bulked-up berserk 'wolfskin' warrior of the kind discussed below. A hallucinatory scene worthy of Wagner depicts a mounted Valkyrie bearing a fallen fighter towards Valhöll, and the mythic archetype of the great sacrificial tree at Uppsala is invoked more than once. Eggers nods to contemporary gender sensibilities; although sexual violence is hinted at, it is not explicitly shown. Women wield considerable agency, often through supernatural power. Extreme masculine violence and uncompromising principles of honour and vengeance are called into question: the usual glamourized action sequences of swashbuckling and courageous raids to gain booty of finely wrought treasures are subordinated to the sordid aim of seizing fellow humans to be brutally trafficked as slaves. Once Amleth is old enough to act, he has at first no qualms as to the rightness of his mission. Yet, like his Shakespearean namesake, he too is forced to choose between more humane, even feminized values and the bleakness of mutual annihilation. Many familiar Viking-movie clichés are overturned or abandoned in *The Northman*'s vision of the early medieval past as radically strange; nevertheless, the film's aesthetic continues to celebrate the white, hypermasculine and uncompromisingly violent ideology that its narrative implicitly critiques.

If Hollywood has tended to both perpetuate and exaggerate prevailing beliefs about the Vikings, so too do medievalist fantasy treatments – consider the Ironborn of George R. R. Martin's books and the wildly popular television series *Game of Thrones*, for example. The Ironborns' proud boast 'We do not sow' traps them within a social system, known as the 'Old Way', that mirrors traditional medievalist ideas about the Viking mindset: seaborne raiding, rather than trading (except for trafficking into slavery those captured in their attacks), is the basis of their economy. Thus, when Theon Greyjoy returns home to the Iron Islands wearing velvet, silk and a gold chain – clothing that is fashionable in the north, where he has been living – his diehard father, King Balon, snarls at him: 'That

Fjölnir returns home to Hrafnsey in Robert Eggers's *The Northman* (2022).

bauble around your neck – was it bought with gold or with iron?' In the Old Way, Theon recalls too late, 'women might decorate themselves with ornaments bought with coin, but a warrior wore only the jewelry he took off the corpses of enemies slain by his own hands'. 'You blush red as a maid, Theon ... Is it the gold price you paid or the iron?' But Balon already knows the answer; he yanks the chain from his son's neck and casts it in the brazier. Balon does not survive for long in the turmoil of the Seven Kingdoms; he is murdered by his ruthless and handsome brother Euron, who succeeds him on the Salt Throne. But change is coming to the Ironborn: by the end of the show, Yara, Balon's daughter, has become their leader. She has promised Daenerys Targaryen that they will abandon their 'reaving, roving, raiding and raping' ways – perhaps, like the Scandinavians of the 11th century, to become traders, farmers and merchants. The Viking way of life no longer seems sustainable in the new world emerging on the continent of Westeros.

## Berserkers

Berserkers were warriors of exceptional ferocity and fearlessness. The limited historical evidence we have suggests that the *berserkir* were a particular elite group of fighters who may have had a ritual role, perhaps in initiating young warriors. They may have worn animal pelts (bear- or wolfskins) and have acted as their war-leader's personal bodyguard, fighting in the frontline of battle in the shield-wall and unleashing terrifying war cries. In medieval literature we find a range of different types of berserker. In sagas of Icelanders, they tend to be depicted as social outsiders; they are often loners or else they roam in small groups, running a kind of protection racket. Typically they arrive at a hall where they demand to be given the householder's wife or daughters; anyone who refuses is challenged to fight a duel. These men become enraged when defied or before they begin a fight: they gnash at the rim of their shields, howl and shout – a display intended to intimidate. The well-known chess pieces discovered on the Outer Hebridean island of Lewis, probably in the early 19th century, illustrate this gesture: four of the figures depict shield-bearing warders, their teeth ostentatiously locked onto the upper rim of their shields.

Berserkers in the literature can sometimes exhibit invulnerability to fire or to swords, although this trait is usually to be found in the later, more fantastic sagas, along with occasional foaming at the mouth. The meaning of the name is much debated: perhaps they were 'bear-shirts', referring to a bearskin garment, or 'bare-shirts' – that is to say, men who fought without a mail shirt, even if, contrary to popular belief, they did not fight naked. Some evidence suggests that groups of berserkers could also be called *úlfheðnar*, 'wolf-coats', cementing the likely connection with animal skins.

Even in the sagas, the berserker was not always taken seriously. When, in *Víga-Glúms saga* (The Saga of Killer-Glúmr), Björn the berserker visits the Norwegian hall where the Icelander Glúmr is staying with his elderly grandfather and challenges every man to admit that he is not as brave as Björn, Glúmr comments that 'Back

The Lewis Chessmen, from the Isle of Lewis, Outer Hebrides (1150–1200).

home, we'd call anyone behaving like you an idiot.' He jumps up, snatches off Björn's helmet with one hand and seizes a brand from the fire with the other, smashing the flaming wood between the berserker's shoulders and driving him out of the hall with blows. Another Icelander, Grettir, deals with a mounted and posturing leader of a berserk band who is biting his shield by slamming the shield upwards so that it breaks the adversary's jaw. He pulls him off his horse, rips off his helmet and beheads him in one easy move. In another saga, an Icelandic chieftain, Styrr, acquires a pair of berserkers in Norway and employs them as enforcers back at home, considerably enhancing his status. But when one asks for the chieftain's daughter in marriage, his boss is quick to dispose of his dangerous assets. First, he sets them to clear a road across a lava field. They achieve this exhausting task in record time thanks to their berserker strength. As a reward, he invites them to take a sauna in his semi-underground bath house, which he heats to an unbearable temperature. As the debilitated men struggle out through the door, Styrr kills them both and has them buried out by the road that they made – a road that can be seen to this day on the Snæfellsnes Peninsula.

The probably erroneous idea that berserkers fought in a frenzy, impervious to pain and semi-naked, has given rise to a good deal of speculation as to what might have underlain the texts' accounts of such behaviour. Various theories have been touted, from the consumption of fly agaric, a kind of mushroom used by Sámi shamans for ritual purposes, or the drinking of large amounts of alcohol, to pre-existing psychopathic tendencies or various kinds of physical illness. However, there is no mention of mushroom nor alcohol use to stimulate berserk behaviour in the medieval sources: when a group of berserkers get drunk in one saga, it enables the hero to kill most of them singlehanded, and neither do the symptoms of a berserk-fit match known pathologies. It seems most likely that berserkers were originally an elite, highly trained

Berserkjahraun (Berserkers' lava field), Snæfellsnes, Iceland.

fighting unit who could turn extremely anti-social if not bound to a leader they respected. The idea that their combat skills were pharmaceutically enhanced has persisted in the modern imagination, however.

## The modern berserker

Berserkers have metamorphosed from the shield-gnashing figures found in the Lewis game-piece hoard into modern fantasy figures: frenzied, bare-chested fighters immune to pain. This is how they were imagined by the Victorians, chiefly following Sir Walter Scott in *The Pirate* (1822), who describes the 'Berserkars' in precisely these terms. Thereafter the word *berserk* is most frequently found as an adjective, with little or no direct relation to its context in the Viking Age. The berserker is not especially common in popular novels, though he may turn up in historical fiction, such as Eric Linklater's *The Men of Ness* (1959) or the explorer Tim Severin's *Viking: Odinn's Child* and *Viking: Sworn Brother* (2005), in which a female berserker, Freydís Eiríksdóttir, is introduced (we will read more about Freydís in Chapter 9). These stories follow in the tradition inaugurated by Scott, though their authors have often read a good deal of popular history and thus incorporate nakedness, howling, frenzy and the consumption of intoxicants into their plots to explain how the berserk loss of control is induced.

Film interest in the berserker is relatively recent. There is no role for them in the major Viking movies discussed above, such as *The Vikings* or *The 13th Warrior*, and not even in the infamous grindhouse movie *The Saga of the Viking Women and Their Voyage to the Waters of the Great Sea Serpent*, directed by Roger Corman (1957). It is unsurprising, however, since Terry Jones was a keen scholar of medieval history, that a berserk father and son, Ulf the Maddeningly Calm and Sven the Berserk, should appear in Jones's *Erik the Viking*. Ulf lectures his son on the tradition: 'I went berserk in every battle I ever fought for him [King Harald Fairhair]. It's a responsibility, being a berserk; you must only let the red rage take hold of you in the thick of battle.' Sven has heard all this many times and anticipates his father's next line, but the old man continues regardless, until his remorseless delivery provokes Sven into a berserk rage exactly when it is least called for. He headbutts a nearby shelter, smashing it to pieces and destroying all around him. This draws criticism from watching women ('That's dangerous!'). His father warns that, if he lets out all his fury now, he will not be able to muster the berserk spirit when he needs it in battle. Sven succeeds at last in appropriately unleashing his rage in combat when his friend Thorfinn is in mortal danger. Foaming at the mouth, he finds his inner berserk, fights off a huge sea serpent and makes his father proud. Jones's treatment of Sven's gradual growth into his true identity is both humorous and touching. The film bears the Monty Python hallmarks of comic inversion – the berserker who can't go mad in battle – and comedy names, such as Ulf's paradoxical sobriquet. Whether or not Sven's grandfather won admission to Valhalla – he must have been quite a cautious berserker, since he died of old age – becomes a key point of contention, resolved when the crew finally make their way to the home of the gods and discover him there. Clearly admission rules to the Hall of the Glorious Ones have been relaxed since Wagner's time.

## Björn, the bear and the berserker

The berserker role is tailor-made for computer games set in the Viking Age. The latest instalment in the Assassin's Creed series *Assassin's Creed: Valhalla* offers a standalone game called *The Way of the Berserker* (2020). In one mode of the game, its heroine, Eivor Varinsdottir, a reincarnation of Óðinn, learns that Björn Bloodtooth, a legendary berserker, is to be found in East Anglia, and so she journeys across the sea to investigate. Björn has retired from the berserk life, and he and his wife, Alfhild, had hoped to lead a peaceful existence in England. They had adopted, improbably enough, a white she-bear cub called Njal (normally a male name). Alfhild was murdered by a Mercian lord, and now Björn seeks vengeance. Eivor offers to help him in his mission, first by finding him some nightshade, the last ingredient necessary for the 'berserker brew' that he must drink to access his full strength and fury. The two warriors consume the drink together as Björn recites the berserk ritual words 'How are you called, you bear-skins, you wolf-shirts, you tasters of blood? We are the shield-biters, wall-breakers, born in battle's flood!' Eivor responds: 'We fight for glory, we shield-biters!' Under the potion's influence, Björn shape-changes into a bear, though when they attack and kill Björn's enemy the two fighters remain in human form. Njal the bear dies, touchingly mourned by Björn and Eivor: with unexpected tenderness, Björn asks Eivor to gather the beast's favourite flowers to lay on its corpse. Njal is dispatched to Valhalla on a funeral pyre where she will be reunited with Alfhild, while Björn joins Eivor's Raven Clan and sets off for new adventures. The game writers are clearly well acquainted with the traditional features of the berserker, including the wolf-pelts worn by the *úlfheðnar*, the shield-chomping villains of the sagas; the pharmaceutically induced frenzy; and the berserker's shamanistic connections with bears (Björn means 'bear', and it is a name that berserkers in the sagas often have).

The Viking and his close cousin the berserker have undergone a number of transformations in the modern popular imagination. The Vikings have metamorphosed from merciless pirates – the 'heathen slaughter-wolves' as they are called in one Old English poem – to more historically nuanced figures: men who combine raiding with trading, who compose poetry, carve runes and have a wife and family. Claims to Viking heritage became desirable in the 19th century, signalling adventurousness and a love of freedom, while in contemporary white supremacist circles they underpin a racist doctrine of Aryan superiority, as we'll see in Chapter 9. Vikings are now understood to include women, those who travelled across the sea to make new homes in the Atlantic archipelago, and even cross-dressing fighters such as the undaunted Hervör. Berserkers have come to stand for an undesirable hypermasculine rage and brutality stimulated by drug-taking. Causing damage to friend, foe and (not least) the berserker himself, he represents a monstrous parody of the noble Viking hero. Keeping heroic rage, personal honour, courage – and openness to romantic love – in balance is a challenge for Sigurðr, the greatest of all the champions of the Old North, as we shall see in the next chapter.

# Sigurðr the Dragon-Slayer

## THE MYTH OF THE MONSTER-KILLER

### The model hero

The myth of the hero and the dragon (or some other variety of dangerous and well-armoured monster) is one of the oldest and most widespread in the Indo-European mythological system. The young man, armed with a special weapon or equipped with a particular technique, confronts the savage creature that no one else can kill and triumphs, reclaiming the monster's territory for human habitation once more. In Old Norse heroic legend, Sigurðr, the posthumously born son of the great hero Sigmundr, descended directly from Óðinn, is the hero who slays the mighty serpent Fáfnir and wins a grand treasure hoard.

We met Fáfnir briefly in Chapter 2, in his Wagnerian form of Fafner – one of the two master architects commissioned by Wotan to build Walhall. This was not his original role in Norse myth. In the accounts given in the *Poetic Edda* and *Völsunga saga*, we learn that Fáfnir had two brothers called Reginn and Otr. Otr was a shape-changer and took on the form of an otter. One day Loki, who was passing along with Óðinn and the god Hœnir, chucked a stone at him. Otr was killed, and Loki skinned him and made the pelt into a bag. The gods fetched up that night – of all places – at the home of Hreiðmarr, Otr's father. When the adventure was related and the bag displayed, Hreiðmarr and his sons were outraged. They seized the gods and demanded a gold ransom. Loki undertook to arrange this; he knew that another shape-changer, a dwarf by the name of Andvari, lived in a nearby waterfall in the shape of a pike and possessed great riches. Loki captured Andvari and made him ransom himself with all his treasure – even the ring that Andvari had hoped to keep for himself. Furious, Andvari placed a curse on the ring. Back at Hreiðmarr's house, the gods piled up the gold, which almost covered the otter-skin bag. Reluctantly Óðinn handed over Andvari's ring too, to conceal the final whisker. The gods departed, but when Reginn and Fáfnir demanded their share of the ransom from their father Hreiðmarr refused. Fáfnir killed him and made off with the treasure to Gnita-heath, where he lay on the hoard in dragon form. This tale provided the kernel that Wagner used for the events of *Das Rheingold*, but there he conflated it with the 'Tale of the Master Builder', and the hoard – including the accursed Ring – originated in the gold of the Rhinemaidens.

Where there is a dragon and a great heap of treasure, there is bound to be a hero. The stories centre around greed: greed as embodied by the dragon who knows to the last goblet what should be in its inventory; the greed of those who covet the hoard but are not courageous or skilled enough to win it; and the hero who is often less interested in the loot than the fame that he will win as a dragon-slayer. However, as we shall see in the next chapter, killing a dragon at the very outset of your career may suggest that you have peaked too soon. There is nothing that can surpass that remarkable feat, and the dragon-slayer's history often takes a turn for the worse thereafter. Hard on the heels of Sigurðr's victory comes a series of moral challenges – not least his relationship with the Valkyrie Brynhildr and, eventually, the circumstances that precipitate his premature and tragic death.

Sigurðr is raised by his foster-father, a skilled smith – and that very same Reginn who was robbed of his father and of his share of Otr's ransom by Fáfnir. Reginn lives for vengeance and urges the young hero to slay the dragon for him. After Reginn has forged him a notable sword from the fragments of his father's weapon – the same sword that was drawn from the tree Barnstokkr, as related in Chapter 1 – creating a blade that befits Sigurðr's extraordinary strength, Sigurðr is ready for the deed. They make their way to Gnita-heath and find the track where the great serpent slithers down to the river to drink. Reginn retreats; a mysterious old man appears, urging Sigurðr to dig a series of pits, to lie in the largest and to stab the dragon from beneath. The extra pits will capture the dying creature's blood and venom. Sigurðr takes his patron's advice – for this is of course Óðinn in disguise – and fatally wounds the serpent. The dying monster warns Sigurðr of the risks involved in trusting Reginn and imparts other wisdom before it perishes.

Reginn orders Sigurðr to roast the dragon's heart for him while he takes a nap. Although treating a dragon-slayer as if he were still an apprentice to be ordered about is entirely inappropriate, Sigurðr obeys – and prods the heart with his thumb to test whether it is done, burning himself. When he sticks the sore thumb in his mouth, he realizes he can now understand the language of birds – and there are some highly opinionated nuthatches sitting in a tree above him. The birds warn him that Reginn will kill him when he awakes; it would be better to slay his foster-father first, then to make his way to the nearby mountain Hindarfjall with the treasure. Up there on the summit he will find a Valkyrie, sleeping behind a wall of flame.

Sigurðr acts on their advice, beheads Reginn, and loads up his faithful horse Grani with the treasure. Soon he is at Hindarfjall, where he awakens the Valkyrie and asks her to teach him wisdom.

In the *Poetic Edda*, the Valkyrie is called Sigrdrífa ('Victory-Bringer'), and she instructs the young hero in runes, spells and common-sense advice. But there is a gap in the manuscript at this point and, when the poems resume, Sigurðr has moved on. Luckily, we have a prose version, *Völsunga saga* (The Saga of the Völsungs), which relates the missing material. The saga tries to make sense of some conflicting traditions and is not always consistent, however; by its account the Valkyrie is Brynhildr, condemned to sleep and forced to marry the man who awakens her by Óðinn. She is the archetype of Wagner's Brünnhilde, whom we met in Chapter 2. Brynhildr had disobeyed Óðinn by awarding victory in battle not to the All-Father's favoured candidate, but to a younger and more handsome hero.

Brynhildr has a complicated backstory in the saga. Not only is she out of favour with Óðinn, but her brother Atli (a legendary figure based on memories of the Migration Age leader Attila the Hun) is very keen that she should marry and ally the family with a powerful dynasty. Brynhildr has sworn to wed only the greatest of heroes, the one who can cross the flames that surround her hall. Brynhildr and Sigurðr pledge themselves to one another, and Sigurðr then journeys on to the court at Worms on the Rhine. There he meets Gunnarr, his brother Högni, their sister Guðrún and their mother Grímhildr. Grímhildr prepares a 'drink of forgetting' for Sigurðr. Soon Sigurðr has indeed forgotten all about Brynhildr and is betrothed to Guðrún, to everyone's delight. Sigurðr is asked to help Gunnarr win the legendary Valkyrie Brynhildr, and they set off for her hall. Gunnarr's horse refuses to cross the flames. Grani will do so – but only if Sigurðr is on his back. What to do? The brothers-in-law magically exchange appearances, and the disguised Sigurðr wins Brynhildr for Gunnarr. Brynhildr is astonished and mistrustful: surely only Sigurðr could have crossed the flames? But she cannot go back on the oath that she had sworn regarding her future husband.

The two weddings are celebrated, but mid-feast the forgetting-drink wears off and Sigurðr remembers his prior feelings for Brynhildr. Thinking it is too late, he resolves to make the best of things. Matters continue thus until Brynhildr and Guðrún have a blazing quarrel, and Guðrún reveals the truth about the appearance-swap. Dishonoured, Brynhildr decides that she cannot live with what has happened. When Sigurðr disguised as Gunnarr breached the flame wall, he slept three chaste nights beside her, laying a drawn sword between them. But Brynhildr tells Gunnarr that Sigurðr has betrayed him; that he was her 'first man'. This is partly true, for they became lovers when they first met on the mountain before Sigurðr went to Gunnarr's court. Now, demands Brynhildr, Sigurðr must pay the price. Gunnarr conspires to have Sigurðr killed. Tradition varies as to how Sigurðr dies: attacked in bed by a brother-in-law who had not sworn an oath of blood-brotherhood; ambushed and killed on the way back from the Þing-meeting (a legal–political assembly); or stabbed in the back during

Left: Sigurðr roasts the dragon's heart, Kirk Andreas Cross (Manx Cross 121), Isle of Man (late 10th century). Right: Sigurðr and the dragon, detail of the carved doors at Hylestad stave church, Norway (c. 12th century).

a hunting expedition (the version Wagner uses). On Brynhildr's recommendation, his and Guðrún's infant son is also murdered, lest he grow up to take vengeance.

Sigurðr's unmerited death has powerful repercussions. Brynhildr commits suicide and shares his funeral pyre. Guðrún goes into exile in Denmark until her brothers and mother fetch her home – and marry her off to Atli, Brynhildr's brother. This does not end well. Atli covets the dragon's hoard and murders Guðrún's brothers when they will not reveal its location to him. Wily Gunnarr has sunk the treasure in the Rhine, and it will never be Atli's. In revenge, Guðrún kills Atli and their two sons.

German tradition knows a different version of the Sigurðr legend, preserved in *Das Nibelungenlied*, an epic poem from around 1200. Here he is called Siegfried, and his nemesis is Brünnhilde; his wife, called Kriemhilt rather than Guðrún, develops from a loving wife into a monstrous figure obsessed with taking vengeance for her husband's death. By the poem's end, Kriemhilt has brought about the death of all her brothers and their chief magnate Hagen, personally cutting off the latter's head. Finally, the famous old warrior Hildebrand cuts the vengeful 'she-devil' into pieces. Wagner chose to adapt the Scandinavian version rather than the medieval German poem, adding some details drawn from a folktale about the youth who knew no fear, and other material from the German ballad tradition.

So perished Sigurðr the Dragon-Slayer, whose fame, as the saga says, was so great that never again would a man like him be born; his name would never be forgotten anywhere that German was spoken, nor in the Northern lands, as long as the world endures. Indeed, the figures of Sigurðr, Gunnarr, Brynhildr and Guðrún have endured in the memories of the north, and their story has often been retold. Images from the Sigurðr legend were carved on stone crosses on the Isle of Man, on rune stones in Sweden, and on the famous church doors from Hylestad in Norway, which depict the whole cycle, from Reginn plotting with Sigurðr to Atli's murder of Gunnarr by imprisoning him in a snake-pit. Ballad versions of the tale were popular in Denmark, but they were often recorded late and contain fragmentary details. The Faroe Islands too have a strong Sigurðr (Sjúrðr) ballad tradition that may date from the medieval period, though the ballads themselves were not written down until the 18th century.

## Wagner's Siegfried

It was Siegfried's undeserved death that first captured Wagner's imagination: the earliest version of the *Ring's* libretto was called *Siegfrieds Tod* (Siegfried's Death). As the epic operatic cycle came slowly into existence, Wagner worked backwards from the hero's demise, establishing how he came to die, the history of his parents and the origin of the hoard. *Siegfried*, the third opera in the cycle, is the most cheerful. It begins at the forge of Mime, the counterpart of Reginn. Mime is the brother of Alberich, who had won the treasure in *Das Rheingold* by forswearing love. Mime has been raising Siegfried since his parents' death in *Die Walküre* and is bent on acquiring Fafner's gold. The boy is now capable of the feat – but only if Mime can forge him a suitable sword. Siegfried is a rambunctious lad, teasing and tormenting his guardian: on his first entrance he is accompanied by a bear that he has captured in the forest. When the sword Mime has forged once again breaks in his grip, Siegfried storms off, but not before hearing a recapitulation of the hoard's history. Mime learns from the Wanderer (a disguised Wotan) that only 'the one who knows no fear' can forge the sword successfully – and that this fearless man will take Mime's head. The dwarf is in a quandary: he must try to instil fear in Siegfried, but only after he has forged the sword. 'The Boy Who Knew No Fear' is a comic Brothers Grimm folk-tale, in which Wagner claimed to recognize the young Siegfried, hence the antics with the bear and the easy confidence with which he

Rock carvings of scenes from the Sigurðr legend at Ramsund, Sweden (c. 1030).

bullies his foster-father and confronts Wotan in his guise as the Wanderer.

Having forged the sword Nothung from the fragments of his father's magical weapon, Siegfried is ready to kill Fafner. On the advice of a woodbird, he also kills Mime, who has shown his bad faith by brewing a poisonous draught that he intends to have the boy drink after the hoard has been won. In Act III, Siegfried sets off to find his future bride, enclosed within the fire wall. Siegfried has never seen a woman before, although the Woodbird has told him something of what to expect, and as he cuts through the sleeper's chain-mail he realizes that here is something different. His exclamation 'Das ist kein Mann!' ('That's not a man!') raises a laugh during most performances. Now at last he learns fear; he dares not awaken this glorious being, yet longing compels him. He ventures to kiss Brünnhilde who, awakening, joyfully calls down the favour of the gods; laughter is dissipated in some of the most sublime music of the whole cycle. They pledge themselves to one another: 'He is mine for ever, mine always, my own wealth, radiant in love, laughing at death,' sings Brünnhilde. The curtain falls as Siegfried echoes her words.

Wagner's treatment of Siegfried's death in *Götterdämmerung* is discussed in detail in Chapter 10, where its consequence is to precipitate at last the end of Wotan's rule. His death also signals the end of the heroic male. Like his father, Siegmund, before him, Siegfried has been in Wotan's sights; he is intended to gain the Ring and restore order in the world as a 'free man'. Siegmund's heroism was compromised not only by his incestuous relationship with his sister, gaining him the enmity of Fricka, but also because Wotan had left the sword Nothung for him at his sister's home as a supernatural aid to achieving victory. Siegfried grows up in innocence, ignorant of his parentage, of Wotan's hopes, of the way that the human world works. Yet, in the end, being a 'free man' – the only man who can cross the fire to find Brünnhilde – is not enough either. His cheerful heroism cannot save him from Hagen's machinations nor from Brünnhilde's vengeance. Once he and Brünnhilde are dead and the waters of the Rhine have reclaimed the Ring, men and women in the ruins of Gunther's hall look up to the heavens 'with the greatest emotion' (according to Wagner's stage directions) as flames consume both gods and heroes gathered in Walhall, and the idea that a hero can save the world perishes with them. What kind of world shall be made now?

Although Wagner wrote optimistically in 1857 that he was sure that *Siegfried* would be tremendously popular, paving the way for the other music dramas of the cycle, strangely it has always been the least loved of the four operas, despite its glorious music. Siegfried's graceless bullying of the wheedling dwarf leaves a nasty taste; the young man's swaggering would grate were it not counterbalanced by his lyrical Act II conversation with the bird in which he laments his loneliness. Tolstoy saw *Siegfried* at Bayreuth and did not enjoy it: 'It was all so artificial and stupid that I had great

Aubrey Beardsley, *Siegfried* (c. 1892–93).

difficulty sitting it out,' he recorded. William Morris, the writer, artist and designer, did not like the sound of the staging described enthusiastically to him by a friend who came 'fresh from Bayreuth': 'Father scoffed at the notion that Fafnir, the man-beast of the savage legend, should be represented by modern stage ingenuity – should be a "practicable, pantomime dragon, puffing steam and showing his red danger-signal like a railway engine",' reported his daughter May. The opera indeed has a good deal of comic business – not only the bear, but also the Act II episode in which the magic of the dragon's heart forces the confused Mime to reveal his true intentions towards Siegfried, laying bare the poison plot and justifying his imminent murder. Nevertheless, the opera's tonal variety and its contrasts of comedy, emotional intensity and grandeur offer a breathing space between the high drama of *Die Walküre* and the coming horror of *Götterdämmerung*.

## William Morris and Sigurd

The first complete performance of Richard Wagner's *Ring* cycle was in 1876. At the same time William Morris was working on his epic poem *Sigurd the Volsung*, published the following year. Morris did not care for Wagner. 'The idea of a sandy haired German tenor tweedledeeing over the unspeakable woes of Sigurd' was more than he could bear, he wrote, and he viewed opera in general as 'the most rococo and degraded of all forms of art'. With his collaborator, the Icelander Eiríkur Magnússon who accompanied him on his two journeys to Iceland in 1871 and 1873, Morris had already published a prose translation of *Völsunga saga* in 1870. For him, the story of the Völsungs was part of the English ancestral heritage: 'the Great Story of the North, which should be to all our race what the Tale of Troy was to the Greeks,' he pronounced.

However much Morris disliked the sound of the *Ring*, his radical views coincided with those of Wagner at several points. His Brynhild warns Sigurd at their first meeting that the gods are not to be trusted, that he was not born to serve them but to be 'their very friend'. Morris's Regin too, crazed by his desire for the gold, sees it as enabling a lust for power that equals that of Alberich. Once he has it in his possession, Regin boasts that he will become like all the gods rolled into one: 'And there shall be no more dying, and the sea shall be as the land, / And the world for ever and ever shall be young beneath my hand.' The dying Fafnir relates how the gods also are fettered by fate, in lines that could be voiced by Wagner's Erda, the seeress who repeatedly spells out to Wotan the limitations of his agency:

> 'I have seen the Gods of heaven,
>     and their Norns withal I know:
> They love and withhold their helping,
>     they hate and refrain the blow;
> They curse and they may not sunder,
>     they bless and they shall not blend;
> They have fashioned the good and the evil;
>     they abide the change and the end.'

Morris makes a good many changes to the saga that he and Magnússon translated, foregrounding the female characters and amplifying their far-sightedness and wisdom, which is generally ignored by the men around them; he also excises some of the many cruelties visited upon children in his source. Furthermore, he completely recasts the poem's final book. Where in the Old Norse tradition Guðrún is both anguished and enraged by her brothers' deaths at the hands of her new husband, Atli, and swiftly takes revenge upon him, Morris draws in part on the *Nibelungenlied* to show his heroine as plotting vengeance upon her brothers. She manipulates Atli, appealing to his greed for the treasure so that he invites her brothers to his hall, there to attack them. The brothers arrive with a sizeable troop of warriors (in the Norse tradition they are almost alone), and a mighty battle ensues between the Huns (Atli's tribe) and the Niblungs, as

Morris calls Gunnarr's clan. In his retelling, Gudrun scarcely reacts to the deaths of Gunnar and Hogni. But during the next night she stabs the husband for whom she no longer has any use, burns his drink-befuddled warriors in their hall, then walks calmly to a cliff overlooking the sea where, invoking her beloved Sigurd, 'brightness unforgotten', she commands the waters to take her life:

> She hath spread out her arms as she spake it,
>     and away from the earth she leapt,
> And cut off her tide of returning;
>     for the sea-waves over her swept,
> And their will is her will henceforward;
>     and who knoweth the deeps of the sea,
> And the wealth of the bed of Gudrun,
>     and the days that yet shall be?

Morris's epic had mixed notices at first. The intellectual Edmund Gosse declared that Morris was 'the interpreter of high desires and ancient heroic hopes as fresh as the dawn of the world and as momentous. The atmosphere of this poem is sharp and cold ... [it has] a solemn and archaic air.' More critically, Morris's friend the poet A. C. Swinburne wrote privately in 1882 to their mutual friend Theodore Dunton: 'It is my belief that you encourage all this dashed and blank Volsungery which will end by eating up the splendid genius it has already overgrown and encrusted with Icelandic moss.' By 1905 the story of Sigurd's triumphs over his scheming foster-father and the dragon, his downfall through the treachery of his brothers-in-law and his complex and anguished relationships with Brynhild and Gudrun had become a school text-book. Here large stretches of Morris's expansive, hypnotic poetry are replaced by prose summaries, and the story ends abruptly with Sigurd and Brynhild's shared funeral pyre.

**Siegfried at the movies**

The first notable film version of the *Nibelungenlied* story, *Die Nibelungen*, directed by Fritz Lang, was released in 1924. It has two parts, *Siegfried* and *Kriemhilds Rache* (Kriemhild's Revenge), which add up to a running time of nearly five hours. It's an extraordinary film, following quite closely the original medieval poem as adapted by Lang's wife, Thea von Harbou. *Die Nibelungen* is an Expressionist masterpiece, with splendid set pieces, stately processions, and contrasting craggy and gloomy landscapes. The actors portraying the Nibelung court, wearing highly stylized, geometrically patterned costumes and accentuated eye make-up, are often grouped in hieratic, striking tableaux. The interiors in the castle at Worms are light, symmetrically arranged and orderly: minstrels play, sweet perfumes fill the air, and lovely Kriemhild sits sewing. These images contrast with outdoor scenes of mist, rocks and bulky tree-trunks in the studio-built forest, the primitive smithy where the loin-cloth-clad, handsome and natural-looking Sigurd is apprenticed at the start of the film, Alberich's cavernous underground lair, and the brooding castle surrounded by a flaming lava-field where Brünnhilde holds sway. There are some surprising non-naturalistic effects, including an impressionistic dream sequence and a moment when a white rosebush suddenly blossoms with death's-heads, foreshadowing Siegfried's end. Lang made use of advanced technology too: the impressive dragon, 20 metres (66 feet) long and designed by Erich Kettelhut, demanded a multi-man team to operate its eyes, tongue, legs and breathing mechanism. Lang aimed to celebrate the *Nibelungenlied* as the 'nation's spiritual, sacred object' by recreating the medieval poem's epic scale and its rich descriptions of courtly interiors and splendid clothing, thus evoking a vision of 'German' civilization.

Lang and von Harbou knew Wagner's work, of course, but they sought deliberately to distance their film from the composer's

IX

Edward Burne-Jones, *Voyage to Vinland the Good*, commissioned
by William Morris for Catherine Lorillard Wolfe's Vinland estate, 1883–84

x

Frank Bernard Dicksee, *The Funeral of a Viking*, 1893

XI
Carl Larsson, *Midvinterblot*, 1915

XII
Bjørn Nørgaard, *The Viking Age*,
from *Tapestries for the Queen of Denmark (Gobelin)*, 1991–97

XIII (*Top*)
Jens Erik Carl Rasmussen, *Erik the Red Discovers Greenland*, 1875

XIV (*Bottom*)
Karl Ludwig Prinz, *Auf Walhall*, before 1911

Norse-derived retelling by returning to the *Nibelungenlied*. Germany was unified in 1871, and Siegfried, the poem's hero, had been a powerful symbol for the kingdom, identified variously with Bismarck and Emperor Wilhelm II. Following the end of the First World War, the *Nibelungenlied* version of Siegfried's death, in which he is stabbed in the back by Hagen during a hunting expedition, was understood as symbolizing the German army's betrayal by left-wing and social democratic Germans. By failing to support, or campaigning against, Germany's imperialist war aims, they had truly stabbed the army in the back, or so the German general Paul von Hindenburg would later claim. On its first release *Die Nibelungen* was by no means a 'Nazi film'; rather it spoke to the hopes and anxieties of the Weimar Republic. When in 1933 the first part, *Siegfried*, was re-released with an added Wagnerian soundtrack, and with the well-publicized approval of Goebbels and Hitler, the film did indeed acquire Nazi propaganda associations: Siegfried, the blond,

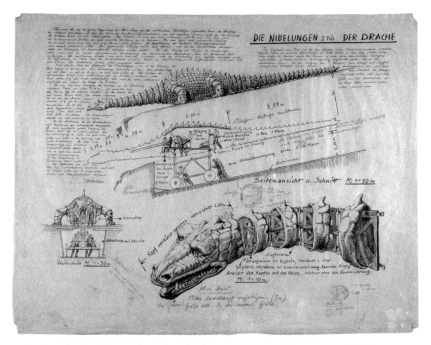

Designs by Erich Kettelhut for the dragon in *Die Nibelungen: Siegfried* (1923).

athletic Aryan hero, could be read – at a stretch – as Hitler, and the Valkyrie he wins represented Germany submitting to his nobility and prowess. One problem remains in this reading, of course: it is those civilized, courtly nobles of Worms – the Nibelungen, who also symbolize the German people – who are responsible for the hero's murder. Germany's reinterpretation of its own medieval past is, and continues to be, conflicted.

There have been surprisingly few later retellings of either Sigurðr or Siegfried's story. The 2004 television film *Curse of the Ring* (also known as *Sword of Xanten*), directed by Uli Edel, boasted a good many well-known British actors: it's a sword-and-sorcery melodrama of love and battle. Perhaps surprisingly, Quentin Tarantino's *Django Unchained* (2012) takes some of its inspiration from the story of Siegfried and Brünnhilde, to which it alludes directly. Dr Schultz (played by the Austrian actor Christoph Waltz), a German bounty-hunter, buys and frees Django (Jamie Foxx), an African-American slave, to help him track down some

The dead Siegfried, still from Fritz Lang's *Die Nibelungen: Siegfried* (1924).

brutal slave-overseers. Django wants to find and rescue his wife, Broomhilda (Kerry Washington). The couple were separated at a slave auction, and she is now the property of the monstrous plantation owner Calvin Candie (Leonardo di Caprio). When Schultz learns Broomhilda's name, he relates a rather mangled version of the plot of *Siegfried*. Brünnhilde, he relates, was a princess, the daughter of Wotan, who banished her to a mountain top for her disobedience. There she is guarded by a fire-breathing dragon and surrounded by hellfire. 'And there Broomhilda shall remain, unless a hero arises brave enough to save her,' concludes Schultz. Django is agog: 'Does a fella arise?' he asks. He is assured that, indeed, Siegfried had the courage to scale the mountain and defeat the dragon: 'He walks through hellfire, because Broomhilda's worth it.' Once Schultz and Django get to Candyland, Candie's plantation, they find Broomhilda confined in the 'hot-box', a coffin-like iron box dug into the ground – a sadistic echo of the fire that surrounded her legendary counterpart. Django finally rescues Broomhilda, kills Candie's remaining henchmen at Candyland, frees the slaves and dynamites the big house – by implication the whole inhuman institution of slavery, in a kind of *Götterdämmerung* – before riding off with his wife by his side. Although Tarantino and Waltz claimed in interviews that it was the Austrian actor who had introduced the director to Wagner's operas, Tarantino was already familiar not only with the *Ring* cycle, but also, given his immersion in film history, Lang's *Die Nibelungen*. There's a strong visual echo of the earlier film when Schultz is telling Django about Siegfried, his mythic counterpart.

### Tolkien, Sigurðr and the dragon

J. R. R. Tolkien protested that the only connection between his epic trilogy *The Lord of the Rings* and Wagner's opera cycle was that 'both rings were round, and there the resemblance ceased'. Yet C. S. Lewis's brother Warnie records in his diary how, in preparation for a visit to the opera in 1934, Tolkien and Lewis spent an evening reading out Wagner's libretto to *Die Walküre* in the original German; Warnie followed along with an English translation. Tolkien's conception of the Ring, then, as an object that grants extraordinary power to its bearer even as it works to corrupt him, owes much more to Wagner than to the ring known as Andvaranaut in *Völsunga saga*. In the Old Norse account, it is the whole hoard that is accursed; the ring functions rather as a recognition token, enabling Guðrún, who now has it, to prove to Brynhildr, from whom it was taken, that it was indeed Sigurðr who crossed the flame wall. Just as in Morris's account of the treasure, Wagner's Ring wields a powerful force that Alberich, Wotan and Fafner all covet: they plan to use it to dominate the world in which they live, to control gods and humans. Tolkien's ring, in contrast, while it kindles an obsessive, even murderous, desire in those who possess it, functions primarily on a symbolic level, figuring the ultimate evil of Sauron: its bearers have no detailed social programme to which they might harness it.

Tolkien had already made detailed use of Old Norse heroic legend, in particular *Völsunga saga*, in his early unfinished story *The Children of Hurin*, which he began as an epic poem during the First World War. Finally completed by Christopher Tolkien, the tale was published in 2007. Here Tolkien created the dragon Glaurung, just as cunning as Fáfnir and a close ally of the Dark Lord Morgoth, along with an evil dwarf called Mîm who betrays the hero, Túrin. Also borrowed from the saga are the motifs of brother–sister incest and the reforging of the ancestral sword. Túrin succeeds in killing Glaurung by stabbing him from below, just like Sigurðr. As he is dying, the dragon reveals to Túrin that Niënor, to whom he is married and who is expecting his child, is his sister. Both the children of Hurin commit suicide in consequence.

Tolkien's most famous dragon, Smaug, appears in *The Hobbit* (1937). Tolkien claimed that the original impetus for *The Lord of the Rings* and *The Silmarillion* was 'fundamentally linguistic', and his ingenuity in naming his characters bears witness to his delight in language, for Smaug derives his name from the past tense of the Old Norse verb *smjúga* 'to creep'. While greed for gold is a common characteristic of Northern dragons, Smaug inherits his fiery nature, his capacity to fly and his propensity for burning down human settlements from the dragon of the Old English poem *Beowulf*. His ability to talk, however, and particularly his fascination with obscure kennings and riddling metaphors, comes from his Old Norse antecedent Fáfnir. Sigurðr engages in a long conversation with Fáfnir after he has dealt the monster his death blow, at first concealing his name and ancestry with mysterious hints. Fáfnir in return imparts arcane knowledge and makes prophetic remarks about the hero's future. Likewise, when Bilbo is reconnoitring the dragon's lair, Smaug tries to entice him to come close enough to be attacked. Bilbo addresses him flatteringly – 'O Smaug, the Chiefest and Greatest of Calamities' – and, like Sigurðr, he hides his identity in kennings: 'I am the clue-finder, the web-cutter, the stinging fly. I was chosen for the lucky number.' As Tolkien observes: 'This ... is the way to talk to dragons ... no dragon can resist the fascination of riddling talk.' Smaug is disarmed enough by Bilbo's cleverness to boast of his invulnerability; he rolls over on his pile of treasure and reveals a large patch 'as bare as a snail out of its shell'. Thus Bard the Bowman, tipped off by a friendly thrush (Tolkien's counterpart to the nuthatches and the Woodbird), knows where to aim. He shoots the fire-breathing monster out of the sky, saving the Dale from his depredations.

## About dragons

Smaug figures in the imaginative ancestry of a good many modern fantasy dragons, and his mixed Old English and Norse heritage gives him a range of useful characteristics. In the 20th century the flying fire dragon, as Tolkien well knew, came to embody fiery destruction rained down from above: the bomb-laden aeroplane, the targeted missile or, indeed, the nuclear warhead. The dragons in Ursula K. Le Guin's *Earthsea* series (1964–2018) can also speak (but only in the Old Speech). Just as Sigurðr instinctively conceals his identity at first from Fáfnir, knowledge of an Earthsea dragon's true name gives a mage power over him. The Earthsea dragons are near invincible and live for a very long time indeed. Thus like Germanic dragons they possess wisdom well beyond that of humans and display remarkable cunning. The young mage Ged is sent to monitor the threat from the Dragon of Pendor, whose eight offspring, now near fully grown, are beginning to fly over and reconnoitre neighbouring islands, for 'the hunger of a dragon is slow to wake, but hard to sate'. Pendor, now 'the dragon-spoiled isle', had been a haunt of pirates and slave-traders for generations, amassing huge gold hoards. This naturally caught the attention of the Old Dragon, who had long ago attacked and incinerated the Lord of Pendor, and then took up his abode in the Sealords' ruined towers. Ged kills some of the young dragons with spells and, by changing himself into a dragon, downs another in aerial combat. To face down the Old Dragon requires more than the usual magic, however. His knowledge of ancient tales and dragon lore acquired at the school for wizards enables Ged to guess the dragon's name, Yevaud:

> When he spoke the dragon's name it was as if he held the huge being on a fine, thin leash, tightening it on his throat. He could feel the ancient malice and experience of men in the dragon's gaze that rested on him, he could see the steel-hard talons, each as long as a man's forearm, and the stone-hard hide, and the withering fire that lurked in the dragon's throat: and yet always the leash tightened, tightened.

Yevaud is constrained to promise that he and his remaining sons will never again fly eastwards of Pendor – indeed, they were never again seen over the archipelago. Later in the series, Ged enters into an alliance with the greatest dragon in existence, Orm Embar, in order to set the world to rights and to nullify the evil caused by the dark magician Cob. Orm's first name is derived from Old Norse *ormr*, meaning 'serpent'; he is descended from the mighty ancestor dragon Orm, who slew one of the most important heroes and dragon lords in Earthsea history: Erreth-Akbe. Orm himself died as a result of the battle – mutual destruction that recalls the fates of Þórr and the Miðgarðs Serpent (in Old Norse, the Miðgarðsormr).

The three huge flying fire dragons of George R. R. Martin's *A Song of Ice and Fire* series (1996–), Drogon, Rhaegal and Viserion, named by their mother, Daenerys, after the three men she has loved most in her life, do not speak. Tyrion, the dwarf son of Tywin Lannister, has always been fascinated by them and, like Ged, he too knows all about them: 'Dragons are intelligent, more intelligent than men according to some Maesters [the learned caste in the Seven Kingdoms]. They have affection for their friends and fury for their enemies,' he observes. In the books, Tyrion witnesses a futile attempt to kill Drogon with crossbow bolts, weapons that are quite ineffective against these comprehensively armoured creatures: '*Dragons are not so easy to kill as that. Tickle him with these and you'll only make him angry.* The eyes were where a dragon was most vulnerable. The eyes, and the brain behind them. Not the underbelly, as certain old tales would have it.' Martin and Tyrion know their dragon lore, of course: the allusion to Smaug and Fáfnir with their vulnerable bellies is deliberate; and the reference to the eye recalls the organ through which Siegfried finally stabs his beast in Lang's *Die Nibelungen* film.

The dragons in *A Song of Ice and Fire* are alive and well – at least at the time of writing. Not so all their counterparts in *Game of Thrones*, the HBO television adaptation of the books. There Viserion falls victim to the Night King, who casts his spear of ice at the beast and transforms him into an ice dragon, the only creature capable of bringing down the great Wall that protects the Seven Kingdoms from the southwards march of the White Walkers and their zombie army of the dead. Rhaegal, shamefully, is slain by two huge, armour-piercing scorpion-bolts, catapulted at him from below by Euron Greyjoy: one sticks in the dragon's belly, while the other passes through his neck (so much for Tyrion's strategic understanding of dragons' weak spots). This grinning, swaggering sea king is almost the last person in the Seven Kingdoms to deserve the illustrious title of dragon-slayer: to my mind this was an outrageously subversive recasting of the greatest of heroic achievements.

### Cyber-Sigurðr

The author Melvin Burgess primarily writes young adult fiction, often with challenging and controversial themes, including sex, drug-taking and violence. He has always been interested in Old Norse myth and legend – an interest that came to fruition in two novels that retell the material in *Völsunga saga*: *Bloodtide* (1999), the beginning of which was discussed in Chapter 1, and *Bloodsong* (2005). The first book deals with the main narrative from the first part of the saga: the tale of Sigmundr, Sigurðr's father, the deaths of his father and brothers through the machinations of his sister's husband, Siggeirr, and the long-delayed vengeance taken for his male kindred by Sigmundr, his sister Signý and their incestuously begotten son, Sinfjötli. Burgess transposes the tale into a futuristic London, one where rival gang lords hold sway and where genetic technology, stemming from the distant city of Ragnor, has allowed strange animal–human hybrids ('half-men') to come to existence and bodies to be modified in disturbing ways. This technology replaces, to a large extent, the supernatural and magical elements in the original legend. By the end of *Bloodtide*, vengeance has been achieved: Conor and Signy (the equivalents of Siggeirr and Signý) are dead. Signy and her twin brother Siggy's incestuous child, Styr (Sinfjötli), has played a significant role in their vengeance and downfall. Cloned, genetically enhanced and with a mind engineered by his mother to think only of revenge, Styr kills his brother and mother in the final slaughter.

*Bloodsong*, the second of the two books, is set a hundred years in the future. Siggy (Sigmundr) is dead, but his son, Sigurd, lives in Wales with his mother, Hjordis. Now everyone has non-human genes: Sigurd is part lion, and his foster-father Reginn is part pig. Reginn urges Sigurd to kill the terrible dragon Fafnir who sprawls across Hampstead Heath. The dragon possesses extraordinary technological powers in the form of 'god machines' that can control emotions – devices that Reginn covets. Fafnir, so it transpires, is not Reginn's brother, but rather Sigurd's, for he is in fact Styr from the previous novel. Hero and dragon share a father, and Styr-Fafnir, who was already largely a product of genetic engineering, has spent the intervening years adapting and enhancing his capabilities. Nothing can pierce Fafnir's hide except the stone knife that Sigurd inherited from his father, that long-ago gift from Odin (see Chapter 1). As in the saga, Sigurd digs a pit at Odin's behest and lies in wait for three nights to kill the monster, Odin keeping him company in this strange underworld. As in the Old Norse stories, Fafnir engages his slayer in a long conversation, but with the aim of distracting the hero from noticing that 'the bastard had two hearts' and is covertly regenerating, ready to attack again. Sigurd is nonetheless victorious and discovers that Fafnir has indeed been hoarding gold, hidden behind the 'tall green machines of the Destiny Corporation'. He loads the gold into his cyberhorse, Slipper (a pun on the name of Óðinn's horse, Sleipnir), kills Reginn in self-defence and blows up Fafnir's lair, including the Destiny machines.

London has been flattened by nuclear attack, but lying beneath it, and parasitic upon it, is the dystopian city of Crayley (a pun on Burgess's birthplace, the unexciting new town of Crawley). It is there that Bryony, the Brynhildr figure, a daughter of Odin, is trapped, behind walls of fire and toxic post-industrial waste. Escaping the shockwaves generated by his destruction of Fafnir's citadel, Sigurd hurtles down into the very heart of the city, surviving thanks to the invulnerability conferred by bathing in Fafnir's blood. There he meets and falls in love with Bryony. She is soon pregnant with his child, but she cannot leave Crayley without protection against fire and toxins. Sigurd leaves her to fetch some of Fafnir's skin to make a fireproof wrapping for her. Once above ground, he becomes enmeshed in the fortunes of the Niberlin family, powerful war-leaders with a good admixture of dog genes. Instead of being given a drink of forgetfulness, Grimhild, the matriarch of the clan, has him cloned, his memory of whom he loves is erased, and the original Sigurd is murdered. The clone then returns to Crayley to destroy the all-devouring city that has now become a terrible threat to everything on the surface. It has cannibalized the neural networks of Bryony and Sigurd's baby, Beatrice, and threatens all life above ground. For this adventure, Sigurd takes on Gunar's shape, for his brother-in-law has tried and failed already, risking the loss of his honour and authority:

> Yes, Gunar was a good man – but he wanted too much. Perhaps his brains had been cooked as well down there. Sigurd, who genuinely did not care for the achievement, only for the doing, gave the glory away without a second's thought, but he would have been a better friend if he had said no. This deed was to carve a wound in many hearts.

Sigurd may have blown up the Destiny Corporation's machines, but he cannot escape destiny itself. Throughout Burgess's novel, Sigurd's decisions – largely motivated by the one part of him that Gunar's evil mother cannot destroy, his powerful capacity to love – lead him further and further into betrayal and deception. Once his memory is erased, the Sigurd-clone's love is turned towards Gudrun. Bryony is claimed by Gunar, but after a quarrel with Gudrun the truth emerges and the domestic situation detonates, destroying all the protagonists in a dramatic climax.

The dragon and the dragon-slayer have taken on a range of new significations over the last 150 years. The dragon himself has come to symbolize the most terrible technologically created threat to human life; from lying quietly on Gnita-heath minding his gold, or popping up to menace Siegfried in Lang's *Die Nibelungen*, he has become capable, as in *Game of Thrones*, of razing a whole city and incinerating its inhabitants. Yet the dragon also embodies ageless wisdom: he knows how to manipulate men through his rhetorical skills, exploiting his capacity to instil fear or revealing a hidden future and imparting vital knowledge. The gift of mastering or wielding temporary control over a dragon is given to very few; study, maturity and wisdom are required, along with nerve and determination. Dragons and humans can exist in a friendly symbiosis. They can be tamed by young children aspiring to true Viking identity, as suggested by Cressida Cowell in the very successful *How to Train Your Dragon* book series, or they can substitute for offspring, as in the queer maternity of Daenerys, Mother of Dragons. These reimaginings of the monstrous creatures work partly to demystify them, but they also underline their powerful imaginative potential.

The dragon-slayer symbolizes the highest form of heroism: the courage to look the embodiment of absolute horror in the face and to summon the resolution to destroy it. The hero often needs key elements of technology – the reforged ancestral sword or Sigurd's stone knife – and he also needs knowledge of the dragon's constraints and vulnerabilities: its tender eyes and belly. Nor does divine help come amiss; Óðinn's quiet advice is heeded by some heroes, but scornfully rejected by Wagner's Siegfried, who has already cast off any allegiance to the gods of Walhall. Superlatively brave though they may be, Sigurðr and his descendants are less well equipped to deal with the machinations of power-hungry humans possessed by envy, greed and fear. Relative innocents, they give their hearts, apparently once and for all, to the fearless Valkyrie who is their heroic equal, only to become entangled in the plots of the Nibelungs and their allies. The hero dies, realizing all too late how he has been deceived and what he has lost to his enemies' flattery and manipulation. This most ancient of Indo-European mythological patterns resonates remarkably with modern preoccupations: our apprehension that the real horror does not emanate from the mythological monster, but rather from the multiple ways in which human beings are prepared to betray one another.

CHAPTER 8

# Ragnarr Shaggy-Breeches

THE MYTH OF VIKING CONQUEST

**Ragnarr, his sons and the serpents**

Ragnarr Loðbrók (Shaggy-Breeches) is a legendary Old Norse hero,
eclipsed only by Sigurðr in terms of fame, whether in medieval
Scandinavia or in later eras. His story – and, importantly, that of
his wife and sons – is told in detail in Saxo Grammaticus's *Gesta
Danorum* (The History of the Danes; *c.* 1200) and in Ragnarr's own
saga, now preserved in the same manuscript as *Völsunga saga*, and
in a very fragmentary manuscript that is nearly illegible. The saga
and a brief continuation relating further adventures of Ragnarr's
sons were composed in the mid-13th century. Ragnarr is the other
great dragon-slayer of the Old North besides Sigurðr. The dragon
he kills is a poison-spewing serpent, the pet of Princess Þóra. Given
the little creature as a present, the girl nurtured it by placing a new
piece of gold beneath it daily; it grew and grew, until it was con-
suming a whole ox every day, was sitting on a sizeable dowry and
had coiled itself around the outside of Þóra's quarters. The creature
allowed her to go in and out freely but repelled others – especially
suitors. Ragnarr heard that whoever slew the serpent would gain
the gold and the girl. He had a special shirt and pair of trousers

made of some kind of shaggy fleece or fur, which were then soaked in pitch. He loosened the nail securing the head of his spear to its shaft and sallied forth against the monster early in the morning when no one was awake to witness his feat. He stabbed it twice with his spear; the final blow pierced its back so deeply that the spearhead was buried in its flesh. Ragnarr then skipped away as the dying beast's death throes unleashed a torrent of poison that would have consumed him utterly had it not been for his protective clothing. Great was the surprise of all in Gautland (in southern Sweden) that the serpent should be so suddenly and mysteriously slain. Ragnarr claimed the victory, proving it by showing that the fatal spearhead fitted his shaft, wedded Þóra and took the gold. He had amply proven his heroic mettle in his very first adventure.

Thereafter, Ragnarr's fortunes were more mixed. Þóra died after bearing two sons, and Ragnarr married again, having the wit to recognize the beauty, cleverness and high breeding of Áslaug, the daughter of Sigurðr and Brynhildr. Áslaug had been rescued from the aftermath of her parents' death by Brynhildr's foster-father, Heimir. On his travels, Heimir unwisely accepted hospitality from two evil Norwegian peasants, who murdered him for his gold and raised the little girl as their own maltreated daughter. Hearing of Áslaug's beauty, Ragnarr posed her a riddle: she must come to him neither clothed nor naked, neither fasting nor fed, neither alone nor with someone. Clever Áslaug solved this by wearing a fishing net, biting on a leek, and taking a dog with her. Ragnarr marries Áslaug, although he does not know her ancestry at this point. Despite her protests, he insists on consummating the relationship straight away, even though she warns that this will mean conceiving a disabled son. The son, Ívarr the Boneless, is indeed born with cartilage instead of bones, but what he lacks in brawn he more than makes up for in brains. More sons are born, but Ragnarr unwisely promises to marry the king of Sweden's daughter, for the king is his friend and there are sound political reasons for

Ragnarr and Áslaug, illustration by August Malmström from Peter August Gödecke's *Sagan om Ragnar Lodbrok och hans söner* (1880).

the match. When Áslaug gets wind of the proposed alliance (like her father, she understands the language of the birds who tattle on her errant husband), she reveals her parentage to Ragnarr and prophesies that the son she is carrying will have snake-shaped pupils as proof of her claims. Her prophecy is fulfilled, and the boy with the unusual eyes is given his maternal grandfather's name: Sigurðr, with the by-name Snake-in-the-Eye.

Ragnarr mostly remains at home, ruling over Denmark, while his grown sons set off campaigning. Ívarr goes along too, borne on a kind of litter. Relations had cooled between Denmark and Sweden after Ragnarr's proposed marriage had come to nothing. His elder sons by Þóra were killed raiding in Sweden, and Áslaug encouraged her own sons to avenge their stepbrothers, herself leading an army to the battle. The brothers conquer Sweden, killing its king, and then expand their raiding activities far and wide across the continent. They even aim to march on Rome but are deterred by meeting an old man wearing worn-out iron shoes and carrying a second pair on his back. He explains that he has used up both pairs walking from Rome – that's how far away it is – and the brothers decide to abandon their plan.

Meanwhile Ragnarr, at home in Denmark, is growing tired of hearing his sons' feats praised above his own. He determines to recover his reputation by mounting an expedition to England, taking only two warships. His wife thinks this is a terrible idea – he needs many more ships to conquer England – but Ragnarr rejects her advice. There is no glory in taking a huge army on such an expedition, he says; and if he is defeated then only two ships will be lost. Áslaug is still doubtful, but she sews for him a magic shirt of invulnerability. Ragnarr lands in Northumbria and is faced by King Ella's huge army. Although he fights mightily, using the spear with which he had killed the serpent, he is captured and placed in a snake-pit, for he refuses to admit his identity to his opponent. The snakes will not bite him, so Ella orders his clothing to be removed – including the magic shirt. Then, famously, Ragnarr remarks, 'The little pigs would squeal if they knew what the old boar was enduring', and the serpents attack. Ragnarr's sons take a speedy and terrible vengeance for their father, conquering the kingdom and apparently agreeing terms with Ella. By a ruse, Ívarr gains from him enough land to found a settlement, the future London. (This is the same trick as was used by Dido to found Carthage: asking for

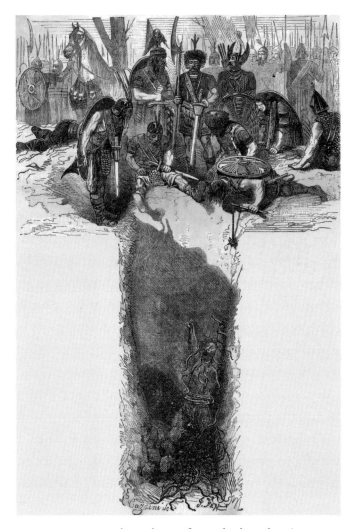

Ragnarr in the snake-pit, from Charles Lahure's
*Histoire populaire de la France* (1864–66).

land equal to a given number of oxhides, then cutting the hides
into thin strips and using them to delineate a vast acreage.) When
Ella attacks again, infuriated by Ívarr's trickery, he is captured and
killed by means of 'the blood eagle', a – likely invented – torment
in which a victim is sacrificed to Óðinn by having his ribcage split
open and his lungs dragged out onto his back, like eagles' wings.
Ívarr remains to rule England while the other brothers disperse.

One dies heroically, raiding in the Baltic; the other two marry high-born women and become the progenitors of important Northern dynasties. Haraldr Fairhair, the king who united Norway, is the grandson of Sigurðr Snake-in-the-Eye; many other Danish kings, including Knútr – England's own King Canute – are also descended from Sigurðr, according to a Danish chronicle.

The saga, therefore, gives Ragnarr very little to do beyond killing his dragon, winning his wives and siring sons until he sets out on his last pig-headed expedition to England. Saxo Grammaticus knew much more about this Danish hero. As king of Denmark, he avenges his grandfather on the king of Sweden with the aid of Lathgertha the shield-maiden, forces her to marry him, but then jettisons her in favour of Thora, who is guarded by two giant serpents whom he kills. She is mother of most of his sons. Ragnarr then subjugates England, Scotland, Norway, Orkney and Sweden, installing his sons as sub-kings as he goes along. Another son gains rule over the Scythians but is killed by the prince of Hellespont in Asia Minor. There are also further raiding expeditions against the Sámi and the Bjarmians, a people in the far north of Europe, as well as repeated attacks on the British Isles. Finally, Ælle of Northumbria successfully attacks Ragnarr's men in Ireland; it is there that he is thrown into the snake-pit and perishes.

**Ragnarr and his sons in history**
The evidence for Ragnarr ever having existed is scanty indeed, but there is some. The *Anglo-Saxon Chronicle*, the principal history of early medieval England, relates that a certain Reginherus or Ragnall led raids along the Frankish coast in the 840s until he was bought off by King Charles the Bald and was granted land there. However, the treaty was broken; Reginherus and his men sailed up the Seine and besieged Paris, lifting the siege only when they were paid 7,000 livres of silver – enough that it would have taken ninety men to carry it all away. Frankish chronicles claim that Reginherus

died shortly afterwards, but other accounts, of varying reliability, record Reginherus/Ragnall as raiding afterwards in Ireland in 851, and then in north-west England. He supposedly played a role in founding Dublin. Ragnarr's historical prototype probably perished somewhere in the area of the Irish Sea in the 850s.

There is better evidence for the men identified in the literary sources as Ragnarr's sons: Ívarr, Halfdan and Ubbi all appear in the historical record, although it is not at all clear that they are the sons of the man who besieged Paris. Ívarr was active in Ireland between 857 and 863 (if, as seems likely, he was the man known as Ímair in Irish chronicles). Along with his brothers Halfdan and Ubbi, he is recorded as leading the Great Heathen Army that arrived in England in 865. This Viking host fought in Northumbria, killing the rival kings of the region, including Ella, and capturing York in 866. They took East Anglia in 868 and killed King Edmund of East Anglia (later canonized as St Edmund the Martyr) in 869 at Thetford. Ívarr seems to have led the army until around 870, following which he may have returned to the Scottish–Irish arena. These were no longer the summer-mounted hit-and-run raids of earlier Viking attacks: the army overwintered at various sites and had a clear intention of conquest and settlement. Bolstered by reinforcements from Denmark (the 'Great Summer Army'), a division of this host went south and fought many battles (nine, says the *Anglo-Saxon Chronicle*) against Wessex before agreeing a truce with Alfred the Great. Ubbi dies in the Battle of Cynuit in Devon in 878.

A mass burial site excavated at Repton in Derbyshire next to the early medieval church of St Wystan, the mausoleum of the Mercian royal family, was found to contain the remains of around 264 Scandinavian men and women who died in the mid-870s. It is thought that they are probably associated with the Great Heathen Army, whose winter camp was established at Repton in 873–74 after the conquest of Mercia. The Mercian king Burghred fled to

Emmanuel O'Brien, sculpture of St Edmund, Bury St Edmunds, Suffolk (2011).

Rome, where he died. The military success of the Great Heathen Army changed the history of the British Isles. In the century that followed its campaign, early English kingdoms were overthrown; an important warrior dynasty was founded in Ireland, whose descendants returned at intervals to attack the English kings; and the army's rank and file found lands, settled down, married local women and became Anglo-Danes, leaving their mark on landscape and language to this day.

**Ragnarr's 'Death Song'**

The figure of Ragnarr was rediscovered in the 17th century when Magnús Ólafsson, an Icelandic priest charged with trying to find material evidence in Iceland to support Saxo's account of early Danish history, laid hands on a medieval manuscript containing Ragnarr's 'Death Song', a poem he was supposed to have recited in the fatal snake-pit. Magnús sent a transcription of the poem, along with his own Danish translation and commentary, to the antiquarian scholar Ole Worm in Copenhagen. In 1636 Worm published a Latin version alongside the Old Norse text, which had been transcribed into runes. Once an Old Norse poem became available in Latin translation, it was, in effect, put into circulation across Europe, and reference was soon being made to the 'Death Song' and its heroic spirit in other countries. Magnús made some errors in his account of the poem that he sent to Worm; these included the infamous mistranslation that gave rise to the idea that Viking heroes would drink from their enemies' skulls in Valhöll. Thomas Bartholin (see p. 157) made Ragnarr and his song a central figure in his book about the ancient Danes' contempt for death, and soon the 'Death Song' was being cited by British scholars as indicative of a particular kind of barbaric courage: the capacity to meet death with insouciance, to look back with satisfaction on a heroic life, to celebrate the savage joys of battle, and to look forward to a glorious eternity in Valhöll. The poem drew much comment, and many versions of it were made over the next couple of centuries before it generally fell out of favour. For devotees of Gothic poetry in the wild and primitive spirit of Ossian, it was this poem, even more perhaps than 'The Incantation of Hervör' or 'The Fatal Sisters', that was the most influential in establishing the conventional idea of the Viking hero.

Bishop Thomas Percy offered a fairly plain translation of the Latin version in his *Five Pieces of Runick Poetry*, published in 1763, which gives a good sense of the tenor of the poem's twenty-nine stanzas. His version of the poem begins with Regner (as he calls the hero) remembering his first exploit: how he killed the serpent and won Thora's hand. Next, he introduces his reminiscences of his other great battles, each introduced with the bald statement: 'We fought with swords.' These conflicts produced 'rivers of blood for the ravenous wolf, ample food for the yellow-footed fowl' – a reference of course to the famous 'beasts of battle' motif: the eagle, raven and wolf who approach the battlefield in anticipation of feasting on corpses. 'The whole ocean was one wound,' Regner boasts, and 'the pleasure of that day was like kissing a young widow at the highest table of the feast.' In fact, the original Old Norse notes that the joys of battle are *not* like the joys of women (a mistake made by Magnús Ólafsson and widely repeated in other translations). Killing is always better than sex for the true Viking hero. Now imprisoned in the snake-pit, Regner anticipates his sons' vengeance: 'Soon shall my sons black their swords in the blood of Ella; they wax red with fury, they burn with rage.' He is bound for Valhöll, where he will quaff 'BEER out of the sculls of our enemies'; 'the goddesses of destiny' (the Valkyries) are coming to fetch him to the highest seat in Óðinn's hall. For, Regner notes, 'a brave man does not shrink from death'; 'Death is not to be lamented.' Finally, although he had not expected that it would be the unworthy Ella who would take his life, nevertheless 'I die laughing.' Regner's 'Death Song' thus offers a wonderfully encyclopaedic collection of the tropes of Viking heroism, a poem that confirmed the 18th-century belief in and admiration for the extreme courage of Northern heroes, who maintained an attitude of proud defiance even in the face of a less than heroic death.

The poem remained popular in the 19th century and was retranslated many times, with flourishes that went well beyond Percy's directness. The vengeance expedition of Ragnarr's sons seemed to receive some material confirmation when the newly discovered runic inscriptions in the Neolithic Maes Howe chambered cairn in Orkney were published in 1862. Most of the inscriptions were carved in the middle of the 12th century; indeed, there is an account of men sheltering in the howe during a severe snowstorm in *Orkneyinga saga* (The Saga of the Orkney Islanders). One of these inscriptions makes a cryptic reference to a certain Lodbrog – and to *her* sons, who were excellent men. The antiquary Professor George Stephens, whose life work was cataloguing the runic inscriptions of the British Isles, was invited, along with two Scandinavian professors, to interpret the inscriptions. He took the view that this carving was indeed the work of 'the celebrated Scandinavian sea-kings' in the 870s, though he did not explain why Lodbrog should be female. The Danish Professor Carl Christian Rafn, on the other hand, thought that the inscription recorded that the mound was 'a sorcery hall' or seeress-platform for Lodbrog. As the word *brók* (breeches) is grammatically feminine, the tradition that Lodbrog was a woman may have become established in Orkney, he argued. It is interesting to see how both experts come up with highly suppositious readings. Stephens determinedly grafts the 'Lodbrog' inscription onto the 'Death Song' tradition, while Rafn, who had studied the legendary sagas in great detail, knew that one relates how a voyage to Orkney was hampered by the spells of some magic-working women sitting on just such a 'sorcery-platform' – albeit one in Norway, not Orkney; this is why perhaps he invents an Orkney-based sorceress with an unusual name.

## Twentieth-century Ragnarrs

The Ragnarr tradition provided the basis for the 1958 film *The Vikings*. The film begins in the aftermath of Ragnar's first attack on Northumbria. Ragnar (Ernest Borgnine) had killed King Edwin and raped his queen. Edwin's cousin, Aella (Frank Thring), has taken the throne. Queen Enid sends her son, born of the rape, to Italy for safety, lest King Aella try to eliminate him. The boy, Eric, has a recognition token, the pommel stone from King Edwin's sword, in his possession. Eric is captured by pirates and sold as a slave, ending up by chance with Ragnar in Norway. Eric and Einar (Kirk Douglas), Ragnar's legitimate son, become bitter enemies. Much later in the plot, Ragnar pursues Eric, who is eloping with Princess Morgana (Janet Leigh) to England, where Morgana is promised as bride to Aella. Ragnar is shipwrecked and rescued by Eric, who then delivers Ragnar to Aella as prisoner. Aella arranges to execute Ragnar by throwing him bound into 'a pit of wolves, half-mad with starvation ... trained to appreciate the flavour of human blood'. Eric is charged with forcing the prisoner into the pit, but he cuts Ragnar's bonds and gives him a sword so that he may die weapon in hand and thus enter Valhalla. For this disobedience, Aella severs Eric's hand.

Eric returns to Einar with the news of the hero's death. Together they mount an expedition to avenge Ragnar, and Aella is himself hurled into the wolf-pit and perishes. Despite uniting in vengeance, the old rivalry flares up once again. Eric had given the princess his recognition stone, and thus she has learned the truth of her beloved's parentage from a priest in Aella's castle. She reveals to Einar that his deadly foe is in fact his half-brother. Thus, as the two men fight to the death over Morgana, Einar fatally hesitates at the moment when he has Eric at disadvantage, and Eric stabs him with the broken stump of his sword. The dying Einar reaches out for his sword so that he may die an honourable death like his father. Eric nobly hands him the sword, bemusedly asking Morgana, 'Why did he hesitate?' No answer is given. With a last cry of 'Odin!', Einar too sets off for Valhalla. He is given a splendid Viking funeral, placed on a longship that is set alight by flaming arrows. This trope recurs at the obsequies of Hoster Tully in *A Song of Ice and Fire* and *Game of Thrones*, even if, embarrassingly, the arrows of Edmure Tully, Hoster's son, fail to find their mark as they should, and his uncle has to fire the boat instead. There is more on longship funerals in Chapter 10.

The outlines of *Ragnars saga* – the hostility between Ragnarr and Northumbria's King Ella, the dishonourable execution, the sons' vengeance – are combined in *The Vikings* with another well-known Germanic legend: that of the half-brothers who do not know their relationship until one has committed fratricide. Many of the key motifs of future Viking movies, from the throwing of axes at a pinioned girl to the spectacle of the longship in full sail and the Viking funeral, along with the frequent invocations of Odin and Valhalla, gained their traction from this splendid Hollywood reimagining of the story of Ragnarr and his intrepid sons.

## Ragnarr and his sons in transmedia franchises

Two enormously successful television series have taken up elements of the saga of Ragnarr and his sons. *The Last Kingdom* is based on the novels of Bernard Cornwell's series *The Saxon Tales*. They are set in 9th-century England and deal with the Scandinavian invasions and the politics of the kingdom of Wessex. The first novel in the series, *The Last Kingdom* (2004), introduced Uhtred of Bebbanburg (Bamburgh), orphaned when his father's stronghold was attacked by Danes but adopted by a Viking jarl called Ragnar. This Ragnar is not our friend Ragnarr Shaggy-Breeches, but rather the son of a man called Ravn (Raven). Uhtred grows up with mixed loyalties, a great love for his foster-father and an understanding of Viking culture, alongside a lifelong ambition to recover his ancestral home at Bebbanburg. He comes to Alfred's court in Wessex, and there fights for his king against the great Danish army led by Ivar, Halvdan and Ubba, the sons of Ragnar Lothbrok, here imagined as king of Denmark and the Swedes. Both Cornwell's novels and the television show give a strong sense of the Danes as an exuberant, fierce and passionate people, rather more attractive than the reserved, God-fearing and dour English.

Of Ragnar Lothbrok's three sons, Ivar is mentioned only briefly: he dies in Ireland, and Ubba leaves the Danish army to go there and avenge him. Halvdan too is absent from the show, though he appears in the novels. It is Ubba (played by the Norwegian actor Rune Temte) who, in the first season, becomes Uhtred's fiercest opponent, bent on taking vengeance on the hero for the death of Ubba's lord, Ragnar Ravnsson, even if Uhtred (Alexander Dreymon) played no part in his murder. 'My advice to you is: never to cross Ubba, and never, never to fight him,' warns Ravn, Ragnar's father, but once he appears to be implicated in Ragnar's death, Uhtred finds himself inescapably in Ubba's sights. The two meet in single combat during the Battle of Cynuit (where the historical Ubbi died), and Uhtred finally gains the victory. As a mark of respect, he makes sure that the dying Ubba has his battle-axe in his hand, ensuring his passage to Valhalla – a tradition we recognize from the script of *The Vikings*.

*The Last Kingdom* was first broadcast in 2015, and its focus is the campaigns of the English against the Danes, Irish, Scots and Anglo-Scandinavians in the British Isles. The History Channel show

Uhtred in a still from season 3 of *The Last Kingdom* (2018).

*Vikings*, which began in 2013, has a much wider geographical scope. Its hero is Ragnar Lothbrok himself, played by the Australian actor Travis Fimmel. One of Ragnar's earliest adventures pits him against King Froh of Svealand, who has invaded Norway and killed its king. In battle Froh drapes himself with tame serpents who will attack his enemies, and it is this threat that Ragnar counters by having special shaggy clothes made for himself. Thus he kills Froh and gains his nickname at the same time. Ragnar wins the hand of Lagertha, whom we met in Chapter 2, by killing a bear and a monstrous hound who guarded her home; the two settle down together and have children – a daughter, Gytha, and a son, Björn. The action of the show begins some years later, when Ragnar has a vision of Valhalla while fighting in the Baltic. When he returns home, he is discontented with his limited prospects as a farmer and retainer to his unsatisfactory lord, Earl Haraldson. When the earl announces yet another raiding season in the Baltic lands and Russia, Ragnar proclaims his intention to raid westwards instead – to universal astonishment and mockery. This marks the beginning of Ragnar's adventures. Along with his sons, he travels and fights widely across the Viking world. He attacks Lindisfarne (the famous raid of 793), thus inaugurating the Viking campaigns in the British Isles. He meets, poses the famous riddle to and eventually sires sons, including Ivar the Boneless, with Aslaug. His next battles are in Wessex, where he becomes increasingly enmeshed in the politics of the kingdom, forever criss-crossing the North Sea and facing the inevitable challenges to his power base at home when he is away on his travels. Ragnar, his sons and his brother Rollo undertake the siege of Paris and indeed successfully sack the city, but Rollo goes over to the Frankish side, being granted the title of Duke of Normandy, and a renewed attack is defeated. An attempted Scandinavian settlement in Wessex fails when the incomers are massacred, and an increasingly despondent Ragnar decides his life is no longer worth living. He is sent to King Aelle in

Northumbria, who tortures him and tries to make him convert – in vain. As he is cast into the serpent-pit, he roars out a truncated but still recognizable version of the 'Death Song':

> It gladdens me to know that Odin prepares for a feast! Soon I shall be drinking ale from curved horns. This hero that comes into Valhalla does not lament his death. I shall not enter Odin's hall with fear. There, I shall wait for my sons to join me. And when they do, I will bask in their tales of triumph. The Aesir will welcome me. My death comes without apology. And I welcome the Valkyries to summon me home!

Ragnar also finds time to deploy his famous line about the piglets – 'How the little piggies will grunt when they hear how the Old Boar suffered' – before the serpents strike at his heart.

Ragnar may have perished and set his feet on the road to Valhalla during the fourth season, but the show continued for two further series. Ragnar's sons Björn (whose mother is Lagertha) and Ubbe, Hvitserk, Sigurd and Ivar (the sons of Aslaug) have many further adventures that take them from Scandinavia and England to Francia, Russia, Byzantine Sicily, North Africa, Islamic Spain, Iceland and even perhaps to North America – the 'Golden Land' rumoured to lie west of Iceland, where Ubbe was last seen heading. Björn leads his brothers in the Great Heathen Army, invading England to avenge his father and subjecting Aelle to the 'blood-eagle'. Hvitserk and Ivar teeter on the edge of madness; Ivar even comes to believe that he is one of the Aesir. When Ivar is killed in battle against Alfred, Hvitserk salutes him in a farewell that splendidly anticipates *ragna rök*. Leaning against the cairn piled over his brother's body, Hvitserk muses: 'So enjoy Valhalla, brother, while it still exists. We can all see the sky darkening, we can all see the twilight of the gods, and I trust to be with you in that great defeat.'

Ragnar, Lagertha and crew, still from season 4 of *Vikings* (2016).

The sons, their rivalries and loyalties, lust for power, blood-thirstiness and strategic genius come to represent the global reach of the Viking world at its greatest geographical extent. The show has many historical inaccuracies, from the initial premise that no one living in late 8th-century Norway would have known of the existence of the British Isles, to the liberal use of bizarre tortures and the self-conscious claims of the characters that they are 'Vikings', treating the occupation as an ethnic identity. As in many medieval shows (and unlike rational real-life military behaviour), the warriors do not wear helmets so that they can be identified in long-shot, thus putting themselves at great risk of fatal head injury from axe or sword.

Nevertheless, the show had a considerable budget, and it paid great attention to detail in its world-building, from the idea that Vikings at home were essentially farmers to the design of ships and the centrality of the hall to early medieval social organization. It also takes seriously the practice and implications of Old Norse religion, and stages revealing encounters between Norsemen,

Christians, Muslims and even Buddhists who have travelled along the Silk Road. Like other medievalist shows, *Vikings* is intensely interested in the politics of power, in particular the fundamental instability of small kingships in a militaristic society where both economics and prestige are heavily invested in continuing tribal warfare against neighbouring peoples. The options available to populations who negotiated with invaders, including the payment of treasure (the Danegeld, for instance) and the surrender of land, are explored, alongside the employment of clever stratagems and newly available technologies. The show also treats emerging ideas about the centralization of power in larger kingdoms versus the possibility of self-determination in Norse colonies such as Iceland. Just as *The Last Kingdom* looks in detail at dynastic politics, alliance-building, religious confrontations between Christian and pagan, and military tactics in the England of Alfred and his successors, *Vikings* takes up similar questions on a continent-wide scale.

It was not just the illusion of historical verisimilitude that drew audiences to these two shows, nor the large-scale battle scenes or close-combat fights. The characters are psychologically interest-ing: they struggle with issues of trust and betrayal, grief and loss, alongside their preoccupations with personal honour. Their prob-lems drive them to alcohol dependence and substance abuse; and their family relationships – particularly issues of sibling rivalry, but also parent–child conflicts – are depicted as shaping their psy-chological and emotional development. Strong female characters are also key (some of *Vikings'* shield-maidens and women warriors were discussed in Chapter 2). *The Last Kingdom* makes space for women with different roles and strengths, such as Brida (Emily Cox), a Saxon woman and skilled fighter who is raised with Uhtred but becomes staunchly loyal to the Danish cause. Their fates, as Uhtred notes, are bound together: 'We are one, you and I. From the moment I took your hand on the steps of the great hall of Eoforwic we were bound as one. You may dislike me, hate me if you wish, despise me at times, but love is immortal; it goes on.' There is also the consummate politician Aethelflaed, Lady of Mercia (Millie Brady), and Stiorra (Ruby Hartley), Uhtred's feisty daughter who claims that she will not marry: 'I will not become a wife … hard work for far too little reward.' However, she looks set to change her mind when she departs with Sigtryggr (Eysteinn Sigurðarson), the great-grandson of Ivar the Boneless, for Eoforwic at the end of the fourth season.

When the *Assassin's Creed* franchise decided to create a Viking Age game, it was unsurprising that it too should alight upon the 9th century and the activities of the Great Heathen Army in England. Ragnarr Shaggy-Breeches appears only in flashback in the game, but three of his sons are significant characters. Halfdan leads the army, sacking London and conquering York. Ivarr and Ubba avenge their father on Ælle in the usual way, attack East Anglia, kill King Edmund for refusing to accept Danish overlordship, and then move on to Mercia. Consolidating victory means coming to terms with Anglo-Saxon dynasties, but Ivarr betrays the interests of the Mercians in order to prosecute his longstanding feud with Rhodri the Great, king of Gwynedd in Wales, and fights Eivor, the game's lead character, in a *holmgang*, or duel to the death.

Ragnarr and his sons were significant figures in the medieval Scandinavian imaginary. They hover between history and legend: their names match those of significant 9th-century war-leaders, but evidence for the father–son relationships is highly unreliable. Nevertheless, whoever their father was, the three brothers who were leaders in the Great Heathen Army left their mark on contemporary chronicles in England and Ireland, while their supposed father is a major figure in Danish tradition. It is not their geopolitical achievements or interventions, even if they radically reshaped 9th-century England, that have triggered modern interest in the Ragnarssons so much as the legend of their father's courageous death in the Northumbrian snake-pit and the grisly vengeance they were believed to have taken on his slayer. Ivarr and Ubbi were involved in the death of Edmund of East Anglia, which probably occurred straightforwardly on the battlefield at Thetford. Nevertheless, clerics who retold the events of Edmund's death, keen to promote the saintly cult that had grown up surrounding his tomb, depicted the two sadistic Viking leaders, 'united through the devil', as tying the blameless king to a tree and peppering him with arrows 'like the bristles of a hedgehog' before decapitating him and hiding his head in dense woodland to prevent an honourable burial.

Magnús Ólafsson's discovery of the 'Death Song' manuscript converted Ragnarr from an ordinary Viking war-leader into the epitome of courage and defiance when confronted with certain death, strengthening the belief that it was the glorious post-mortem existence in Valhöll that underwrote the Viking propensity to laugh in the face of death. Connecting the snake-pit hero with the grand story of his sons' vengeance, the origins of Scandinavian settlement in England and the victories won by Alfred the Great has provided a powerful narrative in the present century. Ragnarr and his sons have been harnessed to storylines that emphasize migration, cultural assimilation and multiculturalism as well as emerging ideas of national identity and political resistance. These complex social processes, so brilliantly imagined as operative in both England and Europe in the 9th and 10th centuries in *The Last Kingdom*, *Vikings* and, to some extent, *Assassin's Creed: Valhalla*, are also culturally central to our present experience.

# CHAPTER 9

# Vínland the Good

THE MYTH OF
AMERICAN COLONIZATION

## Eiríkr Rauði and his children

Eiríkr Rauði (Erik the Red) was a difficult man. Outlawed from
Norway for killing, he made his way to Iceland and soon found
himself outlawed again. As his enemies searched for him to slay
him, he took ship and sailed westwards (see pls IX, XIII), looking,
he claimed, for a land that an Icelander called Gunnbjörn thought
he had glimpsed in the past. He would let people know how he
got on. So it was that he found Greenland. Eiríkr explored the
new land, naming various features after himself, then returned to
Iceland to report on his success, calling the territory 'Greenland'
because, so he said, it would make people keener to move there.
Many did indeed follow Eiríkr over the ocean and set up farms
in the Eastern and Western Settlements. Eiríkr had three sons,
Þorsteinn, Þorvaldr and Leifr, and it was the last of these who,
blown off course when sailing home from Norway, found an
unknown land 'with self-sown wheat, grapevines and huge trees',
which he called Vínland, meaning 'Vineland'. Once he was safely
home in Greenland, accompanied by a shipwrecked crew he had
rescued en route – an action that gained him the nickname 'Leifr
the Lucky' – his thoughts turned to this unknown country. By

this time his brother Þorsteinn was dead, and his brother's widow, Guðríðr, had married a bold Norwegian adventurer called Þorfinnr Karlsefni ('Makings of a Man'), usually known by his nickname.

Eiríkr also had an illegitimate daughter, Freydís, who was married to a rather ineffectual husband called Þorvarðr. These two, along with Leifr, his brother Þorvaldr, Karlsefni, Guðríðr and a good number of other Greenlanders sailed across to Vínland around the year 1010 to see if they could establish a settlement there. They sailed past Markland, a heavily forested area, and Helluland, where the beaches had huge flat stones, and decided to settle further south, where there were vines, plenty of fish to be caught, eggs, various plants to eat and game to be hunted. There they erected buildings and established trading relations with a Native American tribe, probably Beothuks, who are now extinct. The Norse people called them 'Skrælings', identifying them with the Inuit they had encountered and to whom they had given the same name in Greenland. Later, however, the Skrælings attacked the Scandinavians. While the men ran away, the pregnant Freydís stood her ground, shouting insults at those who had left her behind; she bared her breasts and beat them with a drawn sword. The Native Americans retreated at this sight. The Norse settlers concluded that, however attractive the land was, it would not be possible to colonize it given the warlike nature of its inhabitants, and they returned to Greenland. They were confirmed in their decision by the chance shooting of Þorvaldr Eiríksson by a figure whom they identified as a uniped, one of a monstrous race of beings that were believed to live in distant parts of the world.

This is roughly the account of Vínland given in *Eiríks saga*. A second saga account, *Grœnlendinga saga* (The Saga of the Greenlanders) contains further details. It relates how Guðríðr gave birth to a son, Snorri, in the New World – the first European to be born there; how the Native Americans were very willing to trade for dairy products, for the Norse had brought cattle with them; and how one of the Skrælings picked up a Norseman's axe and experimentally struck his companion with it. When the latter fell dead, the Native American hurled the axe away in disgust. Þorvaldr Eiríksson kills a group of Skrælings who are doing no more than peacefully sleeping under their canoes, in the belief that they are outlaws. This provokes reprisals, and he loses his life. Subsequently Karlsefni concludes that the new land is not for him, and the would-be colonists return to Greenland; Karlsefni and his family emigrate to Iceland, where they found a distinguished line, including several bishops. After her husband's death, Guðríðr travels 'south' in Europe, very likely on a pilgrimage to Rome; when she returns to her son Snorri's farm, she lives there as a nun.

There is a disturbing coda to this saga, however. Back in Greenland, Freydís hatches a complex plan. She gets her brother Leifr, the de facto leader of the Greenlanders now that Eiríkr is dead, to lend her the buildings he had erected in Vínland and agrees with two Icelandic brothers that they will all journey to the new land to acquire valuables – most likely furs, timber, dried codfish, grapes and eiderdown. Freydís and her husband agree with the Icelanders that each party – Greenlanders and Icelanders – will take equal numbers of men, along with some women, on their ships. But once she has arrived in Vínland Freydís becomes uncooperative. She will not let the Icelanders use her brother's buildings and, moreover, she has smuggled five extra men among her crew. When spring comes, she picks a fight with the Icelandic captains and then demands that her husband avenge the insults she claims they have hurled at her. The Icelanders and their crew are massacred, but the Greenlanders baulk at killing the women. Freydís demands an axe and kills them herself, for she wants no witnesses to her behaviour. The expedition makes them all a good deal of profit, and Freydís threatens to kill anyone who talks about these events back in Greenland. Leifr nonetheless gets to hear about it, but takes no action against his sister and brother-in-law, opining

Stebba Ósk Ómarsdóttir, cover design for Salva Rubio Gómez
Rubio's *Vinland, la saga de Freydis Eiriksdottir* (2015).

that Freydís and her lineage will come to no good. His prophecy
comes true: unlike with Karlsefni and Guðríðr's splendid offspring,
nothing but bad is related of Freydís's descendants, we are told.

How much truth might there be in these two sagas, written
down only in the 14th century though probably composed considerably earlier? While medieval Icelanders relished the idea that

their courageous ancestors had voyaged into the Western hemi-
sphere, there were troubling details about the saga accounts. Did
the vines that gave the new land its name really grow as far north
as is suggested by the rest of the account? The sagas say that there
was no snow during the winter spent in Vínland, which would rule
out Canada and New England. Furthermore, the story of the grapevines – their discovery by a couple of Leifr's slaves or by a German
who recognized them from the vineyards of his youth – echoes a
biblical anecdote about the Promised Land. Although Karlsefni and
Guðríðr's descendants are well attested in Icelandic genealogies,
there is no independent evidence for Freydís, whether beating her
breasts or slaughtering innocent women with her axe.

These 'Vínland sagas' are the best evidence that we have for the
Old Norse expeditions to North America, but they are unreliable
in all kinds of ways. One of the main aims of *Grœnlendinga saga* is
to establish the illustrious genealogy of Karlsefni and Guðríðr's
descendants, including those high-status bishops, whereas *Eiríks
saga* is primarily interested in recounting how Greenland was
settled and converted to Christianity. They are lively narratives,
incorporating motifs from accounts of exotic travel eastwards,
along with biblical motifs of the Promised Land, and they are often
vague about detail. Clearly the green, fertile North American coast
would look more inviting than the blue-grey glaciers and bare
scree slopes of southern Greenland. Nevertheless, there is more
than a grain of truth in these tales: episodes describing contact
with indigenous inhabitants, their canoes and foodstuffs, the
dynamics of trading and the difficulties of mutual understanding
all concur with more factual accounts of such encounters from
early modern explorers in North America. Markland, Helluland
and Vínland have been identified, with varying degrees of confidence, with Labrador, Newfoundland, the Gulf of St Lawrence
and the northern New England coast – and even further south.
Until archaeological evidence was unearthed that confirmed a

Norse settlement in Newfoundland, however, the historicity of the voyages remained in doubt.

## Chronicles

Vínland's existence, if not its exact location, was reported by some medieval writers, including Adam of Bremen, but they were very confused as to where it might lie. Adam reported that this territory lay in the Atlantic, but other writers placed Vínland between Iceland and Norway, or even to the east of the Scandinavian peninsula. In Old Norse chronicles we hear of a certain bishop who set out from Greenland 'to seek Vínland' in the early 12th century, but he was never heard of again, and a replacement bishop had to be dispatched from Norway. An Icelandic chronicle from 1347 mentions that a ship 'coming from Markland' arrived there after being blown off course; it carried a load of timber, suggesting that the inhabitants of treeless Greenland had in fact continued to fetch supplies of wood from the west rather than waiting for ships from Norway to deliver timber. A Norwegian legal document from the 16th century mentions that a certain man could have no claim to inherit a particular Norwegian farm because he was born and married in Vínland. It is hard to tell from these chance references whether journeys to Markland for wood were so frequent that no one bothered to mention them, or whether early modern Norwegians thought that being born in Vínland was remarkable only from a legal perspective rather than a matter for more general wonder.

## L'Anse aux Meadows and archaeology

In 1960 the Norwegian husband-and-wife team Helge and Anne Stine Ingstad discovered traces of some turf shelters at L'Anse aux Meadows in northern Newfoundland. The site was excavated over a number of years, and many Norse artefacts were found: a bronze ring-headed cloak-pin, iron nails and rivets, and a soapstone spinning whorl, indicating a female presence. The site might have been a temporary camp since the structures are not particularly robust – possibly a spot where iron could be forged to enable ship repairs. However, recent investigation of the peatbogs at the site has uncovered a dense, trampled layer containing woodworking debris, charcoal, and plant and insect remains, pointing to a sustained period of occupation. Some of the plant and insect material originated in Greenland or other parts of subarctic Europe, and the layer was carbon-dated to around the end of the 1st millennium. More recently still, a firm date for the construction of the buildings was determined: close investigation of tree-rings in the timber found at the site using carbon dating and astrophysical data linked to solar storms showed that the buildings were constructed in 1021 – a date that chimes with the accounts given in the sagas.

Since the excavations at L'Anse aux Meadows another possible Norse site has been identified at Point Rosee on the south-west tip of Newfoundland: the presence of bog-iron ore and iron-smelting hearths would be a strong indicator of a Norse presence. However,

Reconstructed buildings at L'Anse aux Meadows, Newfoundland.

the archaeologists have now concluded that what looked like hearths are simply natural features, and the site itself is not well located for ship-travellers. Norse artefacts have been found in various places on Baffin Island, including iron blades, a sword tip, part of an oak barrel, a bronze balance of the type familiar from the British Isles, and a bronze bowl. These finds suggest sustained, if casual, interactions between Europeans and Inuit, chiming with those brief references to Markland and Vínland in the European written tradition. The Norse were indeed present in North America long before Columbus.

## Rediscovering Vínland

The saga accounts and chronicle references to Norse activity in the New World fuelled excited speculation and madcap theories long before the Ingstads found scientific proof of the medieval transatlantic expeditions. Just as tastes for the Gothic and nationalist claims to kinship with the Scandinavian past drove the late 18th- and 19th-century vogue for all things Norse in Northern Europe, so it was in North America. Of vital importance here was the Danish scholar Carl Christian Rafn's compendious study of the history of the North American expeditions, including editions of the key sagas. (We met him briefly in the last chapter, theorizing about the runic inscriptions of Maes Howe.) Called *Antiquitates Americanae*, Rafn's book initially appeared in 1837; an English translation published in 1841 was soon in circulation in the United States and Canada, eliciting much interest. The idea that North America could be claimed not by Catholic, Mediterranean explorers such as Columbus and Amerigo Vespucci, but rather by white-skinned, fair-haired Northerners – pioneers who could be imagined as affiliated with the Protestantism, indeed Lutheranism, of their modern descendants – had considerable emotional appeal in both the US and Canada. The two countries were engaged in developing new, more serviceable myths that allowed them to rewrite their origins at this time, particularly regarding their colonial relationships with Britain and France. There was less excitement and more scepticism about Rafn's theories in Britain. In 1844 the writer and politician Samuel Laing, who himself came from Orkney and had translated Snorri's history of Norway, *Heimskringla*, into English, noted in his preface: 'So much fanciful speculation has been reared upon this foundation [Rafn's work], that it deserves examination.' He does indeed critique Rafn's arguments very thoroughly, as we shall see below.

Meanwhile, the search was on to discover more concrete evidence for a Norse presence in North America than the tenuous claims of the sagas. Rafn mentions the Dighton Rock, a boulder in the Taunton river near Dighton in Massachusetts. It was, as the Reverend Cotton Mather observed in 1690, 'filled with strange Characters: which would suggest as odd Thoughts about them that were here before us, as there are odd Shapes in that Elaborate Monument'. The Rhode Island Historical Society sent a detailed sketch of the rock with its incisions and petroglyphs to Rafn in Copenhagen. He promptly declared that the boulder depicted a scene from *Eiríks saga*, with Guðríðr cradling baby Snorri on her lap, Þorfinnr Karlsefni arriving on his ship and the Skrælings attacking. A runic inscription reading NAM THORFINS ('Þorfinnr's settlement') apparently confirmed the interpretation. Alas, Rafn's theory, which seemed to show that Dighton was Hóp, the site of Karlsefni's sojourn in Vínland, was soon thoroughly debunked. Laing noted that the original sketches of the rock showed nothing that looked either like the runic or the Roman alphabet. It 'would be puerile to dwell on such puerilities', he concluded. In the early years of the 20th century a comparison between the drawings sent to Copenhagen by the Historical Society and the drawings as published by Rafn showed that the Dane had considerably altered the original by sketching in his own lines to indicate what he thought must have been there. That ended once and for all Dighton's claim to be the true Vínland.

The artist Seth Eastman at Dighton Rock, Massachusetts, in 1853.

Dighton Rock was perhaps the earliest identified of many mysterious or bogus artefacts thought to prove the truth of the Vínland story. There is Thorvald's Rock in the Hamptons, supposedly marking the spot where Eiríkr's son was shot by Skrælings (or the uniped), and claims made by a Harvard chemistry professor for the Norumbega area in Cambridge, Massachusetts, as a Norse colony founded by Leifr. The Kensington rune stone, and a map held by Yale University, are notorious forgeries. The former, unearthed in 1898 in central Minnesota by a Swedish immigrant farmer, Olof Öhman, purports to record (in language suspiciously similar to contemporary Swedish) an expedition from Vínland. Some of its members had been killed by local natives. The stone failed to convince any archaeological or rune-stone experts, and it was widely thought that Öhman had created it himself. The Yale map that supposedly depicts Vínland, along with Iceland, Greenland and the rest of Europe, is bound together with two manuscripts from the 15th century, before Columbus's voyages. Its discovery was announced to the world the day before Columbus Day in 1965, to the outrage of New Haven's Italian-American population. Recent investigations have shown definitively that the map is a deliberate modern forgery. It is based on a printed facsimile, produced in 1782, of an earlier map. Comparison of the Yale document with both the original map and the facsimile shows clearly that the Yale map incorporates errors that were introduced in the facsimile. Moreover, the ink that was used contains chemical components that are distinctly 20th century.

## The Newport Tower and other relics

Among the best-known supposed Norse artefacts in the United States is the Newport Tower at Narragansett Bay in Newport, Rhode Island. The enthusiastic local history society sent claims to Rafn and colleagues in Copenhagen that the tower was 'a relic, it may be, of the Northmen, the first discoverers of Vinland!' The sceptical Laing notes, however, that it was clearly designed as a windmill. 'Those sly rogues of Americans dearly love a quiet hoax,' he jokes, poking fun at the New Englanders' pretensions and the Danes' suggestibility. In 1832 another striking find was unearthed, only 20 miles (32 km) away from Newport: a skeleton buried in a sitting position with a bronze plate over its ribcage. The American poet Henry Wadsworth Longfellow connected this discovery with the theories about the tower, observing in his preface to his 1842 poem 'The Skeleton in Armor': 'The following Ballad was suggested to me while riding on the seashore at Newport. A year or two previous a skeleton had been dug up at Fall River, clad in broken and corroded armor; and the idea occurred to me of connecting it with the Round Tower at Newport.' Longfellow's remarks are somewhat tongue-in-cheek: he notes, for instance, that the building has been 'generally known hitherto as the Old Wind-Mill, though now claimed by the Danes as a work of their early ancestors', and quotes Rafn at some length, but he declines to argue the point any further – claiming it is 'sufficiently well established for the purposes of a ballad'. Longfellow's poem, giving voice to the 'fearful guest … Still in rude armor drest', is a stirring tale of a Viking who abducts a prince's daughter and then rams and sinks her father's pursuing ship in a storm: 'Midships with iron keel / Struck we her ribs of steel.' Thereafter,

> Three weeks we westward bore,
> And when the storm was o'er,
> Cloud-like we saw the shore
> Stretching to lee-ward;
> There for my lady's bower
> Built I the lofty tower,
> Which, to this very hour,
> Stands looking seaward.

The girl recovers from the loss of her family and becomes a mother: Longfellow thus reiterates the claim that the first American of European heritage is of Norse stock. Now, however, the lady is dead, and her Viking husband has committed suicide, falling upon

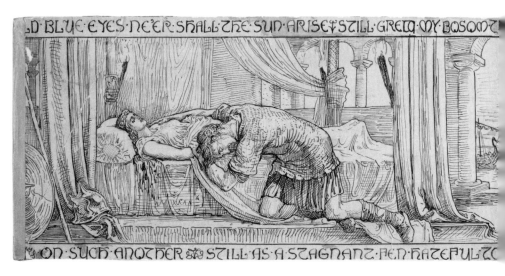

Walter Crane, preparatory sketch for the *Skeleton in Armor* frieze (1883).

his spear. His spirit ascends to his 'native stars', to an indeterminate afterlife that nevertheless sounds more than a little like Valhöll: 'There from the flowing bowl / Deep drinks the warrior's soul / *Skoal!* to the Northland! *Skoal!*'

Approached by the rector of the American Church in Rome in the winter of 1882–83, the British artist Walter Crane was commissioned to create a frieze illustrating 'The Skeleton in Armor' for the dining-room of Vinland, the significantly named Newport mansion being built by the wealthy Catharine Lorillard Wolfe. It was expressly stipulated that Crane should depict the tower in the frieze. He painted seven panels illustrating Longfellow's story – from the Viking's birth in the forest to his suicide in the woods of the New World and the discovery of his body at the base of the tower – and dispatched them to Newport. While the larger panels were painted in a studio in Rome, the smaller ones were completed in London, where *The Viking's Wooing* and *The Viking's Bride* were exhibited in the summer of 1883. After Wolfe's death in 1887, Vinland passed through several different owners and became part of a religious university in 1957. The frieze was

sold at auction in 1987 and is now being restored at the Musée des Beaux-Arts in Rouen.

A 1902 novel, *The Thrall of Leif the Lucky: A Story of Viking Days*, by an American writer of Swedish descent, Ottilie A. Liljencrantz, relates the highly romantic tale of Leif Eiríksson, the fair Helga, who is a bold shield-maiden, daughter of the slave-trader Gilli, and Leif's slave Alwin, actually the son of the earl of Northumbria, captured in a Viking raid. Leif brings Christianity to Greenland, where he comes into conflict with his father, Eirik, and then sets off westwards to seek out the rumoured lands beyond. The expedition arrives successfully, and indeed the new land is green and bountiful:

> To these men from the frozen north, the new world was an earthly paradise. A long clear day under a warm sun was alone a gift to be thankful for. To plunge unstinted hands into the hoarded wealth of ages, to be the first to hunt in a game-stocked forest and the first to cast hook in a fish-teeming river, – to have the first skimming of nature's cream-pans, as it were – was a delight so keen that, saving war and love, they could imagine nothing to equal it ... Snuffing the sweet scent of the sun-heated grapes, they ate and sang and jested as they gathered, in the most innocent carousal of their lives.

Trouble looms in this paradise, however. Unexpectedly, after a period of some months, Native Americans suddenly appear and attack one of the Norse party. Liljencrantz employs the racist stereotypes of the period, describing them as primitive and bestial:

> Skins were their only coverings; and the coarseness of their bristling black locks could have been equalled only in the mane of a wild horse. Though two of the eight were furnished with bows and arrows, the rest carried

only rudely-shaped stone hatchets, stuck in their belts. When they began talking together, it was in a succession of grunts and growls and guttural sounds that bore more resemblance to animal noises than to human speech.

The horrified Europeans who witness the attack note 'the fierce beast-mouth and the small tricky eyes' of one of these men, just before the native band torture to death the hapless slave Kark. Leif does not explicitly link his decision to return home to the hostile presence of the Native Americans, for the expedition is cast as a trading voyage rather than a colonizing venture. The novel concludes with the union of Helga and Alwin, and the mending of the rift between the stubbornly pagan Eirik and his staunchly Christian son, all safely back in Greenland.

A silent early Technicolor film, *The Viking*, loosely based on the novel, was released by MGM in 1928. Directed by Herbert T. Kalmus, it stars Donald Crisp as Leif, Pauline Starke as Helga and LeRoy Mason as the handsome Alwin. Leif is extravagantly moustached – a detail that contributed to the film's unpopularity with the film-going public – and the cast sport splendidly horned or winged helmets, chiming with the largely Wagnerian soundtrack. The latter part of the film is set on the ship sailing towards the unknown west; it dramatizes the rivalry of various suitors, including Leif himself, for the lovely Helga. She of course loves the noble Englishman. The treatment of Vínland is very different from that in Liljencrantz's novel. The intertitle that appears before the closing episode proclaims: 'And so the first white man set foot on the shores of the New World.' Leif plants a cross made of two planks lashed together on a broad, sandy beach and falls to his knees, along with his crew, claiming the land for Christianity. Finally, we learn that Leif built the Newport Tower, 'according to Viking custom', just as Rafn had claimed. There he is seen preaching to a cheerful group of natives and placing a cross and chain around the neck of their gratified leader. Rescripting the book's fudge of the Norse people's reasons for retreating from Vínland, *The Viking* leaves Helga, Alwin and a small, brave band of colonists behind on the New England shore. Their fate is unknown, says the intertitle, but the tower bears witness to the truth of their story. The strains of 'God bless America' are heard as the tower fades into a present-day scene, with the clear implication that Alwin and Helga's descendants, like the offspring of the couple in Longfellow's 'Skeleton in Armor' poem, still inhabit New England to this day.

America, then, so the film asserts, was always already white, Christian and Norse. It builds upon those Norse connections that had already been popularized in the first half of the 19th century, claiming an ideological primacy for Northern white Europeans. These links were cemented by mass immigration from Scandinavia into the American and Canadian Midwest in the latter half of the 19th century. Something like one-quarter of the population of Iceland emigrated westwards between 1870 and 1914, while many more Norwegians, Danes and Swedes exchanged their northern homelands for the open plains of the prairies. Patriotic associations such as the 'Sons of Norway' were formed, while the American-Scandinavian Foundation funded research and publications. They published the first American translation of the *Poetic Edda* in 1923. Henry Adams Bellows's epigraph to this work expresses the hope that 'greater familiarity with the chief literary monuments of the North will help Americans to a better understanding of Scandinavians and thus serve to stimulate their sympathetic cooperation to good ends'. He also implies that 'the glories of that extraordinary past' are the heritage not only of Scandinavian-Americans, but also – in keeping with the understanding of shared Anglo-Germanic identities – of a much larger segment of the white American population.

### 'Immigrant Song', *Lucky Leif and the Longships*, and *American Gods*

In June 1970 the English rock band Led Zeppelin played in Reykjavík as part of a European tour. The opening song on their following album, *Led Zeppelin III* (1970), reflected their experience of 'the land of ice and snow ... the midnight sun where the hot springs flow'. The song imagines a ship sailing westwards, driven by 'the hammer of the gods', seeking new lands, with a crew indifferent as to whether they achieve 'the western shore' or Valhalla. The track's driving rhythm and Robert Plant's wailing shrieks at its beginning reinforce the lyrics' power and self-confidence: 'We are your overlords,' they proclaim.

For many years Led Zeppelin would make this the opening song in live performances. 'Immigrant Song' takes up the familiar tropes of the Vínland myth: the devil-may-care courage of Viking sailors setting out into the unknown, the threat of violence to be visited upon 'soft ... fields of green', the gloriously fertile new land of North America. The 'bulldozer rhythms' and Plant's vocals, commented the music writer Lester Bangs, were 'like some cannibal chorus wailing in the infernal light of a savage fertility rite'. It's perhaps not surprising, then, that the director Taika Waititi should have wanted – and have got – permission to use the song for *Thor: Ragnarok* (2017), where it features both in the trailer and in two key fight sequences. While the track's title may refer to the Viking conquest of Britain – two of the band claim their hometown as Wolverhampton, which formed part of the Danelaw in the 9th century – the inclusion of a live version of the song (recorded at the Long Beach arena in 1972) on the album *How the West Was Won* (2003) strengthens the argument that 'Immigrant Song' taps into the Vínland myth, specifically taking up the suggestion that the Norsemen came there –and stayed, and their descendants continued to venture further westwards.

**LAUGARDALSHÖLL**

**HLJÓMLEIKAR**

**LED ZEPPELIN**

20. júní — 1. júlí 1970

Listahátíð í Reykjavík

The Reykjavik Festival·Festspillene í Reykjavik

mánudag 22. júní kl. 22,30

Ticket to a concert by Led Zeppelin, Reykjavík Arts Festival, 1970.

*Lucky Leif and the Longships* is a 1975 concept album by Robert Calvert, a poet and sometime front man of the band Hawkwind. It was produced by Brian Eno and featured the science fiction writer Michael Moorcock on banjo. Envisaged as a tour of American musical styles as they might have developed if the Norse had remained on the North American continent, it includes a parody of the Beach Boys' song 'Barbara Ann' that swaps in the word 'Barbarian'. The track 'Voyaging to Vinland' evokes the courage it must have taken to sail to the end of the world: 'The mighty Midgard-serpent's tail / Heading for the gods alone know where / Did writhe, and rise up like a flail.' 'The Making of Midgard' imagines surfing Vikings heading for Valhalla, while the album ends with a dramatic account of 'Ragna Rock': 'Clouds of angry blackness rise / And fissures of a mighty size / Appear in both the earth and skies / As Fenrir breaks his shackles.' Although the emergence of a new world is foretold, it's not clear, in this vision of alternative history, that it will be any better than the one we have now.

Neil Gaiman's *American Gods* takes as its starting point the idea that, when people emigrated to the US, their gods came with them.

Tony Hyde, cover of Robert Calvert's *Lucky Leif and the Longships* (1975).

Rather than casting Leifr and his crew as the vectors for the arrival of Óðinn, Þórr and Loki on the North American continent, however, Gaiman invents a much earlier westward journey. He assigns to it a date of 813 CE, long before the Norse had discovered Iceland and Greenland. The exhausted men stumble ashore, fearful that their gods have abandoned them in this place on the edge of the world. Their chieftain assures them that the All-Father is with them. They build a hall using the plentiful timber to be found in this new land and, when it is complete, sing songs of praise to Odin and retell the old myths. The next day (a Wednesday, significantly), they find a Scraeling in the woods, 'his long hair the colour of a crow's wing, his skin the colour of rich, red clay'. That they do not understand his language is cause for wonder rather than (as for Liljencrantz's heroes) a sign that he is somehow subhuman. They lead the man into their hall, feast him and give him mead; but once he is drunk and incapacitated, they hang him on a nearby ash tree as an Odinic sacrifice. When two ravens settle on the corpse, they know that their sacrifice has been accepted. But it is not long before a group of Scraelings descends on their stockade, killing them all, burning both hall and ship, and erasing the Norsemen's presence. Yet what this little band achieved was enough. More than a century later, when Leifr arrives, 'his gods were already waiting for him ... Tyr, one-handed, and gray Odin, gallows-god, and Thor of the thunders'. That earlier sacrifice had rooted these gods in America. Leifr was himself a Christian, according to the sagas, so Óðinn would hardly have accompanied him on his voyage. They relate how the one professed Þórr-worshipper in Karlsefni's crew, Þorhallr, parts company with him and sails homewards. Shipwrecked in Ireland, he is slain there.

Gaiman imagines the world's gods as already present in America, long before any English immigrants set foot on Plymouth Rock. This entails the invention of further prehistoric voyages. No Egyptian migrant to America in recent times would believe in, let alone sacrifice to, the Egyptian gods. Mr Ibis (an avatar of the god Thoth) claims that 'ancient Egyptians came here to trade ... three thousand, five hundred and thirty years ago. Give or take.' He argues that 'there's nothing special about coming to America', for 'this country has been Grand Central Station for ten thousand years or more'. Gaiman's vision, then, even if it takes its inspiration from the Vínland myth and places Óðinn, Baldr and Loki at the centre of its narrative, insists on the speciousness of assertions that only those of Northern white European descent can be 'real Americans': no one ethnicity can claim either priority or superiority.

## Rewriting Vínland's women

Where earlier writers admired Leifr and Karlsefni's determination and good fortune, more recent retellings of the Vínland story have shown a fascination with its two principal female figures: Guðríðr, resourceful and a staunch housewife, the grandmother of bishops; and the dark-hearted, murderous Freydís. The Scots writer Margaret Elphinstone published her acclaimed novel *The Sea Road* in 2000. Here, the character Gudrid relates her life, dictating it to a fictional Icelandic cleric encountered on her pilgrimage to Rome in her final years. Her early life, spent in Greenland, is narrated in detail, but Gudrid's time in Vinland forms the narrative's climax and is shrewdly observed. It is Gudrid, watching quietly with her baby on her lap, who realizes that the skraelings are particularly interested in the Norsemen's weapons and cleverly advises distracting them with the novelty of red cloth. She quickly registers that, once a Norseman has killed one of the natives, the establishment even of a seasonal trading station becomes impossible:

> A man had died because of us, here in Vinland. I hugged
> my innocent baby to me, and I seemed to hear an echo
> of the sound which had never been heard in this country
> before, the clash of sword on sword, and it seemed to me
> that it was the crash of a door closing on us. I knew for
> certain then that we were shut out.

Gudrid, Karlsefni and their son depart from the Eden that they have corrupted. Freydis is not present on this journey (which is largely drawn from *Grœnlendinga saga*'s version of the couple's experiences). Gudrid alludes only in passing to Freydis's 'dreadful expedition ... She made Vinland into a place of hel, a land of murder and betrayal. I wouldn't want to face the ghosts she left behind her.' By the time Gudrid is relating her story in Rome, Vinland has slipped into legend:

> Men talk of Vinland during the winter at every hearth
> in Iceland, but who bothers to go there now? Only
> Greenlanders desperate for timber. It was just a dream,
> I suppose, that it should ever amount to anything else,
> but men like to have their dreams.

Elphinstone's foregrounding of Gudrid's viewpoint allows for a new, more critical perspective on the Vinland venture. From her descriptions of the miserable struggle for existence in Greenland, it is clear why Leif and the other men should have wished to journey to this source of inexhaustible provisions: of wine, timber, fish, furs and game. Yet it is also evident that the patterns of aggressive masculinity embedded in their behaviour and their lack of imagination in trying to understand and communicate with the indigenous inhabitants not only destroy the possibility of peaceful interchange with the North Americans, they also prefigure later European colonial attitudes equally shaped by male violence.

Elphinstone writes from the perspective of a Scots woman, one whose imagination has always been deeply engaged with the history of Scandinavians in the Northern Isles and the North Atlantic more generally. The American writer William T. Vollmann has embarked on a (still incomplete) series of seven novels about the colonization of America, the first of which is *The Ice-Shirt* (1990). Freydis is a central character: illegitimate, cruelly treated by Erik's wife, Thjodhild, who resents her existence, she associates kindness with the little pieces of silver that Erik occasionally gives her, and grows up miserly, obsessive and manipulative. She treks to the Blauserk mountain, which lies at the edge of the central Greenland icesheet, and there pledges allegiance to the demon Blue-Shirt (in Inuit, Amortortak). Blue-Shirt commands her to go to Wineland – 'I expect you will prefer to bring the ice there and extend My kingdom' – and promises her 'all the power that is needful to carry out your wicked designs'. Gudrid and Freydis are strongly contrasted, even if Gudrid is also interested in power, achieved through more indirect means: 'Gudrid, who had always been able to rule (so she fancied) through a beautifully calculated sweetness, intensely disliked Freydis's way of managing her affairs.'

Trying to discover how she can obey her demon master and bring the ice to temperate Wineland, Freydis seeks out Yggdrasill – or its avatar in the new land – and travels deep below its roots to the hall of Hel. There she gives herself sexually to Hel, then to Loki, for they are one and the same – and Loki is also Amortortak. Her palms turn black as a mark of her sojourn with the dead, and she learns that she will have to plant the 'ice-seed' in the blood of her own people. As tensions escalate between Gudrid and Freydis, the latter provokes the killing of the Icelanders and their crew. The narrator signalled in the opening pages that this was the story of Freydis's double-bladed axe, and her deadly weapon is finally deployed against the innocent Norse women. And thus, through this atrocity, the ice finally arrives in this sunlit land of plenty.

Vollmann's novel skilfully interweaves the saga narratives, the early history of Norway as recounted by Snorri in *Heimskringla*, Inuit or Greenlandic myth and the folklore of the Mi'kmaq (the Skrælings) with observations from his own travel journal and accounts of life in the far North from a variety of later sources. Freydis returns to Greenland with riches a-plenty, and Gudrid and Karlsefni too have made their fortunes and emigrate to Iceland. But Wineland the Good will never be the same: 'Along that long low peninsula of grass, snow-patches rose from beneath the tundra like seeping lakes. Ice filmed across the dying eyes of tide-pools and crept up rocky beach-shelves ... the icebergs came closer for nine months of the year now.' The ruin brought about by Freydis is ecological and magical, but it heralds the disasters that will come upon Native Americans in the centuries to come – and in the later books in Vollmann's *Seven Dreams* series.

**Pressing southwards**

What if the Norse voyagers had not been satisfied with landfall in
Canada's maritime provinces and New England and sailed further
south? Quetzalcoatl, the Aztec god, was depicted in ways that
have suggested to scholars that he could be European. Could the
white-skinned enslaved warriors in the murals in the Temple of
the Warriors at Chichen Itza in Mexico represent Norse men?
Even more boldly, Norse descent has been claimed for Paraguayans
and the Incas. These arguments tend to be based on unfounded
etymologies (such as the name *Inca* deriving from the Germanic
suffix -*ing*, meaning 'descendant'), dubious runic inscriptions, and
South American fortresses that supposedly share the ring shape
of the Danish forts built by Harald Bluetooth in the 9th century.
The same ideological impulses – that is, to rewrite the history of
colonialism and to strengthen white European claims to indigenous territory, as in the earlier Vínland myth – are clearly at
work. The Incan theory has recently inspired the wonderfully
ironic counterfactual historical novel *Civilisations*, by the French
writer Laurent Binet, which was published in France in 2019 and
appeared in an English translation by Sam Taylor in 2021.

Binet posits that Freydís does not return to Greenland after
the murders related in *Grœnlendinga saga*, but rather takes off in
the ship belonging to the Icelandic brothers she had deceived,
sailing southwards to warmer and more fertile territory. In their
next encounter with the Skraelings, Freydís pays careful attention
to their language and gestures and goes off with a band for three
days and three nights. She returns with a passable understanding
of their language, a proposal of alliance – and a new pregnancy, giving birth to a daughter whom she names Gudrid, 'after her former
sister-in-law … whom she had always hated'. Peaceful co-existence
with these Native Americans does not last, for the Skraelings begin
to sicken and die, and Freydís comprehends that the epidemic is
connected to the Norse presence. They sail on, coming to Cuba,

where once again the Norse assimilate, settling down and intermarrying. The Cubans teach them about their new habitat – the uses of corn, tobacco and hammocks – while the Norse share the skills of ironworking and introduce horses. When the sickness breaks out anew, the Greenlanders' immunity is obvious: 'They realised they were the disease.' Away they journey, casting the timbers from their dismantled temple of Thor overboard to see where the god wishes them to go. Captured by Aztecs, they are brought to Chichen Itza and made to play the sacred ball game, which, by luck, they manage to win. Freydís again initiates cultural exchange, introducing the Mexicans to the wheel, the iron ploughshare, the draught horse and thus the concept of carts. The strangers' stock rises. Finally, when the epidemic forces them to flee again, they fetch up in Panama. Freydís forestalls a crew mutiny by destroying their ship, and the Greenlanders settle permanently. Once again horses and ironworking enhance the visitors' status: Freydís becomes a high priestess. This time, when the inevitable disease sets in, the natives at last begin to develop immunity. Freydís dies of old age and is buried with full honours; after a season of storms and flooding that suggests Thor is angry, Gudrid leads a group of mixed Skraeling–Norse ancestry southwards and vanishes out of the saga.

The Norse immigration gives the inhabitants of the New World three enormous cultural advantages: metalworking, horses and immunity to Old World diseases. Thus, when Columbus lands in Cuba, he is soon outwitted by the local population. His men are punished for the crimes they commit, their ships are destroyed, and soon all the Europeans except for Columbus himself are dead. He can never return home, and writes a sorry journal of his miserable experiences. Some forty years later, against a backdrop of civil war in his home territory, Atahualpa, the Incan emperor, decides to travel eastwards. Arriving in Cuba, Atahualpa considers massacring the Cubans who do not treat him, he feels, with sufficient deference, but when one deploys an arquebus to shoot down a bird he and his men are impressed: 'Old legends rushed back into memory. Voices yelled "Thor!"' The Incas are descendants of Gudrid's people, and memories of the Norse linger in the Caribbean. In Cuba, Atahualpa learns all about Columbus and his claims; he becomes the lover of a princess who had learned Spanish from the marooned explorer and is thus well placed to venture eastwards across the ocean. Soon he and his tiny army have invaded Europe. After killing the emperor Charles V, they take control of a considerable part of the Holy Roman Empire from their base in Spain. Jews, Moors and Christians are all granted freedom of religious expression, and Atahualpa becomes one of the most powerful men in Europe.

Binet's novel, so he says, was inspired by a moment in Jared Diamond's well-known book *Guns, Germs, and Steel* (1997). Diamond argues that Pizarro and his conquistador associates were able to take control of Peru and other territories in Central and South America because the indigenous peoples lacked horses, iron and antibodies. Freydís develops a savvy and effective model for interaction with the New World natives: she learns their languages, exchanges cultural knowledge and is ready to learn to smoke cigars and drink chocolate as she demonstrates the utility of metalworking and eventually helps confer immunity to European diseases. Her leadership, ruthless though it is, benefits both her followers and the people she meets. Her quick wits save the day on more than one occasion; and, crucially, her long-term (counter-) historical achievement is not only to unsettle, but to reverse, the whole colonizing project, as the Incas take control of the Iberian peninsula in an irrevocable migration that changes the culture of Europe once and for all.

### The 'QAnon Shaman'

On 6 January 2021, a mob stormed into the US Capitol Building in Washington, DC, to protest against the Congressional certification of the November 2020 presidential election result. Among the insurrectionists who featured prominently in media broadcasts was Jacob Chansley, also known as Jake Angeli. His face was painted with the Stars and Stripes, and he wore a furry hat with protruding buffalo horns. He was bare-chested and clearly displayed tattoos that included Þórr's hammer, Mjöllnir; the World Tree; and two symbols sometimes found on early medieval rune stones: the interlocking triangles known as the *valknútr* and the sun wheel. These last two are recognized signs of white supremacist affiliation (the sun wheel or Sonnenrad has particular Nazi associations, although it actually dates back to a time well before the Iron Age). The Mjöllnir and Yggdrasill tattoos, when considered alongside the horns, signalled that this self-styled 'shaman' was laying claim to a white, Scandinavian, Aryan heritage. Subsequently sentenced to forty-one months in prison for his activities in the Capitol, Angeli exemplifies through his theatrical self-presentation how the Vínland myth has come to represent an imaginary place in America's past – one in which violent masculinity and honour

Jake Angeli, also known as the 'QAnon Shaman', during the attack on the Capitol Building, Washington, D.C., 2021.

were supreme values, where whiteness and 'purity of blood' were a given, and where women were obedient and submissive. This 'Viking' imagery has been weaponized in American far-right politics to generate an aesthetic that acts as a dogwhistle for white men who hold racist, misogynist and paranoid views.

The Vinland myth, as we have seen, is in part no myth at all, for Greenlanders and Icelanders did sail to North America and establish settlements there, at L'Anse aux Meadows and perhaps other sites. Although tales of Vinland seem to have slipped into legend in medieval Scandinavia, when they were rediscovered in the 19th century they were harnessed to do powerful ideological work. They allowed parts of US society – particularly in New England, where white, Anglo-Saxon heritage was always at a premium – to sideline Columbus, with his Catholic, Mediterranean affiliations, and permitted a rewriting of the country's origin myths. Although the search for concrete evidence proved vain, at least until the emergence of modern archaeological methods, the idea of the Norse settlement fired imaginations on both sides of the Atlantic and underwrote the legitimacy of the many Scandinavian immigrants who settled the Midwest and the Canadian prairies. More recently, the Vinland myth has become polarized. On the one hand it speaks to the violence and destructiveness of the colonial enterprise, even as it celebrates the courage and vision of the men and women who crossed the sea in the hopes of finding new resources. On the other hand, the alt-right's claim to a fictional and idealized white heritage, rooted in a regressive version of masculinity and a denial of the rights of others, has recast the story of Vinland as a powerful origin myth that shapes the thinking of a significant faction within American far-right politics.

# CHAPTER 10

# *Ragna Rök*

The myth of *ragna rök* (literally 'the doom of the gods'), the end of the world, is perhaps the most influential of all the Old Norse myths. It taps into fears of elemental dislocation and large geological shifts, and it also heralds the rebirth of a splendid new world in which the threats of the giants and the malice of Loki are nullified. We find an elaborated version in Snorri's *Edda*, based very closely on the eddic poem *Völuspá* (The Seeress's Prophecy), and a few allusions in a couple of other poems. The coming end of the world is signalled through a series of catastrophes and evil omens. After the last battle, the earth sinks into the sea as the sun and moon are finally consumed by the two wolves who pursue them. Yet – according to the poem, and to Snorri – a new earth rises once again and the cycle is renewed.

**The death of Baldr**

The first sign that the gods' time is running out is the death of Baldr, the son of Óðinn and Frigg, brightest and most beautiful of the gods. He begins to have evil dreams, and his father rides to Hel to enquire what is afoot. Óðinn does not get as far as Hel's hall; instead he conjures up a dead seeress, buried on the edge of Hel's kingdom, who tells him that Hel is preparing Baldr's welcome: the ale is brewed and fresh rushes strewn on the floor. Frigg springs

Rune stone (Ög 181) at Ledberg churchyard, Östergötland, Sweden (11th century).

into action and gets everything on earth to swear not to harm her son – everything, that is, except the slender mistletoe plant, for it does not seem harmful. Frigg confides this detail to an old woman who questions her about the oaths that have been taken – a mistake, for this is Loki in disguise. The gods amuse themselves by hurling objects at Baldr at their formal council, and all bounce harmlessly off him. Höðr, Baldr's blind brother, cannot take part, but Loki sidles up to him, slides a little dart into his hand and urges him to join in the fun: he will guide the missile.

Baldr is given a grand funeral and cremated on a ship that is launched into the ocean. Before the flames are kindled, Óðinn bends and whispers something in his ear. What does he say? We assume that it is an assurance of resurrection, a promise of return made in line with the prophecy imparted by the seeress in the poem of that name. 'What did Óðinn say in Baldr's ear on the pyre?' is the trick question that the god uses in his wisdom contests (see Chapter 3); it allows him to win every time.

Baldr's wife, Nanna, who has died of grief, is cremated with her husband, and they both enter Hel's hall. Frigg sends Hermóðr – who sometimes appears as a son of Óðinn, sometimes a helpful hero – to Hel to learn if her son can be recovered. Exceptionally, Hel agrees that, if everything in the world will weep for Baldr, then he will be released. And everything does weep for Baldr – except for one old ogress in a cave. Her name, Þökk, means 'Thanks', but she herself is ungracious. 'Þökk will weep dry tears for Baldr / Let Hel hold what she has,' she retorts. And so Baldr must stay in the world of the dead.

**Portents and the great battle**

Not long after these events, Loki finally breaks with the other gods. He marches into a feast and insults each god in turn, leaving only when Þórr arrives and threatens to smash him with Mjöllnir. The outraged gods pursue Loki, who hides in a river in the form

Death of Baldr, manuscript illustration by Jakob Sigurðsson (1760).

of a salmon; he is captured, and his two sons by his wife, Sigyn, are transformed into wolves who tear one another apart. Loki is bound with their guts, and Skaði, who has long hated him, since he played a significant role in the death of her father, Þjazi, hangs a serpent over him. The reptile drips venom onto his face; Loki's devoted wife sits over him with a bowl to catch the poison, but whenever she has to empty it the venom strikes the bound god

Óðinn's last words to Baldr, illustration by William Gershom
Collingwood from Olive Bray's *The Elder or Poetic Edda* (1908).

and his convulsions are the cause of earthquakes. The tableau of
Loki's captivity that Snorri elaborates – the wolf guts; the serpent
hanging over Loki's face, placed there by Skaði; and the attentive
woman holding a vessel – seems to allude to Loki's fatherhood:
his paternity binds him to signs of the monster-siblings he sired,
Loki's most significant contribution to the apocalypse of *ragna rök*.

Next comes the *Fimbulvetr*, or Mighty Winter, in which three
savage winters arrive in close succession, with no summers between.
Human society breaks down, men fight one another and bonds of
kinship are shattered. At last, the great battle begins: Heimdallr
sounds his mighty Gjallarhorn, and the clamour of war is unleashed
across the homes of gods and men. The dead march out of Hel's
kingdom and Loki's children advance to battle. Fenrir is loosed
from his magic bonds and the Miðgarðs Serpent rears up from
the ocean, churning great waves, across which the ship Naglfari
drives onwards; it is made from the uncut nails of the dead and
helmed by the giant Hrymr. Surtr, the fire giant, leads his hordes

Friedrich Wilhelm Engelhard, *Surtur Hurls Fire* (1867).

from the south with a flaming sword, and the mysterious sons of the giant Muspell ride with him. Loki, freed from his chains, allies himself once and for all with his giant kindred. The frost giants, led by Hrímnir, march from the east, and the gods and the Einherjar, ready for action at last, ride out. Men and women tremble; the dwarfs stand at the doors of their mountain fastnesses; and even the great World Tree Yggdrasill groans and shudders.

The gods are matched against their fore-ordained opponents. Óðinn is devoured by Fenrir, but his son Víðarr avenges him, planting his foot in the great wolf's lower jaw and tearing him apart. Þórr strides up to the Miðgarðs Serpent and deals it a mighty blow; as it dies, it spews out poison that kills the Thunderer. Loki and Heimdallr annihilate one another; Týr and the hellhound Garmr kill one another; and Freyr fights mightily against Surtr before he falls. We do not hear of the goddesses: perhaps they watch and wring their hands, or perhaps they too take up arms alongside the Valkyries. The Einherjar plunge from Bifröst, which breaks as they ride over it. Now the wolves at last catch up with the sun and the moon: as they engulf them in their huge maws, the heavens catch fire and the earth sinks back into the sea. It is over.

Óðinn and Fenrir, illustration by Emil Doepler from
*Walhall: Die Götterwelt der Germanen* (c. 1905).

## The return

After some time has passed, however, the earth rises once
again, green, cleansed and beautiful. The second generation of
gods – Þórr's sons, Móði and Magni; Baldr and his brother-slayer
Höðr – enter the golden-roofed hall of Gimlé, where they speak
together about the past. In the grass the golden gaming pieces
that were lost after the end of the first age (see Chapter 1) are
rediscovered. The sun had a daughter, who now takes her mother's
path through the sky; and, dazedly, a couple of humans, Líf ('Life')
and Lífþrasir ('Life-thruster') creep out of the woods (perhaps a
reference to the protective branches of Yggdrasill), where they
have been nourished by morning dew: humanity is regenerated.
Over the waterfall flies an eagle, hunting fish. All seems cleansed,

The world after the battle of *ragna rök*. Top: illustration by William Gershom
Collingwood from Olive Bray's *The Elder or Poetic Edda* (1908). Above: illustration
by Emil Doepler from *Walhall: Die Götterwelt der Germanen* (c. 1905).

renewed – but, notes *Völuspá*, the dragon Níðhöggr flies overhead, bearing corpses in his wings. Do malign creatures still haunt this wonderful new world? Or is there a kind of entropy that means the new heaven and earth will also perish? In one version of the poem, recorded in the early 14th century, the arrival is signalled of 'a mighty one to the judgment of powers, / full of strength, from above / he who rules over all'. Is this Christ – or Baldr? It's a question that provokes a number of answers in later retellings.

## Baldr the beautiful

By the time Sir James Frazer's *The Golden Bough* was published in 1922, Baldr's sacrificial death and resurrection were understood as a typical myth relating to fertility rites, in which the god himself symbolized the mistletoe-bearing oak. He is the year-god who dies at the height of summer, and the traditional bonfires kindled in Scandinavia at Midsummer are folk memories of his funeral pyre, suggests Frazer. For earlier 19th-century poets, Baldr's death was a subject they could treat with epic grandeur. Henry Wadsworth Longfellow visited Scandinavia in 1835, where he became acquainted with Esaias Tegnér's enormously popular poem *Frithjofs saga* published ten years earlier (see Chapter 6). Longfellow's Norse-inspired poems, including 'The Skeleton in Armor' (1842) and in particular 'Tegner's Drapa' (1850), his tribute to the Swedish poet, were charged with displaying a nostalgic inauthenticity by Edgar Allan Poe. Nevertheless, Longfellow finds a distinctive voice that would echo through the century and, indeed, later, with its resonant, repeated phrase: '"Balder the beautiful / Is dead, is dead!"' In Longfellow's vision, Baldr is a sun god: 'I saw the pallid corpse / Of the dead sun / Borne through the Northern sky.' Consolation of a kind comes at the end of the poem, for 'the new land of song' that rises 'out of the sea of Time' is ruled by the 'law of love'; 'Thor, the thunderer' shall no more challenge 'the meek Christ' – these words foreshadowing the poet's bombastic work

'The Challenge of Thor' (1863), discussed in Chapter 4. Longfellow's 'Tegner's Drapa' understands the ending of the myth, the earth rising again from the sea, as metaphorical: the new generation of skalds who walk the green meadows are sustained by a morning dew that has eucharistic overtones, and they will now sing the praise of another, gentler god.

Longfellow's boldly free verse tells a spare version of the myth, cutting away from Baldr's funeral, in which he is likened to the setting sun, to the green plains of the new Christian dispensation. It would prove strikingly influential. The lines "'Balder the beautiful / Is dead, is dead!'" kindled the imagination of the young C. S. Lewis, who writes in his autobiography of how Longfellow's poem first awakened his passion for 'pure "Northernness" ... a vision of huge, clear spaces hanging above the Atlantic in the endless twilight of Northern summer, remoteness, severity'. Alongside the newly published libretto for *Siegfried* and *Götterdämmerung*, with its illustrations by Arthur Rackham, that he saw the same year (and quickly purchased), Longfellow's lines were the starting point for Lewis's enthusiasm for the north, one that powerfully inflected his writing in the *Narnia* series, as we will see.

Matthew Arnold too takes up the Baldr story, addressing it in his three-part epic poem of 1855, *Balder Dead*. Here Arnold starts at the very moment that Baldr falls: 'In his breast stood fixt the fatal bough / Of mistletoe.' The scene is set in Valhalla, where the gods have been sporting with the apparently invulnerable victim as a prelude to their feast: 'On the tables stood the untasted meats / and in the horns and gold-rimmed skulls the wine' (yes, those skulls again!). The gods stand 'weeping and wailing', until Odin rallies them with charges of unmanliness: they must all face the doom that the Norns have spun for them, 'but ours we shall not meet, when that day comes, / With woman's tears and weak complaining cries.' Hoder (Höðr) goes to see his mother to apologize for his unwitting part in his brother's death, and she describes to him the road to Hela's realm, where some god might go to plead for his return. A blind god cannot make this journey, but Hermod (Hermóðr), here another son of Óðinn, agrees to undertake the mission while the gods prepare Balder's funeral pyre. Balder himself appears in a vision to his grieving wife, Nanna, and asks her to join him, though 'dreary, Nanna, is the life they lead / In that dim world, in Hela's mouldering realm; / And doleful are the ghosts, the troops of dead.' All the heroes are of course with Odin in Valhalla, but Nanna and Balder might find some comfort in one another.

In the second part of the poem, Hermod borrows his father's horse Sleipnir and journeys to Hela's kingdom. The dead cluster round him, Arnold notes in one of his many epic similes: just as a flock of swallows gathers at a bulrush-bed, preparing to migrate, so 'around Hermod swarmed the twittering ghosts'. Hermod ignores them – dishonoured cowards drowned in bogs for their failures are among them – and makes his way to Hela's throne.

Arnold omits Snorri's disturbing description of Hela as half-woman, half-corpse, instead making her dignified and stern: she is 'solemn', with 'inscrutable regard'. After rehearsing the wrongs done by the gods to her and her siblings ('Me on this cheerless nether world you threw / And gave me nine unlighted realms to rule') and prophesying her father's role in the last battle, Hela agrees the usual conditions for Balder's return. Balder himself is still no more reconciled to his new dwelling; echoing Achilles in Vergil's *Aeneid*, he complains that he would rather be a slave and alive 'than be a crown'd king here, and rule the dead'. Hermod returns to Asgard, where the gods have gathered for Balder's funeral.

Lok (Loki) sneers as Hermod approaches, noting that he comes alone; Lok's daughter has not released Balder. In another vivid extended comparison, both moving and pathetic, Lok compares Hermod to a farmer who has taken his dog with him to market and lost him in the crowds. Now he returns home, wondering where his dog can be, and the poor canine, exhausted by his search, has collapsed 'before a stranger's threshold, not his home'. Balder's spirit remains exiled in Hela's realm. The gods and heroes take solemn leave of Balder as his corpse lies there; even Regner (Ragnarr Loðbrók, discussed in Chapter 8) touchingly recalls how, whenever Balder sang in Valhalla, instead of evoking battle he would remind the Einherjar of their youth, families and home: 'I heard Thora laugh in Gothland Isle, / And saw my shepherdess, Aslauga, tend / Her flock along the white Norwegian beach.' Arnold dispenses with the undignified elements of Balder's funeral as described by Snorri. The funeral ship does not get stuck on the rollers, capable of being shifted only by a giantess guest at the ceremony; nor does Þórr kick a dwarf into the fire in fury. The ship is soon launched. Arnold's description of the dramatic scene chimes with the well-established Gothic imagining of the 'Viking funeral':

> Soon with a roaring rose the mighty fire,
> And the pile crackled; and between the logs
> Sharp quivering tongues of flame shot out and leapt,
> Curling and darting, higher, until they lick'd
> The summit of the pile, the dead, the mast,
> And ate the shrivelling sails; but still the Ship
> Drove on, ablaze, above her hull with fire.

In fact, the archaeological and textual evidence for fiery ship burials is very slight, but one important testimony is that of the traveller Ibn Fahdlan, who witnessed the shipboard cremation of a chieftain from the Viking Rus' on the Volga at some point in the 10th century (see pp. 168–69). A memorable work by Sir Frank Dicksee, painted in 1893 and now in the Manchester Art Gallery, depicts the launch of just such a flaming vessel bearing an armoured corpse out into stormy waves (see pl. x). The ship has a Viking-style animal figurehead at the prow, and the men on the dark, mountainous shore wear rich clothing; one grey-haired figure, perhaps the dead man's father or a pagan priest, wears a splendidly patterned blue cloak. Another man wears a horned helmet, a signifier of Viking identity that had only just been invented by the costume designers for the *Ring* at Bayreuth in 1876. The men hauling the boat into the waves are bare-chested and muscular; swords and spears are lifted in acclamation and farewell. Just as in Arnold's poem, twilight falls as the ship sets sail, symbolizing the dark unknown into which the warrior must pass. Dicksee, who was a Royal Academician and a distinguished painter of historical genre scenes, declared that *The Funeral of a Viking* was 'the largest and most important work I have yet painted'. While Arnold's poem was composed just as Victorian interest in the medieval Scandinavian past was gathering steam, Dicksee's canvas marks the climax of 'Viking mania'. At the very moment it was being exhibited at the Royal Academy in London, a replica of the only recently discovered Viking Gokstad ship was

Replica of the Gokstad Viking ship on its way to Chicago (1893).

sailing across the Atlantic to be admired and celebrated at the 1893 Chicago World's Fair, a celebration of the 400th anniversary of Columbus's voyage to the New World.

In Arnold's *Balder Dead*, after witnessing how Balder's ship drifts towards the setting sun and the flames are extinguished in an eerie portent of the loss of the sun and moon to come, the subdued gods head to Valhalla for the funeral feast. Odin threatens to invade the realm of the dead to recover his son if Hela's conditions cannot be met, but Frea (Frigg) dissents. The world's order cannot be overthrown, so messengers are sent out to solicit the shedding of tears for the lost: 'So through the world was heard a dripping noise / Of all things weeping to bring Balder back.' But deep in Ironwood, the hag refuses: 'Thok with dry eyes will weep o'er Balder's pyre.' Hermod takes the regrettable news to Hel, where Balder is not only becoming accustomed to his new mode of being, but is actively looking forward to his post-*ragna rök* return: 'And we shall tread once more the well-known plain / Of Ida, and among the grass shall find / The golden dice with which we play'd of yore.' Hermod longs to stay with Balder among the dead and himself wait there for the dawn of the new age, but he may not. Looking wistfully back, he returns to the gods' now increasingly precarious existence.

Unlike Longfellow's confident assertion that the old gods have been displaced by the superior religion of Christ, Arnold's poem takes Balder's prophecy of his return on its own terms. The hope that Balder's future offers is tenuous and pitched at a time beyond the poem's imagining; until then the gods are trapped in the encroaching darkness, in a world that is corrupt, obsessed with violence and doomed to vanish through the machinations of Lok. Arnold had lost his attachment to Anglican Christianity a decade before he composed *Balder Dead*, but he remained interested in religion as a social and individual phenomenon. Within the poem no resolution is possible: as with Hermod, humanity remains trapped within an unsatisfying paradigm, but it is unclear how Balder's millennial vision can be achieved.

Baldr is a strangely underdeveloped figure in more recent treatments of his story. In the original myths he does nothing until his bad dreams start. In Joanne Harris's two *Loki* books, Loki, predictably, finds him annoying: 'Known as Balder the Fair. Handsome, sporty, popular. Sound a little smug to you? Yes, I thought so too.' Loki can't quite account for why he hates him on sight – 'perhaps because people *liked* him so much'. For Loki, Balder (also known as 'Golden Boy') is the archetypal 'most popular boy at school' – the equivalent of the captain of the First Eleven and head boy, adored by girls and idolized by boys. But when Loki learns from his daughter Hel, who also desires Balder, about his dreams, Loki's sense that it is time to act on his growing alienation from the divine community is confirmed, and they strike a deal. Loki stays in the shadows as Balder, bare-chested, stands on a chair at the feast while everyone lobs missiles at him; the goddesses join in by hurling fruit. Hoder, Balder's 'stunted, imperfect sibling', is easy prey for Loki, who slides the dart into his hands. '*Pink!* The gods fell silent. "Did I hit him?" said Hoder, turning his head this way and that.' The tinny sound they hear almost diminishes the effect of the dart, and as an audience we are aligned with Hoder, blindly trying to fathom what has happened. But Loki has vanished, and the gods fall on poor Hoder and tear him to pieces.

Hel is disappointed with her new guest. 'Balder dead was compliant but dull. The spark had gone out of him,' notes Loki, riffing on Arnold's poem. But Balder cannot be wept out of Hel, and that is the last we hear of him. Francesca Simon, in contrast, brings Baldr into focus as a kind, life-loving man who, when he first meets Hel in Asgard, has 'eyes blue like glaciers ... golden light blazed from him'. Baldr, so Hel relates, 'picks me up and whirls me around until I am laughing and dizzy and he is laughing'. 'No one has ever picked me up. No one has ever touched me,' thinks Hel. When

Baldr mentions his wife and child, she reels, but still 'he sees past my deformity; he doesn't see a monster, he sees a girl'. Hel's crush on Baldr becomes an obsession that in no way diminishes once she is consigned to the underworld. Once she has set her realm in order, built a hall and made friends with Modgud who guards the bridge to the kingdom of the dead, she watches and waits. Yet, although Odin comes to question the dead seeress (in fact, Hel's mother) buried at the edge of Hel's kingdom about Baldr's dreams, Hel is as surprised as anyone when the dwarf Litr, kicked in a fury into Baldr's funeral pyre by Thor, arrives as a harbinger of the granting of her heart's desire: 'The great god Baldr is dead. Baldr, god of light, is dead,' he laments. Yet, once again, Baldr dead has eyes only for Nanna when she rejoins him. It is not too long now until *ragna rök*, and as Niflheim empties and the dead march away, to throng the decks of the ship Naglfari, Hel's kingdom collapses around her. She is free to struggle upwards into the new world, her self-loathing and long-nurtured hatreds dissolving as new pink skin begins to emerge from under the black decay of her useless legs. In the second act of Simon and Higgins's opera version of *The Monstrous Child*, Odin prostrates himself before Hel in her hall, begging for his son's return, and she makes her usual stipulation. Then all things are heard weeping for Baldr. Hel resents how much he is mourned – 'How does it feel to be loved? I have never been so loved' – and she takes on the role of Loki:

> 'I do not weep for Baldr.
> If I can't have Baldr no one can.
> Return to Asgard alone.
> Let Hel hold what she has.'

Baldr stretches out his hand in vain to his father as he departs. After *ragna rök*, Hel comes to see the futility of her hatred, which has generated nothing but emotional emptiness: 'I kept Baldr. I kept Baldr. He didn't love me. I should have let him go.' This realization is liberating: emerging into the light of the new world as the last of the gods, Hel begins her work: 'I must remake the world better than before.' It is she who carves new human figures from the toppled trees and breathes life into them. Baldr, along with all the other gods, is erased from this vision of renewal.

In her novel *The Witch's Heart*, Genevieve Gornichec also develops the one-sided romance between Hel and Baldr; here, too, Baldur is a 'blond and bright-eyed boy' who is kind to the little girl when she is brought to Asgard; he tosses her a golden apple as he runs off to play with his friends. Later, in the turmoil of *ragna rök*, Baldur brings Hel back to her mother, Angrboda, in Ironwood, for the divisions between the worlds have collapsed and the dead have left to join Loki in battle. Baldur's presence in Niflheim, as someone already dead, is what has saved him from the fate of the other gods. His salvation is the result of a conspiracy between Odin and Loki that unites their two children in the world to come. Angrboda's sacrifice of her own much-battered heart, as signalled by the book's title, repairs her damaged daughter and, as the new world comes into being, Baldur comes for Hel. Now she, like her mother before her, has become the witch of Ironwood. Hel will not move to Idavoll, where the former gods have built a gold-thatched hall in the place where Asgard once stood, and so Baldur remains with her. They happily raise their children in what had once been a place of horror.

This romance – whether frustrated or fulfilled – between Hel and Baldr is not attested in the surviving mythological sources. Yet the authors who develop this plotline are right to understand Hel as a desiring woman, as we saw in Chapter 5. She is a goddess who wants to gather men to her as her lovers; for her, coming to possess Baldr is the ultimate prize. That Loki should give Baldr to his daughter because it suits his own purposes, as a vital precursor to *ragna rök*, to please her, or because he and Óðinn are working in cahoots are all motives that fit well within the tradition, even if the implications for Hel herself have been explored only in recent young adult and feminist fiction. That a disabled girl, one who thinks and feels like other teenagers and who has done no wrong to anyone, should be exiled into the miserable world of the dead simply on the grounds of her paternity and her appearance opens up vital questions about young women, their capabilities and their bodies: questions that these novels explore very productively.

### Götterdämmerung

In his *Edda* Snorri referred consistently to the final catastrophe as *ragna røkr* (sometimes spelled *ragna røkkr*), meaning 'the twilight of the gods', while the eddic poems use *ragna rök* 'the doom of the gods'. Jacob Grimm – and thus Wagner, who followed him – took up Snorri's term, translating it into German as *Götterdämmerung*. And, indeed, the idea of a gradual sinking into darkness rather than an apocalyptic last battle suited Wagner's vision very well. For ever since Siegfried smashed Wotan's sacred spear, Gungnir, on his way to the mountain top where Brünnhilde lies, the gods have vanished from the stage of the *Ring*; their eclipse is near total. They have withdrawn to Wotan's Walhall, that great fortress for which so high a price was paid. Wotan has ordered the Einherjar to fell the mighty World Ash, already dying because he tore a branch from it to fashion into Gungnir. Now the tree's timbers are to be piled up around his palace in preparation for the final conflagration that will consume the gods utterly. Yet the curse of the Ring must still play out for Wotan's descendant, Siegfried. At the beginning of *Götterdämmerung*, the hero leaves Brünnhilde in search of new adventures. He sails down the Rhine to the hall of the Gibichungs and soon becomes enmeshed in a new scheme to recover the Ring for the Nibelungs. Gunther, his sister Gutrune and their half-brother Hagen (the son of Alberich) are the Gibichungs; Gunther is weak and ineffectual, Gutrune is rather underwritten (unlike Kriemhilt in *Das Nibelungenlied*) and Hagen is pure evil.

Primed by his father, Hagen plots to regain the Ring, which is now on Brünnhilde's finger, for it was given to her by Siegfried. Soon Hagen has cooked up a magic potion that causes Siegfried to forget his beloved and to betrothe himself to the delighted Gutrune.

Meanwhile, Brünnhilde is warned by her sister Waltraute that her father Wotan has abandoned his divine responsibilities and sits silently in Walhall, waiting for the cue for his palace and his rule to be consumed by flames. Only if Brünnhilde returns the Ring to the Rhinemaidens might gods and the world be saved. 'Are you mad?' retorts Brünnhilde. The Ring is a pledge of Siegfried's love for her, and she will never yield it up.

Siegfried swears blood-brotherhood to Gunther and promises to help him win the legendary former Valkyrie as his bride. Using the Tarnhelm to exchange appearances with Gunther, he crosses the flame wall and claims Brünnhilde, placing a sword between them as they lie in bed to assure her chastity and – fatally – taking the Ring from her finger to signify her submission to him as Gunther. A baffled and traumatized Brünnhilde is brought to the Gibichung court and a double wedding is celebrated. But when she catches sight of the Ring now on Siegfried's finger, the extent of his duplicity becomes clear; as a result she, Gunther and Hagen plot his death. Out hunting, Siegfried encounters the Rhinemaidens, who give him a last chance to return the Ring, but he refuses. Reunited with the hunting party, Hagen prompts him to relate his life story, and at the crucial moment gives him a drink containing the antidote to the forgetfulness potion that Gutrune had offered him earlier. Siegfried thus recalls, and guilelessly recounts, his meeting with and passionate love for Brünnhilde. Hagen stabs him in the back, and Siegfried dies, realizing the extent of his deception.

In the opera's final act, Brünnhilde is ready to pull down everything around her as she too understands that Siegfried's treachery was unwitting. She joins Siegfried on his funeral pyre, riding her horse, Grane, into the flames and calling out to the Rhinemaidens to come to reclaim the Ring that she has taken from Siegfried's finger (see pl. v). As the pyre blazes up, the Rhine overflows, and the Rhinemaiden Flosshilde triumphantly holds up the Ring, once more in her possession, as her sisters drag Hagen down to his doom. The flames consume the Gibichung hall as the corresponding pyre that surrounds Walhall catches fire: Loge's last action in the cycle.

What is left after this 'delirious orgy of purification by fire and water', as the critic Tom Service puts it? The *Ring* has revealed to us 'the limits of power and the limitlessness of love', he suggests.

Anselm Kiefer, *Grane* (1980).

The compromised gods and their heroes ranged in Walhall are all gone, leaving us with the men and women in the world's ruins who witness the end 'with the greatest emotion'. *Götterdämmerung's* finale suggests that it is up to us to embrace our liberation from subjection to the corrupt gods and the myth of the hero. Power, the object of Wotan's obsession – until he realizes, as early as *Die Walküre*, that it is both destructive and illusory – has passed from gods to men. But what now? Brünnhilde's ecstatic vision of love is not a programme for rebuilding, even if the Rhine has returned to its bed. Brünnhilde's love can be understood, perhaps, as prefiguring communal and social ideals of *caritas*, a love that values and foregrounds all humanity, some critics have suggested: an egalitarian and communitarian ideology. This is to foreclose the possibilities that Wagner's apocalypse has opened up, however: the point is that there is no programme. The future is ours to shape.

### Retelling *ragna rök*

At last, the long-anticipated battle gets under way. Many modern retellings of the conflict between the gods, giants and monsters are grandly dramatic. Byatt's account in her *Ragnarok* is splendidly written; as the wolves catch up at last with the sun and moon, sinking their fangs into the haunches of the horses that pull them along, 'light in the world went mad, black, blazing white, dark as hell, lurid red'. Full space is given to vivid visualizations of each encounter – 'Odin advanced on the Fenris-Wolf, balancing his ash-spear Gungnir. The wolf's hackles bristled. His mean eyes glittered. He yawned' – and in a series of speedy verbs, as Gungnir is driven into his gaping jaws, 'he shook himself, snapped the spear ... gripped the great god, shook him, broke him, swallowed him.' Wolf and serpent laugh as Thor 'with flailing fists and a thunderous hammer' breaks the serpent's skull but, as Thor turns triumphantly to the other gods, the poison spat from the dying monster pours over him; he takes nine paces, then falls dead. Surtr's fire burns up everything; all that is left is 'a flat surface of black liquid ... a few gold chessmen floated and bobbed on the dark ripples'. Byatt's protagonist, 'the thin child', rejects the possibility of rebirth and renewal; the golden gaming pieces, those powerful symbols of recovery and hope, here mock the illusion that life can begin over again. Even when her father, 'with his red-gold hair shining, gold wings on his tunic', returns alive from the war, like Baldr come again, she clings to that final vision of the 'bright black world' that erased the brilliance of the World Ash and the rainbow bridge.

Joanne Harris's hero, Loki, ever with an eye to the main chance, allies himself with Gullveig the enchantress. Gullveig is also in league with the Oracle – Mímir's head – who both prophesies *ragna rök* and works surreptitiously to bring it about. Loki watches the forces of gods, giants, Einherjar and monsters gather with a sense of horror and anticipation: 'I felt the hairs on my neck stand up like a hedge of upraised spears.' Loki's blood-brother, ally and enemy

Sköll and Hati, from Hélène Adeline Guerber's *Myths of the Norsemen from the Eddas and Sagas* (1909).

Odin falls victim to his son. 'In the end, the Old Man was no match for the wolf's brutal cunning and vigour. Bleeding in two dozen places he fell to one knee, and the wolf closed in to tear out his throat in a single bite.' It is Thor, not Víðarr, who destroys Fenrir in Harris's account, but as the Thunderer pivots next to attack Loki Jormungand strikes: 'Thor saw him coming and turned to fight, but by then the snake had already half ingested him, drawing him into that giant maw as if he were a melon seed. I said: *That's my boy*, or something close.' Loki ticks off all the events that the Oracle has predicted – '*There goes free will*, I said.' And indeed, when he finds himself locked in mortal combat with Heimdallr, the dragon (in fact an aspect of Surtr) sweeps over Loki, and his last protective rune ceases to function. 'I said: "*Oh, crap.*" Then, night fell. *Oh, crap*. As last words go, it wasn't what you'd call memorable.' Even as he is stripped of his illusions that he can indeed make his own fate, that he is not simply playing a part in a preordained course of events foretold by Mímir and appearing in Harris's text as the often quoted poem *Lokabrenna* – a loose version of 'The Seeress's Prophecy' – Loki cannot resist the opportunity for a wisecrack.

Gornichec makes her heroine Angrboda the catalyst that brings about *ragna rök*. It is she who releases Loki from his iron bonds and thus unleashes Chaos, for the sundering of his fetters breaks Fenrir's too. The freed Loki and Angrboda stand on a ledge high above the seashore as Jormungandr, the Miðgarðs Serpent, rears up out of the churning ocean and Fenrir lopes into view. The reunion of mother and sons teeters on the edge of comedy: Fenrir licks his mother, covering her in drool; Jormungandr butts her gently with his massive scaly head, drenching her in seawater. With her prophetic vision, Angrboda sees the great clash between gods and giants, the death of her sons and the many deaths they cause, but she herself remains in Ironwood until Surtr's fire engulfs it, and her too. In contrast, Simon's *Monstrous Child*, both novel and opera, places *ragna rök* offstage. Hel remains in her hall as the dead leave in droves to join the anti-gods' coalition. As she hears the noise filtering down from above, she salutes her brothers who are finally taking vengeance for the wrongs the Æsir have visited upon them. And as the dead flee her kingdom, she senses new possibilities, an instinct that draws her back up towards the light.

Wagner's opera cycle, and in particular his treatment of *ragna rök*, had initiated the shift in which the destruction of the gods came not because they were displaced by Christianity, but because they had become irremediably corrupt. Following their initial act of bad faith – the swindling of the master builder – their ethical position deteriorates. Their cruelty to Loki's children, their plundering of the giants' treasures and their violent oppression of other races escalate into a kind of tyranny. By the time *ragna rök* comes, the Æsir stand convicted of moral bankruptcy – in part because some recent retellings have adopted the perspective of Loki (Harris), his lover (Gornichec) and his daughter (Simon). This represents a radical shift from the earlier but – as Wagner's critique of the gods shows – by no means universal idea that the Old Norse gods were heroes who faced their fates with courage and dignity: their foreknowledge of the last battle imbues their story with a tragic grandeur. The old view is epitomized in the characterization of *ragna rök* and its place in Norse myth by the scholar William Paton Ker, famously quoted by Tolkien in his ground-breaking lecture on *Beowulf* from 1936:

> 'The Northern Gods', Ker said, 'have an exultant extravagance in their warfare which makes them more like Titans than Olympians; only they are on the right side, though it is not the side that wins. The winning side is Chaos and Unreason'—mythologically, the monsters— 'but the gods, who are defeated, think that defeat no refutation.' And in their war men are their chosen allies, able when heroic to share in this 'absolute resistance,

perfect because without hope'. At least in this vision of the final defeat of the humane (and of the divine made in its image), and in the essential hostility of the gods and heroes on the one hand and the monsters on the other, we may suppose that pagan English and Norse imagination agreed.

The gods are on the right side, but it is not the side that wins: it's a formulation that underpins the idea of tragedy, but that old 'stiff upper lip' mentality is too simple and too masculine for many contemporary writers. Tolkien admires the courage and stoicism that animates both the ending of *Beowulf* and the *ragna rök* myth as values that sum up the spirit of 'our northern world beneath our northern sky ... until the dragon comes'. Yet in his own legendarium, *The Silmarillion*, the Dagor Dagorath – 'the Battle of All Battles' – remains a future event. When it comes about, it will herald the destruction of the existing world, the loss of the sun and moon, and then the rebuilding of Arda (Earth), in a post-apocalyptic vision that owes as much to the biblical Book of Revelation as the final verses of *Völuspá*.

C. S. Lewis and Neil Gaiman offer interestingly divergent treatments of the Old Norse 'last battle' tropes. We saw above how Lewis credited Longfellow, Wagner and Rackham with kindling his fascination with the North. The motifs of *ragna rök* bookend his *Chronicles of Narnia* series. In *The Lion, the Witch and the Wardrobe* (1950), the *fimbulvetr*, or Mighty Winter, is the doing of the evil White Witch, Jadis: 'Why, it is she that has got all Narnia under her thumb. It's she that makes it always winter. Always winter and never Christmas; think of that!' the faun Mr Tumnus explains to Lucy. Evil wolves stalk the frozen land, key operatives in the White Witch's secret police. Fenrir metamorphoses into Maugrim, the wolf-chief of the secret police force who is eventually killed by Peter. Towards the end of the book, however, spring comes to Narnia: 'The sky became bluer and bluer, and now there were white clouds hurrying across it from time to time. In the wide glades there were primroses. The trees began to come fully alive.' As the White Witch's dwarf observes, this is no thaw, but spring – and it is Aslan's doing. Lewis postpones the battle in the first book, bringing together the White Witch's evil horde for Aslan's sacrifice:

> A great crowd of people were standing all round the Stone Table and though the moon was shining many of them carried torches which burned with evil-looking red flames and black smoke. But such people! Ogres with monstrous teeth, and wolves, and bull-headed men; spirits of evil trees and poisonous plants; and other creatures whom I won't describe because if I did the grownups would probably not let you read this book – Cruels and Hags and Incubuses, Wraiths, Horrors, Efreets, Sprites, Orknies, Wooses, and Ettins.

When they realize that the resurrected Aslan and his reinforcements have joined Peter, Edmund and their army in the battle against the White Witch, her inhuman hordes 'squealed and gibbered' in dismay. Matters are settled very quickly, and the violence is kept to a minimum. Once Aslan has leapt upon and crushed Jadis, her wicked cohorts are either slain or flee. A mopping-up operation after the children are crowned sees off the rest: 'In the end all that foul brood was stamped out.' In the final book of the series, however, *The Last Battle* (1956), the apocalyptic events that destroy Narnia are unleashed. Summoned by Aslan, the giant Father Time blows his horn, 'high and terrible, yet of a strange, deadly beauty'. Then the stars begin to fall from the sky. Dragons and giant lizards consume the vegetation until the land is bare. The sea rises to cover the land, and the sun begins to come up: 'A streak of dreary and disastrous dawn spread along the horizon, and widened and grew brighter.' But soon the sun – much larger than it should be, and a dark red, swallows up the moon. 'Great lumps of fire came dropping out of it into the sea and clouds of steam rose up.' Finally, the giant snuffs out the sun, and all is darkness. Ice begins to form around the mystical Doorway through which Aslan and the saved are witnessing the end, and Peter pulls it shut. Aslan and his people walk away from the Doorway, 'and as they went they talked to one another about old wars and old peace and ancient Kings and all the glories of Narnia'.

Lewis's treatment is, as ever, allegorical, and the last novel depends fundamentally on the Christian concept of the Antichrist (the false prophet 'Tashlan') and the Day of Judgment. Yet his staging of the end of Narnia owes as much to the Norse mythological sources as to the Book of Revelation. Father Time's mighty horn is the Gjallarhorn, the horn of Heimdallr that blows to mark the onset of that final phase. And although there are no wolves to swallow the sun and the moon, the scene recalls this verse from *Völuspá*:

The sun turns black, land sinks into the sea,
the bright stars vanish from the sky;
steam rises up in the conflagration,
hot flame plays high against heaven itself.

The humans mourn for the Narnia that they have loved, and that has now vanished for ever. *Völuspá* relates how 'earth [arises] from the ocean, eternally green, / the waterfalls plunge, an eagle soars above them, / over the mountain hunting fish'. At the end of the Norse poem the surviving gods gather in the gold-roofed hall of Gimlé after the world is renewed and talk about the past: 'and they converse about the mighty Earth-girdler [Miðgarðs Serpent] / and Óðinn's ancient runes'. The new world in *The Last Battle* is similarly a transfigured Narnia: a prelude to Aslan's country, heaven itself, that must be reached by passing through the Great Waterfall – a symbol of baptism, but also a nod to the landscape of the reborn earth in *Völuspá*. The descriptions of snow-covered mountains and deep fjords in Lewis's pristine landscape spring from that deep Northern wellspring in his imagination: what he called 'my whole Norse complex – Old Icelandic, Wagner's Ring and (again) Morris'.

Gaiman's treatment of the last battle topos in *American Gods* is ironic. Like Wagner's ending to his cycle, it places the onus back on humans to decide how – or whether – to live with the old gods or the new. The gods assemble at Lookout Mountain in Tennessee, in the heartland of America – old gods such as Mama-ji, the Morrigan and Mr Anansi, and new ones who include Media, airplane- and drug-deities, and the car-gods, 'with blood on their black hands and on their chrome teeth: recipients of human sacrifice on a scale undreamed-of since the Aztecs'. Yet, after an initial skirmish, the great battle itself fizzles out when the book's hero, Shadow, reveals that the whole conflict is a scam, a long-term grift dreamed up by Odin (Mr Wednesday) and Loki between them to bring about a huge sacrifice, one that will restore the two gods to power through the shedding of huge quantities of blood. Shadow addresses the deities drawn up in their battle-lines. He begins by noting that America is 'a bad country for gods', that the old ones are swiftly forgotten and even the new ones last only briefly, after which they are 'cast aside for the next big thing'. Thus, says Shadow,

> The battle you're here to fight isn't something that any of you can win or lose. The winning and the losing are unimportant to him, to them. What matters is that enough of you die. Each of you that falls in battle gives him power. Every one of you that dies feeds him. Do you understand?

The gods realize the truth of Shadow's story, underpinned as it is by the revelation that he is Mr Wednesday's son. But he is no Baldr come again, no better kind of god, for he too lays claim to humanity as preferable to divinity: 'I think I would rather be a man than a god. We don't need anyone to believe in us. We just keep going anyhow. It's what we do.' A bolt of lightning crashes into the mountain top, and in the darkness the gods begin to leave silently, without grand declarations or opportunities for heroic posturing. Shadow has prevented *ragna rök* by showing the two sets of opponents that they are being manipulated by forces they cannot recognize: by fake news and staged standoffs.

Gaiman understands that Baldr's death need not be cast as a terrible accident, nor a strange twist of fate, nor final evidence of Loki's malevolence. Rather, Shadow's ordeal on the tree – his death and journey through the underworld – not only ritually replays Óðinn's own self-sacrifice to gain wisdom and power, but it also represents the death of the innocent, the father's sacrifice of his own son. Radiant Baldr is god of light, of joy and goodness; Shadow's name labels him as Baldr's dark double. As Nanna dies to follow Baldr to Hel's hall, so Shadow's wife, Laura, is killed in a car accident, arranged by Mr Wednesday, in order to free Shadow to play his role in the great plan. But Shadow walks away from Lookout Mountain to finish up his other, human, business, first setting his wife's soul free.

### Fire and ice

George R. R. Martin's *A Song of Ice and Fire* series and the HBO television show *Game of Thrones* draw their narrative of apocalypse from the *ragna rök* myth. The imaginative origins of the forces of ice, embodied by the Others or the White Walkers – the super-natural creatures who are led, in the television adaptation, by the Night King, an updated version of a Norse frost giant – seem very clear. That the Night King can marshal an army of the dead speaks also to the popular idea that we have seen above: that the dead will abandon Hel's realm to crew the ship made of their dead fingernails (though in fact neither Snorri nor *Völuspá* mobilize them in this way). The three dragons, hatched into existence through the power of fire and Daenerys Targaryen's affinity with that element, breathe flames and might be expected to destroy the Night King and his cohorts. In *Game of Thrones*, at least, it is not in fact the dragons that prevail – particularly since one, Viserion, has been killed by the Night King and revived as an ice dragon capable of bringing down the great Wall that protects the Seven Kingdoms. Whether Martin's final vision for the battle for the survival of humanity will be resolved in the same way in his novels remains to be seen.

Martin also draws on other *ragna rök* elements for his world-building project. The Seven Kingdoms are prone to irregular and prolonged winters, which humans struggle to survive. In one such winter from the distant past, the Long Night was (according to Old Nan, the oldest inhabitant of Winterfell) a time

> when the snows fall a hundred feet deep and the ice wind comes howling out of the north. Fear is for the long night when the sun hides its face for years at a time, and little children are born and live and die all in darkness while the direwolves grow gaunt and hungry, and the white walkers move through the woods ... riding their pale dead horses and leading hosts of the slain.

This great mythic winter of the past, and its restaging in the eternal winter that the White Walkers seem bent on bringing about, have their roots in the *fimbulvetr*; it is a portent of horror for all men. Martin also draws on other medievalist fantasy developed from Old Norse myth: far beyond the Wall, in the extreme north, lies the likely home of the Others, the Lands of Always Winter – an appellation that is clearly borrowed from Narnia. Yet Martin also subverts Norse mythic motifs: the cosmic wolves that pursue the sun and the moon, Fenrir, and the brood of evil wolves raised in Ironwood are reconfigured in his writing as the direwolves, the fiercely faithful animals who are devoted to the Stark children and who symbolize the strength and loyalty of House Stark itself. Their resonant House Words, 'Winter is coming!', evoke the spirit of the *fimbulvetr* and the mysterious and terrifying icy world beyond the Wall, for Martin makes very clear how far the mythic North still haunts our imaginations.

### *Ragna rök* and Thor

The Marvel Universe decided, in the third *Thor* movie, to face head on the doom of the gods and the destruction of Asgard. It opens with a variation of the 'Loki bound' motif: Thor lies in chains as the prisoner of Surtur, the great fire demon. His character here also reflects aspects of Baldr, for he has, he says, been having terrible dreams: 'Asgard up in flames, falling to ruins, and you, Surtur, are at the centre of them all.' Surtur assents: 'Then you have seen Ragnarok, the fall of Asgard, the great prophecy.' Thor summons Mjolnir, frees himself from his bonds and rips Surtur's crown, with its diabolical horns, from his head, nullifying the fire demon's power. As we saw in Chapter 5, Thor proves unable to protect Asgard from the vengeful fury of his older sister, Hela, and the final battle plays out on Bifrost. There is no Miðgarðs Serpent, only Fenris, the giant wolf who was revived by Hela. Since Odin died earlier in the movie, the beast now has a new role. Snarling ferociously, he stands between Heimdall (Idris Elba), who is shepherding the Asgardians and the ship in which they hope to escape the doomed planet. Valkyrie fires over and over again at Fenris: 'This stupid dog won't die,' she cries in frustration. The Incredible Hulk takes on the role of Víðarr, the Wolf-Slayer; he leaps upon the monster and, as the adversaries tumble off the rainbow bridge into the water below, Fenris seizes the Hulk in his great jaws. The Hulk smashes the beast in the snout, and as they slide towards the edge of the realm Fenris plummets into the void while Hulk scrambles to safety. That's one enemy down, but Hela remains, invincible. Thor now realizes that *ragna rök* is inescapable: 'This was never about escaping Ragnarok, it was about *causing* ragnarok.'

Asgard must be abandoned, surrendered to a revived Surtur who destroys first Hela and then the whole planet. Thor feels more than equivocal about his role in fulfilling the prophecy but, as Heimdall reminds him, 'Asgard is not a place, it's a people.'

The film's director, Taika Waititi, makes knowing play with the familiar elements of *ragna rök*: placing Hela at the centre instead of leaving her offstage in Hel, and reimagining the fight against Fenrir with the Hulk (once the fight is relocated to the water, there are strong hints that the monster symbolizes Jormungandr too). Surtur the fire demon is unstoppable and the planet is destroyed, but Loki, as is traditional in Marvel movies, redeems himself, retrieving

Massacre of the Valkyries, still from *Thor: Ragnarok* (2017).

Surtur's skull, allowing Surtur to exterminate Hela, and helping
Thor save the Asgardians. That the last shot of the movie shows the
*Ark*, the Asgardians' ship, falling into the shadow of the ironically
named *Sanctuary II*, the warship of Thanos, a genocidal warlord, sets
up the survivors and the gods for the next adventure narrative.

### Starting over

In Snorri's *Edda*, Líf and Lífþrasir stepped cautiously out of the
ruins of the old world to begin the work of human regeneration,
reconfiguring the original story of Askr and Embla (see p. 39).
So too in Francesca Simon's *The Monstrous Child*, Hel takes up

two pieces of wood to shape into new humans. Purged of her self-hatred and her pitiless contempt for the dead who were her subjects, now she promises the humans her loving tenderness. Where the Æsir cared little for humans, except for heroes, Hel, the last surviving divinity, vows a new start – in an environment that once more looks like Eden. Harris's Loki survives the cataclysm by being subsumed back into the Chaos from which he emerged, and then becomes trapped in a video game, as we saw in Chapter 5; since *ragna rök* has already happened in Harris's universe, the new human world has turned out very much like the one we all live in. In *The Witch's Heart*, the gods are gone and only humans survive; Baldur and his kindred return after *ragna rök* to a universe where the Nine Realms have merged into a space where there are no gods, and a utopian community is established. Odin and the old order are definitively destroyed, but it is not clear that there is any place for gods – not even Christ – in the contemporary vision of a universe that is reborn. The human has triumphed.

Will the new world be an improvement on the old? On the whole, the move from religious veneration to a secular humanism seems promising. The new world offers an environment restored to its pristine condition, where nature – with its waterfalls, eagles and fish – seems whole and healed once more. Yet the sight of the dragon Níðhöggr flying overhead 'with corpses in his wings' that concludes *Völuspá* unsettles this vision: is he a dire portent, or is he merely tidying up the last remnants of the old order? There is real optimism that this time, with no Óðinn, Þórr nor Loki, and no catastrophic end to be warded against, humans can create a better world. For Neil Gaiman, however, that astute reader of Norse myth, when the gods find the golden gaming pieces once more in the lush grass of Iðavellir and set up the chessboard, the same moves are repeated, the same patterns reiterated: divine history repeats itself. *Ragna rök* is, paradoxically, always in our past – and in our future.

# Postscript

The Norse gods and heroes we have encountered in this book are certainly having a moment, but it is a moment that has lasted a good 300 years. And it is clear that they have turned out to be particularly vital and effective in the last fifty or so years in British and American culture, shaping the popular imagination. Why should that be? Part of the answer must lie with the belief that they do seem – in some ways – like our gods. They are not the elite Greek and Roman gods who stroll through the sunny olive groves of the Mediterranean, nor the mysterious part-animal deities of ancient Egypt, nor yet the dimly perceived Irish deities who leave their names embedded in the soft, green Irish landscape. The Norse gods belong among forests and mountains, like our own northern landscapes; they walk along the wild seashore or wait for passage by a steep-sided steel-blue fjord. In the British Isles they are understood as close cousins to the gods of the Angles and Saxons who settled in this archipelago more than a millennium and a half ago; and indeed the Scandinavians, who formed the next wave of invaders, brought them here in the 9th century. When Leifr Eiríksson stopped off in Orkney on his way from Norway to Greenland, just as Neil Gaiman proposes for America, his gods were already here.

'I feel I need to further my education', says Jacob in Elizabeth Knox's *The Absolute Book*, 'about how gods can be changed by the nature of their worshippers.' The Norse myths have been used in both past and present to lend support to ideologies of racism, toxic masculinity and white entitlement. Those of us who love and study the myths must counter this by reminding those coming to them afresh that the myths are historically contingent. They mean largely what they are made to mean at different times, and we can never know how they signified in the distant era when they took shape. They are supple, strange, radically different, and yet they engage, as we have seen, with far larger questions than the limited and self-serving obsessions of far-right politics, nationalism and the ravings of conspiracy theorists.

The Norse myths enable us to think critically about the climate crisis and humanity's place in the green world, about death and its place in life, about the inevitable end of the old order and the emergence of the new. We've seen how idealism and a keen sense of honour can be maintained in the face of deception and cynicism, and how the exclusion and oppression of those who are different leads to paralysis and social collapse. These stories allow us to explore the paradoxes of hybridity and the limits of time, space and mortality. Revisiting the tales of Vikings and their culture's greatest heroes has illuminated some of the changing ways that we think about masculinity, its positives and its drawbacks, and the ways in which women inflect and reconfigure the familiar social roles. Our apprehension of how medieval Scandinavians moved freely across much of the then-known world emphasizes how human beings are ceaselessly in motion, travelling, settling, integrating and telling stories that frame and mediate their sense of where they come from. And, at the end of this book, we have returned, inevitably, to the spectre of planet-wide destruction, the question of how – or whether – it can be prevented, and the ways in which we must work to imagine a brand-new world if one is to arise, green and hopeful, out of the old.

# Pronunciation Guide

Old Norse names are cited in their Old Norse forms except in cases where, in specific modern works, their names have been anglicized. Thus I talk about 'Óðinn' when referring to the god in his Old Norse form. Usually in modern iterations he is called 'Odin', as his son is called 'Thor', and Baldr may be 'Balder' or 'Baldur'.

The Old Norse alphabet uses two unfamiliar letters (still employed in modern Icelandic and Faroese) called 'eth' (ð / Ð) and 'thorn' (þ / Þ). The first is pronounced like the 'th' sound in 'this', for example in the name of Óðinn. The second is pronounced like the 'th' sound in 'thorn', for example in the name of Þórr.

Scholars usually pronounce Old Norse words as if they were modern Icelandic. Stress falls on the first syllable. Most consonants are pronounced as in English, though the letter *g* is always hard, as in 'gate', but *j* is pronounced as 'y', as in 'yes'. Note that the double consonant *ll* is pronounced as 'tl': Valhöll = 'VALhertl'. Vowels are pronounced as in southern British English when short, but a short *a* is like the 'a' of 'father', not as in 'cat'; *y* is the same as 'i': Gylfi = 'GIL-vee'. Long vowels (marked with an acute accent) are mostly just a longer version of the short, although *á* is like 'ow', as in 'how'. So Ásgarðr, the home of the gods = 'OWs-garther'. Diphthongs are somewhat different: *ei* or *ey* is 'ay' as in 'hay', so Freyr = 'FRAY-er'; *au* is a little like 'oh', but longer than in English: *draumar* (dreams) = 'DROH-mar'. The letter *æ* is pronounced 'eye', so that the Æsir, the main group of gods = 'EYE-seer'. The letters ö and ø are like German 'ö', something like the southern British English 'er'. Thus Jötunheimar (the lands of the giants) = 'YER-tun-HAY-mar'.

# Further Reading

An extensive guide to the myths and legends discussed in this book is Carolyne Larrington, *The Norse Myths: A Guide to Viking and Scandinavian Gods and Heroes* (London: Thames & Hudson, 2017). There you'll find more detail on the myths and legends explored here, and a good number of further myths too.

You can read the original stories in Carolyne Larrington (trans.), *The Poetic Edda* (Oxford: Oxford World's Classics, 2nd edn 2014) and Snorri Sturluson's *Edda* in the translation by Anthony Faulkes: *Edda* (London: Everyman, 2005). This is also available for free download from http://vsnrweb-publications.org.uk/. The original Old Norse text of the *Prose Edda*, edited by Anthony Faulkes, is available from the same site, as is a translation of *Heimskringla* by Alison Finlay and Anthony Faulkes.

An excellent history of the reception of Old Norse myths, focusing in particular on the medieval period, is Heather O'Donoghue, *From Asgard to Valhalla: The Remarkable History of the Norse Myths* (London: Bloomsbury, 2008). Jón Karl Helgason, *Echoes of Valhalla: The Afterlife of the Eddas and Sagas* (London: Reaktion Books, 2017) looks at more modern treatments of myth and legend. Thomas Birkett and Roderick Dale's essay collection *The Vikings Reimagined: Reception, Recovery, Engagement* (Kalamazoo, Mich.: Medieval Institute Press, 2020) has some very interesting chapters, including Neil Price's thoughts on *Vikings* and my own piece on the Ironborn in *A Song of Ice and Fire* and *Game of Thrones*.

The magisterial two-volume *The Pre-Christian Religions of the North*: *Research and Reception*, ed. Margaret Clunies Ross (Turnhout:

Brepols, 2018), gives an exhaustive overview of the history of myths and their reception. Andrew Wawn, *The Vikings and the Victorians: Inventing the Old North in Nineteenth-Century Britain* (Cambridge: D. S. Brewer, 2002), remains unsurpassed as a readable account of the rebirth of interest in Norse myth and history in the long 19th century.

An interesting study of Yggdrasill and its place in Old Norse myth is Christopher Abram, *Evergreen Ash: Ecology and Catastrophe in Old Norse Myth* (Charlottesville, Va.: University of Virginia Press, 2019). For more on cosmology and archaeology, see Anders Andrén, *Tracing Old Norse Cosmography: The World Tree, Middle Earth and the Sun in Archaeological Perspectives* (Lund: Nordic Academic Press, 2014).

Howard Williams has written an illuminating series of blog posts about the Bj. 581 grave at: https://howardwilliamsblog.word-press.com/ (search under 'Viking warrior women'). He has also written a good deal about funerals in *Vikings*, along with some other fascinating reflections on the series.

Martin Arnold, *Thor: Myth to Marvel* (London: Continuum, 2011), is a wide-ranging history of Thor in medieval and modern times.

A very readable and up-to-date account of historical Vikings is Neil Price, *The Children of Ash and Elm: A History of the Vikings* (London: Allen Lane, 2020). Eleanor Barraclough's engaging *Beyond the Northlands: Viking Voyages and Old Norse Sagas* (Oxford: Oxford University Press, 2018) offers fascinating insights into the ways in which the Viking world is reimagined in the sagas, in the context of the author's own travels in Northern lands.

Also entertaining and informative, particularly on Vikings in literature, is T. A. Shippey, *Laughing Shall I Die: Lives and Deaths of the Great Vikings* (London: Reaktion Books, 2018). A very much up-to-date and archaeologically well-informed book is Cat Jarman, *River Kings: A New History of Vikings from Scandinavia to the Silk Roads* (London: HarperCollins, 2021). Perhaps the last word on berserkers is the authoritative book by Roderick Dale, *The Myths and Realities of the Viking Berserkr: Studies in Medieval History and Culture* (London: Taylor and Francis, 2021).

Jóhanna Katrín Friðriksdóttir has written a wonderfully comprehensive account of Viking Age women: *Valkyrie: The Women of the Viking World* (London: Bloomsbury, 2020).

Elizabeth Ashman Rowe's *Vikings in the West: The Legend of Ragnarr Loðbrók and His Sons* (Vienna: Fassbaender, 2012) is an exhaustive study of the historical sources about Ragnarr and his offspring.

A good introduction to Richard Wagner's *Ring* cycle is Stewart Spencer and Barry Millington, *Wagner's Ring of the Nibelung: A Companion* (London: Thames & Hudson, 2010).

Bettina Bildhauer's books, *Filming the Middle Ages* (London: Reaktion Books, 2011) and the essay collection edited with Anke Bernau, *Medieval Film* (Manchester: Manchester University Press, 2011), are good introductions to the various ways in which medieval material has inspired films.

For more on Vínland and the particular interest of North Americans in the Viking past, see Tim William Machan and Jón Karl Helgason, *From Iceland to the Americas: Vinland and the Historical Imagination* (Manchester: Manchester University Press, 2020). See in this collection in particular Heather O'Donoghue's chapter on *American Gods* and the account by Kevin J. Harty of the Newport Tower, on which I draw for my discussion.

# Sources of Illustrations

# Acknowledgments

This book owes its genesis to Colin Ridler. My thanks to him, Ben Hayes and the rest of the team at Thames & Hudson, in particular Jen Moore. Sam Wythe and Nikos Kotsopoulous did splendid work, copy-editing and undertaking picture research. Warm thanks to those who read the book in draft: Dave Larrington, whose fingerprints are clear in places, Tim Bourns, doubtless relieved not to have to index this one, and Jóhanna Katrín Friðriksdóttir. Will Brockbank, Caroline Batten and Felix Taylor all played a part in forming my thoughts about Norse fantasy. Heather O'Donoghue, Jón Karl Helgason, Tom Shippey, Tom Birkett, Roderick Dale and David Clark have done outstanding work on the reception of Old Norse myths that helped shape this book. Bettina Bildhauer kindly sent copies of her work on film that were hard to get hold of in lockdown. Joanne Harris and Francesca Simon shared their thoughts about rewriting Norse myth for different kinds of audience in our joint podcasts and on other occasions. Neil Price fixed errors of archaeological fact just in time, while Cat Jarman kindly sent a vital copy of *River Kings*. Any remaining errors are of course all mine.

# Index

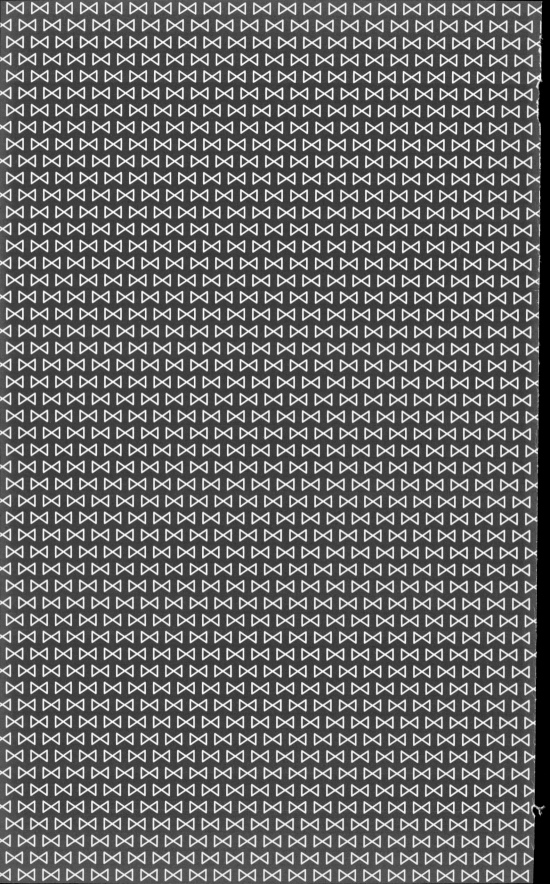